First to Arrive

The BCSIA Studies in International Security book series is edited at the Belfer Center for Science and International Affairs at Harvard University's John F. Kennedy School of Government and published by The MIT Press. The series publishes books on contemporary issues in international security policy, as well as their conceptual and historical foundations. Topics of particular interest to the series include the spread of weapons of mass destruction, internal conflict, the international effects of democracy and democratization, and U.S. defense policy.

A complete list of BCSIA Studies appears at the back of this volume.

First to Arrive

State and Local Responses to Terrorism

Juliette N. Kayyem and Robyn L. Pangi, editors

BCSIA Studies in International Security

in cooperation with the Executive Session on Domestic Preparedness

The MIT Press
Cambridge, Massachusetts
London, England

This book was typeset in Palatino by Wellington Graphics and was
printed and bound in the United States of America.

Library of Congress Control Number: 2003109630
ISBN 0-262-11281-7 (hc); 0-262-61195-3 (pbk)

Printed in the United States of America

10   9   8   7   6   5   4   3   2   1

On the cover: We gratefully acknowledge John Axon for his cover image design.

Contents

Acknowledgments

Work on this book began out of deliberations regarding the newly created Department of Homeland Security (DHS). As a response to the terrorist attacks of September 11, 2001, and the growing recognition that the federal government's structure was too diffuse to be effective, the DHS was eventually proposed and, soon after, established.

In the fury of activity regarding the DHS, it became clear that state and local responses to domestic preparedness planning were either ignored, or a mere afterthought. In the world of national security thinkers, that should come as no surprise as the focus tends to be on federal responses to international threats. But, by and large, domestic preparedness is a "ground up" response, since it is local responders who will be the first to arrive. We came to regard this book, an edited volume about domestic preparedness planning on the state and local level, as a necessary contribution to the vast amount of literature related to terrorism and homeland security.

The thoughts behind this book were truly grounded in the biannual meetings of the Executive Session on Domestic Preparedness (ESDP) at the Kennedy School of Government at Harvard University. The ESDP, funded by the Department of Justice, is a joint project of two distinct research centers at Harvard University, two centers that rarely combine their intellectual efforts: the Belfer Center for Science and International Affairs and the Taubman Center for State and Local Government. The ESDP has brought together key leaders in domestic preparedness planning, national security, and public health, since 1999 when the idea of homeland security was rarely considered in government or policy circles. The goal of the ESDP was to combine the operational insights of members out in the field (police officers, firefighters, elected officials, etc.) with the contributions of Harvard faculty to provide a unique forum to address the challenges of domestic preparedness. Their thoughts and contributions are memorialized at www.esdp.org. This book has benefited from these continuing conversations, publications, and the Kennedy School's efforts in this urgent arena.

We are indebted to our contributing authors who provided their thoughts, and words, for this effort. We are equally indebted to the members of the ESDP, a list certainly too long to list here, but each, over the course of the last few years, has been an invaluable resource. In addition, we would like to thank the Harvard faculty and scholars who assisted the ESDP and us in this project, particularly: Graham T. Allison, Alan Altshuler, Ashton Carter, Frank Hartmann, Steve Miller, Philip Heymann, Arnold Howitt, Matthew Meselson, and Jessica Stern. Kennedy School Dean Joseph Nye has been a vocal and supportive player in all our efforts. We also would like to thank Richard Falkenrath, who initiated the ESDP with Arnold Howitt before leaving to serve at the Office of Homeland Security.

Andy Mitchell and Sue Obuchowski at the Department of Justice's Office of Domestic Preparedness have been patient partners in our efforts. Sean Lynn-Jones and Karen Motley at the Belfer Center for Science and International Affairs have assisted tremendously in producing this book. We thank Richard Dill, a former *Boston Globe* editor, and Susan Lynch for their thoughtful editing and proofreading of this book. In addition, John Axon provided the powerful cover image, and John Grennan prepared the index. We also want to thank Rebecca Storo, Assistant Director of the ESDP, who helped with this book at various stages along the way.

While this book has taken a tremendous effort, it truly could not have been completed without the always helpful, and always willing work (both substantive, and not so substantive) of ESDP researcher Patricia Chang. She has been an invaluable resource for us. We could not thank her more.

Finally, on a more personal level, we would like to thank our respective spouses, David Barron and Corey Sassaman, who have provided calm and surety for us. It is not easy to work in the field of terrorism, and it may certainly be less easy to be married to someone who does. Our heartfelt thanks to both of them.

Juliette N. Kayyem
Robyn L. Pangi
Cambridge, Massachusetts

Introduction

It is difficult to remember what this nation was like before September 11, 2001. The date itself, now simply referred to as 9/11, represents more than the terrorist attacks on the World Trade Center and the Pentagon and the crashing of a fourth aircraft into a field in Somerset, Pennsylvania. It has come to represent the day the United States fundamentally changed, when military-scale violence returned to our shores and distant lands and different religions began to have greater implications within the nation's borders.

The amount already written about 9/11 and its implications for U.S. policy and governance is too vast to measure. Yet much of it merely casts blame or pinpoints failures. In contrast, this volume contains advice from a standing task force of experts, government officials, and academics who recognized the growing terrorist threat against the United States long before September 11, 2001. Before the attacks there was steady low-key interest in terrorism, leading to piecemeal measures, congressional commissions, and an occasional academic conference, but terrorism failed to capture the public's attention or sustain high-level government interest until the unimaginable happened.

The essays in this book highlight the best of what has been learned in the time since 9/11 concerning homeland security. They address the question: what are the most effective methods and means to protect the United States? These essays emerged from discussions and insights of the Executive Session on Domestic Preparedness (ESDP) at the John F. Kennedy School of Government at Harvard University. Since 1998, the Kennedy School has hosted a series of ongoing conferences, bringing together a diverse group of practitioners, first responders, and academics to discuss what were at first "developing issues" confronted in the early days of domestic preparedness. That the ESDP existed before 9/11 has been beneficial to the evolution of the group's thinking because it has allowed for more deliberate and less reactionary analysis. The contributors to this book have been committed to homeland security for much of their professional lives; 9/11 changed them and their profession, permanently.

First to Arrive: State and Local Responses to Terrorism is unique for a variety of reasons. First, most of the contributors are first responders or emergency managers who work daily in the field of domestic preparedness. They come from a variety of professions—fire, emergency management, public health, law enforcement, and politics. They are not all necessarily terrorism experts; fires still occur, people still get sick, mayors still need to govern, and, on some days, terrorism receives little attention. But since 9/11, there has been a tremendous evolution in their professions, changes that have led to the new insights that are evidenced in these contributions.

Second, this book does not seek to fix blame nor does it focus on what went wrong. Perhaps because so many of the contributors spend their days in the field, actually stopping fires or making arrests, they are more interested in identifying what the nation is still missing, what lessons it has learned, and how it can best maximize its security. Their experience may be a valuable guide to what the nation needs to do to realize security in the post-9/11 world.

Third, this book addresses major themes and issues that have not been adequately explored in the day-to-day changes occurring in domestic preparedness planning and homeland security since 9/11. While much focus has been devoted to the federal government's response (for example, the creation of a new Department of Homeland Security), most federal changes will have little impact on the local and state responders who will be the first called to an incident. In this sense, what these contributors see as significant lapses in government planning should help the nation is its long-term struggle to protect U.S. interests.

Finally, this book represents a cross section of interests in that it takes a serious look at the operational, financial, structural, political, and even psychological aspects of domestic preparedness planning. It does not confine itself to one profession or one issue, because homeland security is too vast for this type of simplification. Readers can begin to understand how interrelated the different aspects of homeland security and relevant disciplines are, and how a truly comprehensive domestic preparedness program depends on each of them to function properly.

The articles contained in this volume can be grouped loosely into five categories: protecting the nation; press, politics, and the polity; extra-governmental concerns; response operations; and political and operational hurdles. Many potential terrorist scenarios are unprecedented, and so the probability of an attack and consequences of such an attack are unknown. Yet, these authors have developed pragmatic approaches that peel off some layers of complexity, revealing feasible and forward-looking approaches to dealing with terrorism.

Protecting the Nation

Counterterrorism comprises myriad issues and actions that are relevant at different times and places. The first priority, of course, is to identify probable threats and prevent an attack. Because not all attackers can be thwarted, however, counterterrorist strategies also seek to mitigate the effects of an attack, minimizing the "success" a terrorist can achieve. The first two articles in this book are concerned with the former goal: to understand and prevent an attack by identifying the threat and hardening possible targets.

In "The New Containment: An Alliance Against Nuclear Terrorism," Professor Graham Allison, of Harvard's Kennedy School of Government, and Andrei Kokoshin, of the Russian Academy of Sciences, discuss the renewed nuclear threat. They urge leaders to "ask today what governments will be doing urgently on the day after the first nuclear terrorist assault," and to use that hypothetical as a basis for taking actions necessary to prevent nuclear terrorism. Led by a proposed U.S.-Russian "Alliance Against Nuclear Terrorism," some preliminary methods to preempt nuclear terrorism include: preventing the theft of nuclear fissile material, reinventing a robust regime of controls on the sale and export of weapons of mass destruction, and fostering international cooperation in counterproliferation efforts.

In his article "Assessing Infrastructure Vulnerability and Security," Indianapolis terrorism preparedness coordinator Peter Beering complements the previous analysis of the terrorist threat with an attempt to simplify issues of vulnerability to an attack—in particular, infrastructure vulnerability. He notes some of the inherent, but not insurmountable, challenges to securing infrastructure: prioritizing likely targets, setting an acceptable level of risk, and evaluating and acting on threat assessments.

Press, Politics, and the Polity

Terrorists seek to instill fear in the populace and to alter our way of life. The three articles in this section stress the importance of planning for an attack in ways that involve the people, work with the press, and recognize the competing demands on politicians. Simultaneously, they attempt to fit the recommended actions into norms of democracy. They advocate using our system to meet the needs of people rather than compromising it or misleading the public.

"In Defense of the Law" notes the trade-offs that have been made between civil liberties and public safety. Juliette Kayyem, Executive Director of the Executive Session on Domestic Preparedness, notes that, "before September 11, the United States fought terrorism primarily by arresting perpetrators and trying them in an American courtroom after the fact. Since September 11, law enforcement has given way to military power and the lawyers have been superseded by the generals—and, along the way, the values of war are transforming American law." Kayyem emphasizes that the legal approach needs to be used not in isolation from other approaches but as part of our overall strategy against terrorism.

Clarence Harmon, former mayor of St. Louis, Missouri, uses his vantage point as a statesman to emphasize the importance of the polity in his article, "Turning a Popular War into a Populist War: Preparing the American Public for Terrorism." Harmon encourages political leaders to involve the citizenry in domestic preparedness *beyond* simply telling them to be vigilant. Building on the model of civil defense systems that originated in the late 1940s in response to the perceived threat of a Soviet nuclear attack, Harmon notes that citizens constitute a vast resource that can be mobilized to protect themselves and their neighbors in the event of an attack with a biological weapon.

Director of the Office of Emergency Services in San Jose, California, Frances Edwards-Winslow, also emphasizes the importance of communicating with the populace in "Telling It Like It Is: The Role of the Media in Terrorism Response and Recovery." The article charts a course for government officials and the media to build relationships and convey critical information. After an attack (as with any disaster), communicating critical, life-saving information requires media participation. Getting the facts across and the appropriate experts on the air cannot be done unless both sides make fact-based communication the top priority in a crisis.

Extra-Governmental Concerns

Not all solutions lie with government action. Unfortunately, domestic preparedness planning tends to focus on local, state, and federal capacities at the expense of private sector planning. As this nation looks forward to long-term domestic preparedness plans, it must look beyond the traditional government roles and responsibilities.

"Is Density Dangerous? The Architects' Obligations after the Towers Fell" is architect David Dixon's exploration of the challenges inherent in providing safer places for Americans to work and live in. The easiest security solutions often involve erecting physical barriers and closing off public spaces, changing the nature of U.S. communities. Dixon argues that by barricading buildings and cordoning off sections of the city, we risk destroying the vitality of downtown areas and permanently altering our work environments in ways that could be avoided with careful urban planning.

In "Beyond Business Continuity: The Role of the Private Sector in Preparedness Planning," Juliette Kayyem and ESDP research assistant Patricia Chang also look to the involvement of non-governmental actors in domestic preparedness. They emphasize that private sector involvement in homeland security has tended to focus only on ensuring that business operations continue smoothly; yet there is a vital and often overlooked role for the business community in protecting their employees. The chapter examines the danger caused by a lack of integration of the private sector in domestic preparedness programs as well as the need for integrated public-private emergency planning.

Response Operations

The later sections of the book concentrate on elements of response that are critical to mitigating the effects of an attack. The first two articles in this section look at types of health care treatment that may be called for and analyze the population that may require treatment in a crisis. The last two articles ask the question: who should be responsible for the domestic military response?

In "Inside and Outside the Loop: Defining the Population at Risk in Bioterrorism," Rear Admiral Robert F. Knouss, former Director of the Office of Emergency Preparedness, Department of Health and Human Services, prioritizes three goals for the health care response to a bioterrorist attack. First, protect those who were not initially exposed so that they do not become infected after being exposed to a sick individual. Second, identify those who have been exposed so that appropriate prophylaxis can be applied to prevent them from becoming symptomatic. Third, provide timely treatment for those who have been exposed and have already become symptomatic. Knouss offers recommendations for building a system that can achieve these goals. Monitoring and surveillance as well as public education may play a big role. Each biological agent can cause distinct symptoms over varying periods of time; familiarity with the effects can save thousands of lives.

ESDP research associate Robyn Pangi uses data from the sarin attack in the Tokyo subway system in 1995 as the basis for "After the Attack: The Psychological Consequences of Terrorism." Her article highlights the need to plan for likely psychological responses to terrorism, instead of preparing only for worst-case scenarios. Data from Tokyo suggest that panic is relatively rare, but psychiatric disorders, such as short- and long-term anxiety disorders, may affect not only the immediate victims but also a large number of others, such as volunteers and worried healthy people. The article argues that this relatively new component of disaster preparedness, dubbed "fear management," must become an integral part of disaster plans if we are to deny terrorists their underlying goal of instilling fear and terror throughout the nation.

Two articles in this section answer the question: how can the United States best use existing military resources to protect the homeland? Major General Phillip Oates, former Adjutant General of Alaska, presents his recommendations in "Supporting the National Strategy for Homeland Security: The Role of the National Guard." Since response agencies cannot politically, operationally, or financially start from scratch, Oates argues that all levels of response should build upon existing capacity, including the Department of Defense. The article concludes that the National Guard is the appropriate component of the military to spearhead homeland defense efforts for several reasons, including experience, capability, availability, familiarity with response operations, and legal authority.

In "Homeland Security and War-Fighting: Two Pillars of National Guard Responsibility," Major General Paul D. Monroe, Adjutant General of the California National Guard, addresses the possibility that the military might start to see homeland security as its primary mission and therefore overlook the National Guard, the logical agency to assume primary responsibility for this mission. He notes the many complexities involved in preparing to meet new challenges to national security, while transforming the military to meet these and other demands.

Political and Operational Hurdles

Much like operations to prevent an attack, responding to an attack involves finding solutions to a complex set of issues with many inherent obstacles. The closing articles in the book reveal some of these obstacles and recommend feasible solutions to important problems in response operations.

In the article "The Two-Hat Syndrome: Determining Response Capabilities and Mutual Aid Limitations," Fire and Emergency Services Chief for Cobb County, Georgia, Rebecca Denlinger, with Kristin Gonzenbach, uncovers a logistical nightmare—many first responders hold multiple, and often conflicting, critical jobs. The survey that provides the data for the article found that in 16 fire departments, an average of 22.2 percent of employees hold two (or more) public safety positions. Emergency response plans assume that personnel are either on duty and, therefore, at hand or off duty and ready to report on short notice. In reality, however, police often serve as firefighters and Emergency Medical Technicians (EMT)s, EMTs work part-time in hospitals, and firefighters staff police Special Weapons and Tactics (SWAT) teams. Public safety officials sometimes claim the title of Emergency Management Director. The chapter asks important questions concerning which roles first responders will play in a disaster and who can fill the empty duties in the event of an emergency.

Senior congressional policy advisor David Grannis looks at the operational and political challenges of domestic preparedness. "Sustaining Domestic Preparedness: Challenges in a Post-9/11 World" closes the volume by asking the question: how might we sustain both the materials needed to respond to terrorist attacks and the attention required to continue vital programs and funding? Grannis provides five recommendations: designate a clear organizational home for domestic preparedness issues, develop metrics to gauge the readiness of responders and plans, aggregate budget data, continue utilizing an all-hazards disaster management approach and invest in dual-use materials where possible, and create protocols or automated tasks to increase response effectiveness within communities.

The articles in this volume consider, through a variety of professional lenses, critical questions about our nation's preparedness to prevent and face terrorist attacks. All of the contributors who have come together in this book—whether first responder, politician, private sector specialist, civil servant, or academic—are aware of the need to address the nation's response to terrorism within the framework of disaster preparedness. All are mindful of the spirit of democracy that is fundamental to American society. *First to Arrive: State and Local Responses to Terrorism* goes a long way toward preparing to fight the *next* war, instead of the *last*.

Chapter 1

The New Containment: An Alliance Against Nuclear Terrorism

Graham Allison and Andrei Kokoshin

During the Cold War, American and Russian policymakers and citizens thought long and hard about the possibility of nuclear attacks on their respective homelands. But with the fall of the Berlin Wall and the disappearance of the Soviet Union, the fears of a nuclear conflict faded from most minds. This is ironic and potentially tragic, since the threat of a nuclear attack on the United States or Russia is certainly greater today than it was in 1989.

In the aftermath of Osama bin Laden's September 11, 2001, assault, which awakened the world, especially Americans, to the reality of global terrorism, it is incumbent upon national security analysts everywhere to think again about the unthinkable. Could a nuclear terrorist assault happen today? Our considered answer is: yes, unquestionably, without any doubt. It is not only a possibility but, in fact, the most urgent unaddressed national security threat to both the United States and Russia.[1]

Consider this hypothetical: a crude nuclear weapon constructed from

---

This article is reprinted with permission from *The National Interest*. It appeared as: Graham Allison and Andrei Kokoshin, "The New Containment: An Alliance Against Nuclear Terrorism," *The National Interest*, Vol. 69 (Fall 2002), pp. 35–45.

---

1. This judgment echoes the major finding of a Department of Energy Task Force on nonproliferation programs with Russia led by Howard Baker and Lloyd Cutler: "The most urgent unmet national security threat to the United States today is the danger that weapons of mass destruction or weapons-usable material in Russia could be stolen and sold to terrorists or hostile nation states and used against American troops abroad or citizens at home." *A Report Card on the Department of Energy's Nonproliferation Programs with Russia*, January 10, 2001.<http://www.hr.doe.gov/seab/rusrpt. pdf.>

stolen materials explodes in Red Square in Moscow. The blast of a bomb made from just 40 pounds of highly enriched uranium would instantaneously destroy tens of thousands of lives as well as the Kremlin, Saint Basil's Cathedral, the ministries of foreign affairs and defense, and the Tretyakov Gallery. In Washington, D.C., an equivalent explosion near the White House would completely destroy that building, the Old Executive Office Building, and everything within a one-mile radius, including the Departments of State, Treasury, the Federal Reserve—and all of their occupants (as well as damaging the Potomac-facing side of the Pentagon).

Psychologically, such a hypothetical is as difficult to internalize as are the plot lines of a writer like Tom Clancy, whose novel *Debt of Honor* ends with terrorists crashing a jumbo jet into the U.S. Capitol on Inauguration Day and whose *The Sum of All Fears* contemplates the very scenario we discuss—the detonation of a nuclear device in a major American metropolis by terrorists. That these kinds of scenarios are physically possible is an undeniable, brute fact.

After the first nuclear terrorist attack, the Russian Duma, U.S. Congress, and the press will investigate: who knew what and when? They will ask what could have been done to prevent the attack and demand vigorous action to prevent future nuclear terrorism. Most officials will no doubt seek cover behind the claim that "no one could have imagined" this happening. But that defense does not ring true. Today, we have unambiguous warnings that a nuclear terrorist attack could happen at any moment. Responsible leaders should be asking hard questions now. Nothing prevents the governments of Russia, America, and other countries from taking effective action today—except, a lack of determination.

The argument here can be summarized in two propositions: first, nuclear terrorism poses a clear and present danger to the United States, Russia, and other nations; second, nuclear terrorism is a largely *preventable* disaster. Preventing nuclear terrorism is a large, complex, but ultimately finite challenge that can be contained by a bold, determined, but nonetheless finite response. The current mismatch between the seriousness of the threat and the actions governments are now taking to meet it is unacceptable for American, Russian, and global security. Below, we assess the threat and outline a solution that begins with a U.S.-Russian-led "Alliance Against Nuclear Terrorism."

Assessing the Threat

A comprehensive threat assessment must consider both the likelihood of an event and the magnitude of its anticipated consequences. As described above, even a crude nuclear explosion in a city would produce devastation in a class by itself.[2] A half-dozen nuclear explosions across the United States or Russia would shift the course of history. The question is: how likely is such an event?

Security studies offer no well-developed methodology for estimating the probabilities of unprecedented events. Contemplating the possibility of a criminal act, Sherlock Holmes investigated three factors: motive, means, and opportunity. That framework can be useful for analyzing the question at hand. If no actor simultaneously has motive, means, and opportunity, no nuclear terrorist act will occur. Where these three factors are abundant and widespread, the likelihood of a nuclear terrorist act increases. The questions become: is anyone *motivated* to instigate a nuclear attack? Could terrorist groups acquire the *means* to attack the United States or Russia with nuclear weapons? Could these groups find or create an *opportunity* to act?

Motive: There can be no doubt that Osama bin Laden and his associates have serious nuclear ambitions. For almost a decade they have been actively seeking nuclear weapons, and, as President Bush has said, they would use such weapons against the United States or its allies "in a heartbeat." In 2000, the CIA reportedly intercepted a message in which a member of al Qaeda boasted of plans for a "Hiroshima" against America. According to the U.S. Justice Department indictment for the 1998 bombings of American embassies in Kenya and Tanzania, "at various times from at least as early as 1993, Osama bin Laden and others, known and unknown, made efforts to obtain the components of nuclear weapons." In addition, a former al Qaeda member has described attempts to buy uranium of South African origin, repeated travels to three Central Asian states to try to buy a complete warhead or weapons-usable material, and discussions with Chechen criminal groups in which money and drugs were offered for nuclear weapons.

Bin Laden himself has declared that acquiring nuclear weapons is a religious duty. "If I have indeed acquired [nuclear] weapons," he once said, "then I thank God for enabling me to do so." When forging an alliance of terrorist organizations in 1998, he issued a statement entitled

---

2. Although biological and chemical weapons can cause huge devastation as well, "the massive, assured, instantaneous, and comprehensive destruction of life and property" of a nuclear weapon is unique. See Matthew Bunn, John P. Holdren, and Anthony Wier, "Securing Nuclear Weapons and Materials: Seven Steps for Immediate Action," Nuclear Threat Initiative and the Managing the Atom Project, May 20, 2002, p. 2 or <http://www.nti.org/e_research/securing_nuclear_weapons_and_materials_May2002.pdf>. This report provides extensive, but not overly technical detail on many of the points in this essay.

"The Nuclear Bomb of Islam." Characterized by renowned Middle Eastern scholar Bernard Lewis as "a magnificent piece of eloquent, at times even poetic Arabic prose," it states: "It is the duty of Muslims to prepare as much force as possible to terrorize the enemies of God." If anything, the ongoing American-led war on global terrorism is heightening our adversary's incentive to obtain and use a nuclear weapon. Al Qaeda has discovered that it can no longer attack the United States with impunity. Faced with an assertive, determined opponent now doing everything it can to destroy this terrorist network, al Qaeda has every incentive to take its best shot.

Russia also faces adversaries whose objectives could be advanced by using nuclear weapons. Chechen terrorist groups, for example, have demonstrated little, if any, restraint in their willingness to kill civilians and may be tempted to strike a definitive blow to assert independence from Russia. They have already issued, in effect, a radioactive warning by planting a package containing cesium 137, an extremely radioactive isotope and potential ingredient for a "dirty bomb," at Izmailovsky Park in Moscow and then tipping off a Russian reporter. Particularly as the remaining Chechen terrorists have been marginalized over the course of the second Chechen war, they could well imagine that by destroying one Russian city and credibly threatening Moscow, they could persuade Russia to halt its campaign against them.

All of Russia's national security documents—its *National Security Concept*, its military doctrine, and the recently updated *Foreign Policy Concept*—have clearly identified international terrorism as the greatest threat to Russia's national security. As President Vladimir Putin noted in reviewing Russian security priorities with senior members of the Foreign Ministry in January 2001, "I would like to stress the danger of international terrorism and fundamentalism of any, absolutely any stripe." The proliferation of religious extremism in Central Asia, relating directly to the rise of the Taliban in Afghanistan, and the illegal drug trade threaten Russia's borders and weaken the Commonwealth of Independent States. The civil war in Tajikistan, tensions in Georgia's Pankisi Gorge, and the conflicts in South Ossetia, Abkhazia, and Nagorno-Karabakh—all close to the borders of the Russian Federation—provide feeding grounds for the extremism that fuels terrorism. Additionally, Russia's geographical proximity to South Asia and the Middle East increases concerns over terrorist fallout from those regions. President Putin has been consistent in identifying the even darker hue that weapons of mass destruction add to terrorism. In a December 2001 interview in which he named international terrorism the "plague of the 21st century," Putin stated: "We all know exactly how New York and Washington were hit. . . . Was it ICBMs? What threat are we talking about? We are talking about the use of mass destruction weapons terrorists may obtain."

Separatist militants (in Kashmir, the Balkans, and elsewhere) and messianic terrorist groups (like Aum Shinrikyo, which attacked a Tokyo subway with chemical weapons in 1995) could have similar motives to commit nuclear terrorism. As Palestinians look to uncertain prospects for independent statehood—never mind whose leadership actually increased that uncertainty in recent years—Israel becomes an ever more attractive target for a nuclear terrorist attack. Since a nuclear detonation in any part of the world would likely be extremely destabilizing, it would threaten American and Russian interests even if few or no Russians or Americans were killed.

Means: To the best of our knowledge, no terrorist group can now detonate a nuclear weapon. But as Secretary of Defense Donald Rumsfeld has stated, "The absence of evidence is not evidence of absence." Are the means beyond terrorists' reach, even that of relatively sophisticated groups like al Qaeda?

Over four decades of Cold War competition, the superpowers spent trillions of dollars assembling mass arsenals, stockpiles, nuclear complexes, and enterprises that engaged hundreds of thousands of accomplished scientists and engineers. Technical know-how cannot be uninvented. Reducing arsenals that include some 40,000 nuclear weapons and the equivalents of more than 100,000 nuclear weapons in the form of highly enriched uranium and plutonium to a manageable level is a gargantuan challenge. Providing gainful employment for those that comprised what once was a million-man nuclear establishment is a critical challenge as well.

Terrorists could seek to buy an assembled nuclear weapon from insiders or criminals. Nuclear weapons are known to exist in eight states: the United States, Russia, Great Britain, France, China, Israel, India, and Pakistan. North Korea's admission, in October 2002, that it has an active uranium-enriching program signifies that it may soon become part of the nuclear threat. Security measures, such as "permissive action links" designed to prevent unauthorized use, are most reliable in the United States, Russia, France, and Great Britain. These safeguards, as well as command-and-control systems, are much less reliable in the two newest nuclear states—India and Pakistan. But even where good systems are in place, maintaining high levels of security requires constant attention from high-level government officials.

Alternatively, terrorists could try to build a nuclear weapon. The only component that is especially difficult to obtain is the nuclear fissile material—highly enriched uranium or plutonium. Although the largest stockpiles of weapons-grade material are found in the nuclear weapons pro-grams of the United States and Russia, fissile material in sufficient quantities to make a crude nuclear weapon can also be found in many civilian settings around the globe. Some 345 research reactors in 58 nations together contain about 20 metric tons of highly enriched ura-nium, many in quantities sufficient to build a bomb.[3] Other civilian reac-tors produce enough weapons-grade nuclear material to pose a prolifera-tion threat; several European states, Japan, Russia, and India reprocess spent fuel to separate out plutonium for use as new fuel. The United States has actually facilitated the spread of fissile material in the past—over three decades of the Atoms for Peace program, the United States exported 749 kg of plutonium and 26.6 metric tons of highly en-riched uranium to 39 countries.[4]

Terrorist groups could obtain these materials by theft, illicit purchase, or voluntary transfer from state control. There is ample evidence that at-tempts to steal or sell nuclear weapons or weapons-usable material are not hypothetical, but a recurring fact.[5] In the fall of 2001, the chief of the directorate of the Russian Defense Ministry responsible for nuclear weap-ons reported two incidents in which terrorist groups attempted to per-form reconnaissance at Russian nuclear storage sites but were repulsed. The 1990s saw repeated incidents in which individuals and groups suc-cessfully stole weapons material from sites in Russia and sought to ex-port them—but were caught trying to do so. In one highly publicized case, a group of insiders at a nuclear weapons facility in Chelyabinsk, Russia, plotted to steal 18.5 kg (40.7 lbs) of highly enriched uranium, which would have been enough to construct a bomb, but were thwarted by Russian Federal Security Service agents.

In the mid-1990s, material sufficient to allow terrorists to build more than 20 nuclear weapons—more than 1,000 pounds of highly enriched uranium—sat unprotected in Kazakhstan. Iranian and possibly al Qaeda operatives with nuclear ambitions were widely reported to be in Kazakhstan. Recognizing the danger, the American government itself

---

3. See U.S. Department of Energy, *FY 2003 Budget Request: Detailed Budget Justifica-tions—Defense Nuclear Nonproliferation* (Washington, D.C.: DOE, February 2002): p. 172. <http://www.cfo.doe.gov/budget/03budget/content/defnn/nuclnonp.pdf>.

4. Jeffrey Fleishman, "Sting Unravels Stunning Mafia Plot," *Philadelphia Inquirer,* Jan-uary 12, 1999. Summarized in NIS Nuclear Trafficking Database <http://www.nti.org/db/nistraff/1999/19990110.htm>.

5. The Nuclear Threat Initiative maintains a database of cases and reported incidents of trafficking in nuclear and radioactive materials in and from the former Soviet Union, at <http://www.nti.org/db/nistraff/index.html>.

purchased the material and removed it to Oak Ridge, Tennessee. In February 2002, the U.S. National Intelligence Council reported to Congress that "undetected smuggling [of weapons-usable nuclear materials from Russia] has occurred, although we do not know the extent of such thefts." Each assertion invariably provokes blanket denials from Russian officials. Russian Atomic Energy Minister Aleksandr Rumyantsevhas has claimed categorically: "Fissile materials have not disappeared." President Putin has stated that he is "absolutely confident" that terrorists in Afghanistan do not have weapons of mass destruction of Soviet or Russian origin.

For perspective on claims of the inviolable security of nuclear weapons or material, it is worth considering the issue of "lost nukes." Is it possible that the United States or Soviet Union lost assembled nuclear weapons? At least on the American side the evidence is clear. In 1981, the U.S. Department of Defense published a list of 32 accidents involving nuclear weapons, *many of which resulted in lost bombs.*[6] One involved a submarine that sank along with two nuclear torpedoes. In other cases, nuclear bombs were lost from aircraft. Though on the Soviet/Russian side there is no official information, we do know that four Soviet submarines carrying nuclear weapons have sunk since 1968, resulting in an estimated 43 lost nuclear warheads.[7] These accidents suggest the complexity of controlling and accounting for vast nuclear arsenals and stockpiles.

Nuclear materials have also been stolen from stockpiles housed at research reactors. In 1999, Italian police seized a bar of enriched uranium from an organized crime group trying to sell it to a law enforcement agent posing as a Middle Eastern businessman with presumed ties to terrorists. On investigation, the Italians found the uranium originated from a U.S.-supplied research reactor in the former Zaire, where it presumably had been stolen or purchased *sub rosa.*

Finally, as President Bush has stressed, terrorists could obtain nuclear weapons or weapons material from states hostile to the United States. In his now famous phrase, Bush called hostile regimes developing weapons of mass destruction and their terrorist allies an "axis of evil." He argued that states such as Iraq, Iran, and North Korea, if allowed to realize their nuclear ambitions, "could provide these arms to terrorists, giving them the means to match their hatred." The fear that a hostile regime might transfer a nuclear weapon to terrorists has contributed to the Bush administration's development of a new doctrine of preemption against such

---

6. U.S. Department of Defense, "Narrative Summaries of Accidents involving U.S. Nuclear Weapons: 1950–1980," April 1981.

7. Joshua Handler, Amy Wickenheiser, and William M. Arkin, "Naval Safety 1989: The Year of the Accident," *Neptune Paper No. 4,* April 1989.

regimes, with Iraq as the likely test case. It also adds to American concerns about Russian transfer of nuclear technologies to Iran. While Washington and Moscow continue to disagree on whether any civilian nuclear cooperation with Iran is justified, both agree on the dangers a nuclear-armed Iran would pose, and Russia is more than willing to agree that there should be no transfers of technology that could help Iran make nuclear weapons.

Opportunity: Security analysts have long focused on ballistic missiles as the preferred means by which nuclear weapons would be delivered. But today this is actually the least likely vehicle by which a nuclear weapon will be delivered against Russia or the United States. Ballistic weapons are hard to produce, costly, and difficult to hide. A nuclear weapon delivered by a missile also leaves an unambiguous return address, inviting devastating retaliation. As Robert Walpole, a National Intelligence Officer, told a U.S. Senate subcommittee in March 2002, "Nonmissile delivery means are less costly, easier to acquire, and more reliable and accurate."[8] Despite this assessment, the U.S. government continues to invest much more heavily in developing and deploying missile defenses than in addressing more likely trajectories by which weapons could arrive.

Terrorists would not find it difficult to sneak a nuclear device or nuclear fissile material into the United States via shipping containers, trucks, ships, or aircraft. The nuclear material required is smaller than a football. Even an assembled device, like a suitcase nuclear weapon, could be shipped in a container, in the hull of a ship, or in a trunk carried by an aircraft. After 9/11, the number of containers currently arriving daily at the port of New York/New Jersey that are X-rayed has increased to about 500 of 5,000, approximately 10 percent. But as the chief executive of CSX Lines, one of the foremost container-shipping companies, put it: "If you can smuggle heroin in containers, you may be able to smuggle in a nuclear bomb."

Effectively countering missile attacks will require technological breakthroughs well beyond current systems. Success in countering covert delivery of weapons will require not just technical advances but a conceptual breakthrough. Recent efforts to bolster border security are laudable but just begin to scratch the surface. More than 500 million people, 11 million trucks, and two million rail cars cross into the United States each year, while 7,500 foreign-flag ships make 51,000 calls in U.S. ports. That's

8. Statement of Robert Walpole before the Senate Subcommittee on International Security, Proliferation, and Federal Services, March 11, 2002. <http://www.senate.gov/ <gov_affairs/031102walpole.pdf>.

not counting the tens of thousands of people, hundreds of aircraft, and numerous boats that enter illegally and are uncounted. Given this volume and the lengthy land and sea borders of the United States, even a radically renovated and reorganized system cannot aspire to be airtight.

The opportunities for terrorists to smuggle a nuclear weapon into Russia or another state are even greater. Russia's land borders are nearly twice as long as America's, connecting it to more than a dozen other states. In many places, in part because borders between republics were less significant in the time of the Soviet Union, these borders are not closely monitored. Corruption has been a major problem among border patrols. Visa-free travel between Russia and several of its neighbors creates additional opportunities for weapons smugglers and terrorists. The "homeland security" challenge for Russia is truly monumental.

In sum: even a conservative estimate must conclude that dozens of terrorist groups have sufficient motive to use a nuclear weapon, several could potentially obtain nuclear means, and hundreds of opportunities exist for a group with means and motive to make the United States or Russia a victim of nuclear terrorism. The mystery before us is not how a nuclear terrorist attack could possibly occur, but, rather, why no terrorist group has yet combined motive, means, and opportunity to commit a nuclear attack. We have been lucky so far, but who among us trusts luck to protect us in the future?

Chto Delat—What is to be Done?[9]

The good news about nuclear terrorism can be summarized in one line: no highly enriched uranium or plutonium; no nuclear explosion, no nuclear terrorism. Though the world's stockpiles of nuclear weapons and weapons-usable materials are vast, they are finite. The prerequisites for manufacturing fissile material are many and require the resources of a modern state. Technologies for locking up super-dangerous or valuable items—from gold in Fort Knox to treasures in the Kremlin Armory—are well developed and tested. While challenging, a specific program of actions to keep nuclear materials out of the hands of the most dangerous groups is not beyond reach, *if* leaders give this objective highest priority and hold subordinates accountable for achieving this result.

The starting points for such a program of specific actions are already in place. In his major foreign policy campaign address at the Ronald Reagan Library, then-presidential candidate George W. Bush called for "Con-

---

9. *Chto Delat* is a proverbial Russian refrain meaning, "What is to be done?"

gress to increase substantially our assistance to dismantle as many Russian weapons as possible, as quickly as possible." In his September 2000 address to the United Nations Millennium Summit, Russian President Putin proposed to "find ways to block the spread of nuclear weapons by excluding use of enriched uranium and plutonium in global atomic energy production." The Joint Declaration on the New Strategic Relationship between the United States and Russia signed by the two presidents at the May 2002 summit stated that the two partners would combat the "closely linked threats of international terrorism and the proliferation of weapons of mass destruction." Another important result yielded by the summit was the upgrading of the Armitage/Trubnikov-led U.S.-Russia Working Group on Afghanistan to the U.S.-Russia Working Group on Counter-terrorism, whose agenda is to address the threats posed by nuclear, biological, and chemical terrorism.

Operationally, however, priority is measured not by words but by deeds. A decade of Nunn-Lugar Cooperative Threat Reduction Programs has accomplished much in safeguarding nuclear materials. Unfortunately, the job of upgrading security to minimum basic standards is mostly unfinished: by U.S. Department of Energy accounts, two-thirds of the nuclear material in Russia remains to be adequately secured.[10] Bureaucratic inertia, bolstered by mistrust and misperception on both sides, leaves these joint programs bogged down on timetables that extend to 2008. Unless implementation improves significantly, they will probably fail to meet even this unacceptably distant target. What is required on both sides is personal, presidential priority measured in commensurate energy, specific orders, funding, and accountability. This should be embodied in a new U.S.–Russian-led "Alliance Against Nuclear Terrorism."

When it comes to the threat of nuclear terrorism, many Americans judge Russia to be part of the problem, not the solution. But if Russia is welcomed and supported as a fully responsible nonproliferation partner, the United States stands to accomplish far more toward minimizing the risk of nuclear terrorism than if it treats Russia as an unreconstructed pariah. As the first step in establishing this alliance, the two presidents should pledge to each other that his government will do everything technically possible to prevent criminals or terrorists from stealing nuclear weapons or weapons-usable material, and do so on the fastest possible timetable. Each should make clear that he will personally hold accountable the entire chain of command within his own government to assure

---

10. Matthew Bunn, John P. Holdren, and Anthony Wier. "Securing Nuclear Weapons and Materials: Seven Steps for Immediate Action." Nuclear Threat Initiative and the Managing the Atom Project, May 20, 2002.

this result. Understanding that each country bears responsibility for the security of its own nuclear materials, the United States should nonetheless offer any assistance required to make this happen.[11] Each nation—and leader—should provide the other sufficient transparency to monitor performance.

To ensure that this is done on an expedited schedule, both governments should name specific individuals, directly answerable to their respective presidents, to co-chair a group tasked with developing a Russian-American strategy within one month. In developing a joint strategy and program of action, the nuclear superpowers should establish a new "international security standard" based on President Putin's Millennium proposal for new technologies that allow production of electricity with lowly enriched, non-weapons-usable nuclear fuel.

A second pillar of this Alliance would reach out to all other nuclear weapons states—beginning where the threat of theft is currently greatest: Pakistan. Each should be invited to join the Alliance and offered assistance, if necessary, in assuring that all weapons and weapons-usable materials are secured to the new established international standard in a manner sufficiently transparent to reassure all others. Invitations should be diplomatic in tone but nonetheless clear that this is an offer that cannot be refused.

A third pillar of this Alliance calls for global outreach along the lines proposed by Senator Richard Lugar of Indiana in what has been called the "Lugar doctrine."[12] All states that possess weapons-usable nuclear materials—even those without nuclear weapons capabilities—must enlist in an international effort to guarantee the security of such materials from theft by terrorists or criminal groups. In effect, each would be required to meet the new international security standard and to do so in a transparent fashion. Pakistan is particularly important given its location and relationship with al Qaeda, but, beyond nuclear weapons states, several dozen additional countries hosting research reactors—such as Serbia, Libya, and Ghana—should be persuaded to surrender such material (almost all of it either American or Soviet in origin) or have the material secured to acceptable international standards.

A fourth pillar of this effort should include Russian–American-led cooperation in preventing the spread of nuclear weapons to additional

---

11. A U.S. Department of Energy Task Force estimated that this would cost about $30 billion over several years, an amount the president could surely persuade Congress to appropriate, if he made this goal his highest national security priority.

12. Speech by Richard Lugar, May 27, 2002, at the Moscow Nuclear Threat Initiative Conference, < http://lugar.senate.gov/052702.html>.

states, focusing sharply on North Korea, Iraq, and Iran. The historical record demonstrates that where the United States and Russia have cooperated intensely, aspiring nuclear actors have been largely stymied. It was only during periods of competition or distraction, for example in the mid-1990s, that new nuclear weapons states openly declared the realization of their ambitions. India and Pakistan provide two vivid case studies. Recent Russian-American-Chinese cooperation in nudging India and Pakistan back from the nuclear brink suggests a good course of action. The new alliance should reinvent a robust nonproliferation regime of controls on the sale and export of weapons of mass destruction, nuclear material, and missile technologies, recognizing the threat to each of the major states that would be posed by a nuclear-armed Iran, North Korea, or Iraq.

Finally, adapting lessons learned in U.S.-Russian cooperation in the campaign against bin Laden and the Taliban, this new Alliance should be heavy on intelligence-sharing and counterproliferation efforts, including disruption and preemption to prevent acquisition of materials and know-how by nuclear wannabes. Beyond joint intelligence sharing, joint training for preemptive actions against terrorists, criminal groups, or rogue states attempting to acquire weapons of mass destruction would provide a fitting enforcement mechanism for alliance commitments.

As former Senator Sam Nunn of Georgia has noted: "At the dawn of a new century, we find ourselves in a new arms race. Terrorists are racing to get weapons of mass destruction; we ought to be racing to stop them."[13] Preventing nuclear terrorism will require no less imagination, energy, and persistence than did avoiding nuclear war between the superpowers over four decades of the Cold War. But absent deep, sustained cooperation between the United States, Russia and other nuclear states, such an effort is doomed to failure. In the context of the qualitatively new relationship Presidents Putin and Bush have established in the aftermath of 9/11, success in such a bold effort is within the reach of determined Russian-American leadership. Succeed we must.

---

13. Sam Nunn, "Our new security framework," *Washington Post*, October 8, 2001.

Chapter 2

Assessing Infrastructure Vulnerability and Security

Peter S. Beering

"The water supply in Johnson County has been contaminated with dihydrogen monoxide. Side effects of this contamination include increased urination, profuse sweating, and wrinkling of the hands and feet." Intended as an "April Fool's" gag by a pair of suburban Kansas City, Kansas, radio hosts, it backfired. After the April 1, 2002, broadcast, the local water company received 120 calls and there were 30 additional calls to the emergency number 911, highlighting the sensitivity of a frightened nation.[1]

Threats to attack structures or contaminate water systems are not unusual. Hundreds of threats are made against municipal water systems each year. "No one really knows how many incidents there are because before the September 11, 2001, attacks, there were not a lot of people interested in water system security."[2] Movies, television, novels, and news stories have depicted water supplies as a potential terrorist target.

Water systems are just one example of the utilities and other vital infrastructures that have become the focus of the media, law enforcement, the public, and our adversaries. Infrastructure represents vast and almost indefensible targets. Some of the utility infrastructures deliver vital com-

---

1. Watertech Online, April 3, 2002, <www.watertechonline.com/archives>.

2. Frank Blaha, Director of Research for the American Water Works Association Research Forum, interviewed by the author, April 18, 2002. Estimates of water threats vary widely. This is due in part to the lack of a comprehensive reporting mechanism, failure to recognize incidents as malicious, a tendency for utilities to dismiss incidents as "vandalism," a lack of interest from academia prior to September 2001, and a general lack of interest from law enforcement agencies.

modities that may burn, explode, or wreak havoc if unleashed. Natural and liquid propane gas are examples of products that may be used as weapons, used to create disruptive incidents to divert attention from other attacks, or used to compromise the public safety response to a terrorist incident by interfering with water service or by making roadways impassable. Interference with communications and transportation infrastructures can paralyze or isolate communities, making attacks on the infrastructure even more tantalizing to an enemy bent on instilling fear or chaos. Because "the critical infrastructure has become increasingly more concentrated, more interconnected, and more sophisticated . . . [with] very little redundancy in [the] system, " it has become easier to affect a community by attacking even one infrastructure site.[3] In addition, most of the physical plant, telecommunications, power, water supply, and transportation infrastructure lies unprotected or is equipped with security sufficient to deter only amateur vandals, thieves, or hackers.

The way our infrastructure is designed and installed also makes it vulnerable to attack. Most local governments organize their utility infrastructures in corridors, legal rights-of-way, or easements to make their locations more uniform and to limit the likelihood of accidental damage from digging activities and failures of nearby utilities. Utility infrastructure is not only in predictable locations; it is often in plain view. Wires, cables, and conduits hang overhead and fire hydrants dot the landscape at regular intervals. Information technology systems have also proven vulnerable to terrorism; they have been both targeted and attacked.[4] These and other vulnerable networks may present attractive targets to those bent on mass disruption.

The range of potential attackers, the array of weapons available to them, and the ruthless creativity of many of them complicate terrorism in the new millennium. Technology, particularly the vast collections of information about how to assemble, acquire, or deploy various weapons on the Internet, has eliminated many of the barriers that historically have limited the likeliness and impact of attacks. Weapons that were once solely under the control of governments—chemical, biological, or even nuclear weapons—may now be in the hands of terrorists. Local utility operators whose greatest concern has traditionally been service interrup-

---

3. Steven E. Flynn, "America the Vulnerable," in James F. Hodge and Gideon Rose, eds., *How Did This Happen? Terrorism and the New War* (New York: Public Affairs Press, 2002), pp. 185–186.

4. Additionally, hacking attempts on information systems have increased significantly, though until recently many of these attacks may not have been reported. Charles Pillar, "Hackers Target Energy Industry," *Los Angeles Times*, July 8, 2002, p. A1.

tions and outages from natural causes must contend with these weapons as well as new, emerging threats.

Throughout modern history, radical groups have considered using unconventional weapons to achieve their goals. In 1972, for example, the eco-terror group R.I.S.E. that was based in Chicago obtained *Salmonella typhi* (typhoid fever), *Shigella sonnei* (dysentery), *Corynebacterium diptheriae* (diptheria), *Clostridium botulinum* (botulism), and *Neisseria meningitides* (bacterial meningitis) from a variety of hospital and university sources.[5] The group intended to kill by using aerosols to disperse biological organisms in the air and water. Chicago police recovered maps from the group that detailed plans to release contaminants into reservoirs containing drinking water for millions of people.[6] If R.I.S.E. could have acquired access to the information resources of the Internet, it may have been able to overcome the engineering obstacles such as how to culture, grow, weaponize, and disseminate the biological organisms that prevented the attack's success. In 1985, a survivalist group called The Covenant, Sword, and Arm of the Lord acquired 30 gallons of potassium cyanide that they intended to use to contaminate the water systems of several U.S. communities.[7] Much like R.I.S.E., this effort failed in part because the group could not determine an effective way to deliver the poison to their intended target.

Yet these attempts were isolated and typically the province of fringe groups. Today, well-organized and well-funded terrorist networks are seeking advanced capabilities. Attempts to attack the water supply at the U.S. Embassy in Rome during the spring of 2002, the discovery of sodium cyanide secreted in a Chicago railway tunnel on March 10, 2002, and the discovery of ricin, a lethal poison derived from castor beans, in London on January 6, 2003, are examples that underscore how contemporary the threat is.

This chapter seeks to provide real tools for evaluating and acting on infrastructure vulnerability. It begins with an examination of what constitutes critical infrastructure and why it poses such an attractive target for terrorists. Next, it deals with the difficulties of deciding what should be protected—specifically, focusing on vulnerability assessments, risk analysis, and professional assessment review. Finally, recommendations are offered for protecting critical infrastructure.

---

5. Jonathan Tucker, ed., *Toxic Terror: Assessing Terrorist Use of Chemical and Biological Weapons* (Cambridge, Mass.: MIT Press, 2000), p. 69.

6. Ibid., p. 150.

7. Tucker, *Toxic Terror*, pp. 55–70.

Elements of Infrastructure Vulnerability

A discussion of vital infrastructure must begin with an analysis of the enormous and diverse range of utilities and resources that are considered to be infrastructure. Roads, rail lines, subways, tunnels, and bridges are key components of the transportation infrastructure. Traditional utilities including water, energy, telecommunications, and sewer systems are also key infrastructures. Traditional utilities deliver critical commodities via pipeline, wire, cable, or conduit. There are many types of utilities, transportation structures, and data systems that are critical to the operation of the nation and, in many respects, to life itself.

Vital infrastructures can be characterized either by physical attributes or by function. Transportation structures, utilities, information technology, communication links, and agricultural and food processing facilities are key components of the infrastructure. Municipal structures; "surname targets" (named stadiums and places of assembly); university, educational, and research facilities; and symbolic structures, some with significant historic importance, are all parts of an infrastructure that is highly concentrated.

Electricity is also among the critical infrastructures vulnerable to attack. Electric outages are common, particularly in regions where storms disrupt the distribution network. A short-term interruption of electricity is an inconvenience but is not generally considered life threatening. A longer-term outage or an outage that is produced by a coordinated attack against key points in the transmission, retransmission, or distribution grid can create cascades across several other critical infrastructures and produce widespread physical and economic consequences.[8]

Indeed, infrastructure is vulnerable on several levels: it can be attacked as a direct target; it can be attacked to create a diversion so that another attack goes longer without detection or response; or it can be attacked as part of a simultaneous attack on a number of targets.

What Complexities Underlie Infrastructure Vulnerability Assessments?

GATHERING, PROCESSING, AND SHARING INFORMATION

Infrastructure managers have had tremendous difficulty finding information about the risks, vulnerabilities, and threats from terrorists. Much of

8. Committee on Science and Technology for Countering Terrorism, National Research Council, *Making the Nation Safer: The Role of Science and Technology in Countering Terrorism* (Washington, D.C.: National Academy Press, 2002), p. 4, <www.nap.edu/books/0309084814/html.>

the spring of 2002 was consumed by questions about what various officials knew—and when—with respect to the 9/11 attacks. While it is not clear whether any particular information could have prevented the attacks, it is clear that more efficient information sharing and alerting systems need to be developed. Some of these systems have recently been developed and are in the process of being deployed. Electronic mail, facsimile, and voicemail networks have arisen within a variety of utilities and industries in the wake of the attacks. These systems typically alert participants to unusual events and threats to specific or related industries.[9]

Managing threat information is made more complicated by the fragmented nature of the utility industry and the lack of a formal warning mechanism from the government.[10] For example, there are 54,065 public and private water utilities in the United States.[11] Many smaller utilities have limited access to information technologies, including the Internet and electronic mail, making comprehensive alerting and warning difficult.

WORKING WITH THE PRIVATE SECTOR

One challenge associated with infrastructure considerations is ownership. Much of the vital infrastructure in the United States is privately owned and operated. Unlike their municipal counterparts, few private sector utility and infrastructure managers have more than limited familiarity with security matters, and fewer still are able to put the terrorist threat in perspective. Even though much of the vital infrastructure is privately owned, most improvements are bid in a public process. Plans, specifications, and engineering drawings are often included in bid packets made available for potential bidders. Prior to the September 11, 2001, attacks, little thought was given to vulnerabilities presented by such practices. Potentially more problematic is the prospect of inadvertent disclosure of security methodology or design during the assessment and upgrade process. Actions as simple as indicating the contents of an envelope or shipping pouch for submission or transmittal could result in theft or disclosures that could yield disastrous consequences.

Many organizations have removed sensitive information from their

---

9. See generally Peter S. Beering et al., "Winning Plays: Essential Guidance From the Terrorism Line of Scrimmage," BCSIA Discussion Paper 2002–6, ESDP Discussion Paper ESDP-2002–02, John F. Kennedy School of Government, Harvard University, February 2002.

10. Office of Homeland Security at <www.whitehouse.gov/homeland>.

11. Brock Meeks, "U.S. Water Supply Vulnerable," MSNBC, January 17, 2002, <www.msnbc.com/news/685645.asp>.

websites such as system diagrams, plant locations, addresses, and telephone numbers and have restricted pre-employment tours, plant access, and contractor activities. Many more have also limited disclosures and require confidentiality agreements prior to sharing sensitive information such as the security systems that are in place and whether or not there have been past breaches in security. Several organizations have pushed for greater protection from these types of disclosure. Newer federal legislation such as the Public Health Security and Bioterrorism Preparedness and Response Act of 2002 (PL107–188) provides penalties for disclosure, but state freedom of information and public records statutes may not have similar provisions and may even require disclosure.

BALANCING PROBABILITIES AND CONSEQUENCES

A third challenge is balancing the huge consequences of an attack with the low probability that any specific site will be targeted. This debate lies close to the heart of vulnerability and security discussions. While the consequences of a significant attack can be catastrophic, the probability of such an event remains low. Balancing consequences means prioritizing different values; for instance, the loss of human life, business and economic disruption, and symbolic meaning are all considerations one faces when making a judgment regarding security. Measuring the probability of a specific target being attacked against these varied consequences is often a difficult task. Based solely on probability analysis, one might conclude that doing nothing is an appropriate response. If there are no attacks and thus, no disasters or catastrophes, then the investment in security may seem unwise and costly. Unfortunately, attacks that are prevented are often unlikely to be known.

Recognizing the Potential Pitfalls of Automation

The increasing use of automation to manage infrastructure raises issues of security. Some computer experts believe that system control technologies represent great vulnerabilities from hackers or employee misconduct. Insertion of false data, data manipulation, tampering, denial of service, and unauthorized monitoring are potential threats to electronic controls. Some systems that rely on wireless and telephone control are potentially susceptible to similar penetrations. Al Qaeda funded many of their activities through electronic stock trading and has transmitted coded messages using steganography, the use of seemingly random dots hidden in pictures that can only be decoded by someone with the decryption key. Terror groups have also employed more traditional forms of computer crimes including theft, fraud, using host systems to attack other systems, and even the Internet itself. The technology, hardware, and software industries have been responsive to security concerns, but systems using these architectures must be frequently updated, monitored, and inspected to prevent unauthorized use.

WHAT IS VULNERABILITY?

Assessing the vulnerability to any given threat is a function of weighing the probability of the threat against the consequences of the threatened action. Given the size and nature of utility infrastructure and the interrelationships and dependencies between utilities, the analysis of consequences becomes one of identifying critical components, hardening or securing those that can be reasonably hardened or secured, and developing response plans for all types of emergencies, including terrorism. Assessing vulnerability is a crucial step toward protecting that which is deemed to be most important; planning responses to events involving structures that are deemed vulnerable; and determining budget and spending priorities. "For a utility, one of the most significant challenges will be to direct its often limited resources to protecting its most important elements. This prioritization must take into account possible threats, probability of attack, consequences of attack, and response capability."[12]

Vulnerability analysis is at once both instructive and ineffectual; instructive because it constitutes an important preliminary step in identifying key elements that must be hardened, duplicated, or secured and ineffectual because of the size, scope, and complexity of the infrastructure. Few targets are as vulnerable to attack as pipes, wires, transformers, or transportation structures that are left unattended, unprotected, and designed, built, or installed with some redundancy but often little security.

The dilemma is one of determining "what next" once the vulnerability is defined. In May 2002, Congress passed legislation that provided funds for water and sewer utility managers to conduct vulnerability assessments.[13] This legislation, which has been heralded as a good "first step" in determining specific vulnerabilities, funds an analysis of facili-

---

12. Committee on Science and Technology for Countering Terrorism, *Making the Nation Safer*, p. 6.

13. Public Health Security and Bioterrorism Preparedness and Response Act of 2002 (PL 107–188) which amended the Safe Drinking Water Act by adding Section 1433 which requires all utilities serving 3,300 people or more to conduct a vulnerability assessment. Large utilities (those serving more than 100,000) must complete these assessments prior to March 31, 2003, medium-sized utilities prior to December 31, 2003, and small utilities prior to June 30, 2004. Once completed, the vulnerability assessments must be submitted to the Environmental Protection Agency or EPA (who must protect the assessments from disclosure). The legislation requires system operators to certify

ties using a matrix originally developed by Sandia National Laboratories to assess risks to the nuclear power industry.[14] The matrix reviews physical security, chemical handling, computer and data security, and personnel procedures. Theoretically, once vulnerabilities are identified, they can then be systematically "hardened" or eliminated. "It becomes a risk management exercise," says Joel Meihle, head of the New York City water system. "You must evaluate the risk from various sources and determine which risk you can live with, and which risk you cannot."[15]

WHAT IS RISK?

Traditionally risk has been defined in insurance terms—events that may lead to damage or destruction that can be quantified, measured, and predicted based on historical data. Insurance shifts risk to the insurer for a fee or premium. It is difficult to rate the risk of terrorist attacks due to the scope and amount of damage that they can create. In the days after the 9/11 attacks, casualty carriers and reinsurance firms were reeling from staggering losses. The attacks left risk managers with dramatic, often draconian choices about continued insurance coverage. David Gadis, a claims manager for an Indianapolis utility, related that, "our insurance premiums for terrorist attacks increased exponentially following September 11 in spite of a stable loss record across more than 100 years of insurance history for our utility."[16] Terrorism changes risk analysis because it is difficult to determine with any actuarial certainty the frequency and scope of attacks.

Terrorism also affects risk analysis by extending the focus of risk management beyond the damage that a more "generic" disaster might cause to an organization's business operations, reputation for safety, political standing, and even its continued existence. The challenge for the operators of vital infrastructure is to examine the total risk picture and

---

to the EPA what changes are made in response to the vulnerability assessments, requires the system operator to update their emergency response plans to incorporate the findings of the assessments, expands the EPA's emergency powers, expands system tampering penalties, and makes it a crime to release vulnerability information.

14. RAM (Risk Assessment Method) is an analysis which prioritizes facilities; assesses threats; characterizes facilities; assesses security system effectiveness; analyzes risk and mitigation methods; updates the facility emergency response plan; and recommends security and facility upgrades and enhancements.

15. Joel Meihle, PE, Commissioner, New York Department of Environmental Protection, Presentation to American Water Works Executives, March 9, 2002.

16. David Gadis, Insurance Claims Manager for an Indianapolis Utility, interviewed by the author, June 24, 2002.

determine if the risk can be managed and, if so, how to accomplish risk management.

With all of these unknowns, the one predictable fact is that failing to prepare for an attack carries not only the risk of casualties but also an extreme political (for appointees and those in positions of responsibility), image (public relations and perceptions), and legal risks for all those responsible for the infrastructure, whether as owners, operators, or even tax- or ratepayers. As Senator Richard G. Lugar of Indiana, co-author of the landmark Nunn-Lugar-Domenici counterterrorism legislation, warned, "We will lose persons in the initial attack, but failure to prepare for these attacks, and failure of people in responsible positions to know what to do, will be indefensible."[17]

Risk Shifting

Unlike legal risk shifting employed in the insurance industry, physical risk shifting is a very real concern for infrastructure operators. Utility operators in rural areas must contend with a risk that has been pushed out geographically from higher-secured urban areas. In an era of satellite television, terrorists need not attack a metropolitan area in order to have an impact on the people of our nation. Attacking a rural target may actually instill more fear by delivering the message that no one is safe. Terrorism can affect any community. Thus, the process of protecting the infrastructure and measuring risk poses two problems—the nearly infinite number of feasible targets and the fact that protecting some sites would simply shift risk to other unprotected areas, negating much or all of the benefit despite significant costs of protection. This displacement effect has many implications. A protective strategy for critical infrastructure should not push risk onto other areas but should raise the "threshold of competence, capability, and inventiveness that terrorists would need to carry out a successful attack" in any area.[18]

How to Assess Infrastructure Vulnerability

WHAT SHOULD BE ASSESSED?
The short answer to this question may be "everything," but such a facile answer leads to potentially overwhelming assignments. A more success-

---

17. Senator Richard Lugar, interview with the author, December 8, 2001.

18. Michael E. O'Hanlon et al., "Protecting the American Homeland: A Preliminary Analysis," Brookings Institution (Washington, D.C.: Brookings Institution Press, 2001), p. 51.

ful approach is to consider vulnerabilities based on the specific organization being assessed. An electrical interruption may be the greatest vulnerability for an enterprise that is totally dependent upon electricity, while an ice storm may be the greatest vulnerability for an electric utility.

Assessments are best managed by dividing them into logical components. Physical facilities; security and business procedures; systemic design and operation; suppliers of goods and services; chemical suppliers; employees; administrative functions and activities; procedures; and data and technology are all categories that may be vulnerable to natural and man-made disasters. The assessment must evaluate what assets or systems exist, and how secure or hardened they are, and determine what systems are in place to deter, detect, delay, or even deny an attacker.

Once the vulnerabilities are identified, a consequence analysis must be performed to determine the potential impact of an attack or incident targeting a particular vulnerability. The most important components of a utility system are often the most vulnerable, and when considering the complexity of generation, storage, or filtration plants, transportation structures, and other key infrastructures, the consequences of even a short interruption can be disastrous. As a result, some organizations build redundancy into their systems. Others develop robust response capabilities.

WHO SHOULD CONDUCT VULNERABILITY ASSESSMENTS?

Many infrastructure managers are not trained, staffed, equipped, or funded to conduct vulnerability assessments. Understanding the risk of a fire, flood, or tornado is relatively easy. Assessing a national security threat is far more complicated. Infrastructure executives must now consider a host of risks that they may not have even previously known existed from actors with whom they are unfamiliar. Many infrastructure providers turn to engineering, security, or consulting firms to conduct or assist with the assessments. Decisions about whom to hire to conduct assessments have often been made based upon which firm has an open purchase order or contract with the hiring jurisdiction or organization. In other cases, infrastructure managers were overwhelmed by the consultants, vendors, and engineering firms that began to market security solutions after the 2001 attacks. It is very important to engage in a vetting process to confirm the credentials, experience, and expertise of security or other professionals.

Once an assessor is selected, the utility manager must consider what to do with the assessment. Axiomatic though it seems, infrastructure managers must exercise common sense in their evaluation of assessments and dire predictions. They must answer such questions as, "Do we really need a fence?" or "Would building a redundancy in the system be a better investment?" For some circumstances, bridges and tunnels for example, such a determination can be made easily, based upon economic factors such as the high cost of building another bridge or tunnel. The dollars equivalent to the fencing of a raw water reservoir are better invested in improved monitoring, filtration, or treatment. Investments in redundancy allow systems to withstand incidents regardless of cause.

WHO SHOULD EVALUATE REVIEWS?

Once an assessment is performed and a report written, its regulatory review, or lack thereof, raises difficult issues. Government regulators prone to political criticism must balance the need to review with the risk that such a review would make the assessment a public document subject to disclosure. Public disclosure could allow adversaries free access to a compiled list of vulnerable places and means to attack. Many regulators are not likely to be versed in security and may be poorly equipped to evaluate the assessments, forcing reliance on additional consultants. "There are specific things one must be trained to look for in evaluating security assessments," relates Richard Hahn, former Federal Bureau of Investigation (FBI) agent and terrorism expert.[19] Some environmental and citizen groups believe that there should be disclosure while most industry leaders and security experts cite a need to prevent adversaries from easily obtaining vulnerability analyses. One solution to this problem is for legislatures to enact statutory exclusions to open records statutes, allowing vulnerability assessments to be confidential, as they have done for some types of intelligence and proprietary information. Some regulatory bodies have opted to have third parties review assessment documents to avoid disclosure problems.

Challenges to Vulnerability Assessment

IS EVERY THREAT CONSIDERED A CREDIBLE THREAT?

Credibility of potential attacks is evaluated by security professionals. Using a combination of analytical tools and intelligence information may determine whether the person or organization making the threat has the technical ability and the behavioral resolve to carry out the attack.[20] Evaluating the various threats to the infrastructure is a far more complicated

---

19. Richard S. Hahn of R.S. Hahn & Associates, Los Angeles, California has assisted the author in the conduct of utility assessments.

20. De Becker, *Fear Less*, p. 76.

undertaking than it first appears. The analyses have many significant challenges, many of which can cause inaccurate conclusions, exacerbate vulnerabilities, or produce a false sense of security, fooling managers into dangerous complacency.

Threats are an integral part of terrorism. "Terrorism is not an ideology or a political doctrine, but rather a method—the substate application of violence or the threat of violence to sow panic."[21] Terrorism is manipulation, and threats are manipulative behavior designed to force unwilling participants to take actions they otherwise would not be disposed to take. Some threats come with warnings issued by the terrorists themselves; some threats have warnings issued by the government. Other threats have no warning but come in the form of leaked information or tips to the media.

One difficulty associated with threat credibility analysis is determining how believable a threat is: threats must be evaluated to determine if they should be ignored or if they merit a response. Threats that are not credible will not elicit the desired response. Prior to the 9/11 attacks, many people believed that a significant terrorist attack in the United States was highly improbable and thus threats were often discarded as non-credible and no remedial actions were triggered. Afterward, the nation began reacting to numerous threats—regardless of credibility—differently. Credibility analysis after the 9/11 attacks has changed dramatically to include threats that might have been considered to be hoaxes or science fiction absent the surprise attacks.

There are myriad possible threats, but possibility is not the same as credibility. It is possible that it will rain regularly in the desert, but it is not probable, nor is it a particularly credible scenario. Credibility analysis hinges on the technical capacity (can they do it?), feasibility (will it work?) and behavioral resolve (are they motivated enough to do it?) of an adversary.

Simplifying Assessments: Math Problems

There are several models for vulnerability assessment; some employ computer analysis evaluating threats in hierarchical fashion and prioritizing based on that evaluation. Other models score risk based on probabilities and consequences and then rank risks as they relate to one another. The inherent limitation with all such risk analyses is that their

---

21.   Walter Laqueur, "Left, Right and Beyond The Changing Face of Terror," in James F. Hodge and Gideon Rose, eds., *How Did This Happen? Terrorism and the New War* (New York: Public Affairs Press, 2002), p. 71.

underlying assumptions may lull managers into a false sense of security. Contemporary terrorists do not "play by the rules"; they are smart, ruthlessly creative, and savvy in their selection of targets and tactics. This makes mathematical prediction difficult, if not impossible.

Mathematic analyses rely on the use of statistical data collected over periods of time. Generally, the larger the data set, the more accurate the predictive ability. Many naturally occurring phenomena such as weather patterns lend themselves to trending; vulnerability to a specific weather threat can be loosely determined by examining incidence of weather events over the course of the statistical sample. Data from the past can be used to make predictions and forecasts about future weather.

Applying this model to terrorism is difficult. Although terrorism has existed for centuries, its incidence is statistically not patterned. Terrorists deliberately change their activities to thwart pattern creation and thereby limit their own vulnerability to capture. These behaviors make statistical interpretation of terrorist incidents difficult and prediction very difficult or impossible. Furthermore, terrorists who are unconcerned with their own safety or escape—for example suicide terrorists—add additional challenges to mathematical modeling because they have more freedom to change the timing, method, and even the target.

The most important recommendation for improving security is to make preparedness part of the organizational culture. Many organizations have named a senior executive as the chief preparedness officer, the person who will manage and coordinate preparedness efforts. Infrastructure security can be improved once vulnerability assessments are conducted and security shortcomings are revealed. Prudent management of important assets, facilities, and infrastructure includes assessment of vulnerabilities, policy review, countermeasure development, response planning, budgeting for improvements, and training.

Managers should develop response plans for all types of emergencies. They should build responsive systems to address routine threats that can flex to address the extraordinary. They should establish relationships with those persons, agencies, and organizations that may be called to assist in times of difficulty. Infrastructure managers should be aware of new threats (which may use existing systems) against possible targets and should then develop appropriate countermeasures. They should share information about specific threats across disciplines and departments. Infrastructure managers should also limit discussions about vulnerability and catastrophic events with the media to prevent the seeding of ideas and to maintain public confidence in the infrastructure.

Policies and procedures should also be reviewed with an eye toward the new security imperative. Deliveries should be restricted to finite hours from branded delivery services, known contractors, vendors, and shippers. Drivers should be identified, and sensitive shipments should employ some form of "pre-approval" process that verifies driver identity. Mail, packages, and deliveries should be carefully screened. Mail handlers should be trained in proper screening and handling of suspect mail and parcels. Environmental testing should be conducted regularly at potential target sites. Both untreated and treated water supplies should be tested frequently for contamination.

Facilities should be protected using the security systems and measures that are already in place (locking the doors and gates that already exist costs nothing). Public access to plants, facilities, and administrative offices should be limited to prevent unauthorized activities. Websites should be reviewed to ensure that adversaries are not able to access information that could be used to support an attack. Facilities, distribution systems, and grids should be regularly inspected and patrolled. Surveillance and alarm systems should be installed and utilized.

Employees and contractors should be subject to regular background, driving record, and criminal history checks and immigration checks when appropriate. All employees, contractors, and visitors should be required to wear photo identification at all times. Employees should be encouraged to participate in trade organization and government sponsored security programs. Executives responsible for vital infrastructure should encourage government and industry sponsored research supporting various security initiatives including chemical, biological, and radiological methods of attacking the infrastructure. Call center personnel should be trained in threat management, including information-gathering techniques. Infrastructure customers and the public should be educated about what activities are unusual, and they should be provided with easy ways to notify police or utility officials about suspicious activity. Infrastructure managers must also maintain relationships with the news media. Training must be provided for utility personnel in how to deal with the media. Training must also be provided to the media about the specific threats facing the infrastructure and the limits on those threats. There should also always be a television tuned to one of the cable news networks and the local media as means of warning the organization about developing events and emergencies.

Planning and Response

The U.S. capacity to respond well in times of difficulty has been proven repeatedly. The attacks on 9/11 have stimulated emergency and contingency planning. Relationships are being forged with those who will be called upon in times of difficulty; politicians and managers are building systems to respond to routine events that also have the capacity to address extraordinary situations. Emergency response planning is critically important to successful responses to all types of emergencies. In many cases, particularly where vulnerability is difficult to mitigate, a vigorous emergency response may be the best investment of resources.[22]

Funding Necessary Improvements

It is tempting for budget-strapped infrastructure operators to wrap necessary improvements to their systems, networks, and structures in a counterterror blanket capitalizing on fear to obtain funding that political systems are often unwilling to provide without such urgency. Infrastructure decay is a significant problem that must be addressed regardless of a terrorist threat. Infrastructure investment is difficult largely due to its unseen nature. Indianapolis Mayor Bart Petersen explains, "People don't get excited about things that are buried, that they don't see, no matter how important they may be to their lives. Much of our vital infrastructure is crumbling beneath our feet and it is difficult to get enough money in the budget to fund repairs or replacement. Without some crisis, taxpayers want more police officers instead of more pipes."[23] System improvements can be funded through direct federal or state funds, as is the case with Environmental Protection Agency (EPA) funded assessments, via revolving fund loans, from utility ratepayers, or from the tax base.

Physical Security

Physical security seeks to deter attacks before they happen, deny an attacker access to a target, detect intrusion, delay the attacker to increase chances of interception, and disable the attacker. Whether trying to secure a water plant, a conduit, or a telephone wire, the basic principles of physical security apply. The dilemma facing the infrastructure manager is that a security system is often designed to deter vandals and other amateurs, not trained adversaries or suicide bombers.

Securing infrastructure is a complicated exercise. Physical security is more of an engineering exercise than a police function. It is expensive to renovate or build structures that are able to thwart or withstand attack. Complicating the engineering analysis is the wide array of types of po-

---

22. See Beering et al., "Winning Plays."

23. Indianapolis Mayor Bart Petersen, interviewed by the author, June 26, 2002.

tential attacks. Those responsible for the infrastructure must study past attack methods and employ solutions to address both past methods and means of attack that are most likely to be employed in the future. Explosives, chemicals, biological agents, nuclear weapons, and suicide-bombing techniques must now join the already lengthy list of "natural" catastrophes like fires, floods, and various weather events for which utilities must be prepared.

It is prohibitively expensive to secure anything with guards. Although guards can be deployed quickly, maintaining their vigilance is a very difficult proposition. Moreover, removing guards once the threat is believed to have passed can prove difficult politically or practically. Guards are predictable and can easily be monitored, overpowered, or even killed. Short term, high risk events are completely appropriate assignments for properly trained and equipped guards, but long term assignments should employ engineered security solutions such as hardening, barriers, alarms, and surveillance systems.

For most utilities, security will come from combinations of traditional security elements, awareness of security vulnerabilities, development of and adherence to security procedures, surveillance of critical sites and equipment, hardening selected sites, installation of barriers to prevent intrusion, and masking of selected equipment.[24]

Educating the Public

Educating the public about what to report, when to report, and how to report suspicious or unusual activity is a key tool in promoting security. Richard Reid, the shoe-bomber who attempted to light a plastic explosive on a trans-Atlantic flight on December 22, 2001, was first noticed and thwarted by a flight attendant onboard, then subdued by passengers and crew. Theodore Kazcynski, the Unabomber, was turned in by his brother after he had read Kazcynski's manuscripts that were published in the newspaper. Elected and appointed officials from the President of the United States to the beat patrolman have encouraged the nation to be on "high alert" and to be vigilant. This methodology has been repeatedly proven effective by neighborhood crime watch programs across the nation.

9/11 ignited a major response within the United States regarding its internal security. The attacks were a "call to action." America faces threats from highly motivated and technically sophisticated adversaries. Ameri-

---

24. Committee on Science and Technology for Countering Terrorism, *Making the Nation Safer,* p. 6.

cans must assess their infrastructures, determine and prioritize their vulnerabilities, develop countermeasures, revise their response plans, and build relationships with those whom can be called upon to help in times of trouble. Developing response systems and plans that can address the "mundane" threats but that can also flex to deal effectively with the "spectacular" are crucial.

The United States must take action quickly. Some have waited for guidance and assistance from federal or state governments that may not come for years, if at all. Although assistance will always flow freely after an attack, prudence and judgment require action now. Our adversaries will not wait for deliberation and appropriation processes. Great trust has been placed in the hands of those responsible for the vital infrastructure and that trust requires proactive, thoughtful measures to ensure its protection.

Chapter 3

In Defense of the Law

Juliette N. Kayyem

When the United States began bombing in Afghanistan in the fall of 2001, the Bush administration had effectively decided that military action would be the dominant way to respond to the September 11, 2001, attacks on the World Trade Center and the Pentagon. The turn to military action generated relatively little debate and, indeed, was not surprising given the severity of the attacks. Nevertheless, the use of military force signaled a major shift in U.S. counterterrorism policy. Before 9/11, the United States fought terrorism primarily by arresting perpetrators and trying them in an U.S. courtroom after the fact. Since 9/11, law enforcement has given way to military power and the lawyers have been superseded by the generals—along the way, the values of war are transforming U.S. law.

This shift has generated a relatively predictable debate—whether the fight against terrorism has shunted aside a hallmark of U.S. law: the protection of individual rights. During the debates of the comprehensive counterterrorism law, the U.S.A. Patriot Act, critics were concerned that in rush to pass the legislation, too much authority was being offered to the government with too few checks.[1] With an emphasis on "prevent first, prosecute second," the government has attempted to explain away criticism leveled at the Department of Justice's (DOJ) new antiterrorism measures.[2] Critics of the administration's policies—which include lengthy detentions, increased surveillance, and the potential use of military tribunals against suspected terrorist leaders—have questioned the

---

1. Public Law 107–56, 107th Cong., 1st sess., October 26, 2001.

2. Karen Branch-Brioso, "Ashcroft orders redesign of FBI; Reorganization reflects hard focus on terrorism," *St. Louis Post-Dispatch*, November 9, 2001, p. A1.

very premise of pitting liberty against security.[3] After all, it has not been proven that some of the more aggressive legal measures that the Bush administration has utilized thus far in the war on terrorism, including increased surveillance or tougher immigration standards, would have resulted in the capture of those responsible for 9/11, as most after action reports suggest that it was the failure of our agencies to actually share information with one another that may have been the cause of the intelligence failure.

This debate, though significant, overshadows a far greater and more long-term danger emerging from the U.S. war against terrorism. While the limitations of countering terrorism through law enforcement were made abundantly clear on 9/11, the U.S. failure to utilize existing laws successfully had less to do with the laws, per se, and more to do with the nation's lack of attention and resources devoted to fighting terrorism prior to 9/11. Unfortunately, there has been, since 9/11, a strategic abandonment of lawyering as one of many tools to counter the emerging threat. Ironically, it is the Justice Department that has promoted this abandonment.

Before 9/11, various government agencies—the Departments of Defense, Justice, and State and the Central Intelligence Agency (CIA)—worked, sometimes cooperatively and at other times competitively, to counter the terrorist threat. Where there was agreement, it was that terrorism was a problem, but not one that should consume the government's agenda. Since 9/11, the Bush administration has made legal, diplomatic, and intelligence interests somewhat subservient to the military efforts as the military campaign initially took precedence over any other tool to disrupt terrorist cells and, though unsuccessful, capture Osama bin Laden. What this has meant for law enforcement is that it has been subordinate to the military role, almost a sideshow. As the war on terrorism continues, however, it will look less like the bombings in Afghanistan and more like a series of international police actions. If the government fails to recognize the import of the law enforcement role, we will lose support and ultimate victory in the efforts against terrorism.

An understanding of U.S. historical campaigns against terrorism is essential to ensure that law takes equal footing with war. For decades after World War II, the United States had no significant counterterrorism policy because Americans had not been, by and large, the target of terrorist attacks. That changed on December 21, 1988, with the explosion of Pan

---

3. David Cole, Testimony Before the Subcommittee on the Constitution, Federalism, and Property Rights of the Senate Judiciary Committee, October 3, 2001, at <www.cdt.org/security/011003cole.pdf>.

Am Flight 103 over Lockerbie, Scotland, that killed 189 Americans.[4] In the wake of the Pan Am bombing, the U.S. government devised four guiding counterterrorism principles: strike no deals with terrorists, bring terrorists to justice for their crimes, isolate and pressure terrorist-sponsoring states; and bolster the counterterrorism capabilities of countries that cooperate with the United States.[5]

With the growing recognition that terrorism was a threat, the government permitted 46 federal departments or agencies to have some jurisdiction over countering the threat or responding in the event of a terrorism incident. This number, however, is misleading. Four actually dominated: Defense, Justice, State, and the CIA—the soldiers, lawyers, diplomats, and spies. The lawyers were an integral part of the effort. In 1984, Congress had given the Federal Bureau of Investigation (FBI) authority to operate overseas to investigate cases involving Americans. Again, in the 1990s, the FBI for the first time set up permanent Legal Attache offices abroad to assist foreign nations investigating international crime. By 1999, Legal Attache offices existed in 35 countries, including Israel, Jordan, Russia, and South Africa.[6]

This legal approach to countering terrorism served U.S. interests for three reasons. First, it allowed the government to fight terrorism without interfering too much with other U.S. diplomatic or strategic goals. Lawyers can be annoying, but they are not often threatening. Thus, after the 2000 bombing of the USS Cole, the FBI could begin an investigation (much to the chagrin of the government of Yemen), but a U.S.-led investigation there never threatened our relationship with Yemen, a country in an oil-rich area. When the U.S. investigators began to question Yemen's cooperation, as the Yemeni officials made access to sites and witnesses more difficult, the U.S. Ambassador simply barred the FBI's top investigator from returning to Aden, a port city in Yemen.[7] By contrast, military force could prove to be more unwieldy, sometimes inaccurate, and certainly not an option in allied countries. When President Clinton ordered

---

4. "Lockerbie bombing suspects arraigned in Netherlands," CNN, April 6, 1999, at <www.cnn.com/WORLD/Europe/9904/06/lockerbie.suspects/>.

5. Report from the National Commission on Terrorism, *Countering the Changing Threat of International Terrorism*, June 7, 2000, p. 17.

6. 30 Years of Terrorism: A Special Retrospective Edition, "Terrorism in the United States 1999," U.S. Department of Justice, FBI, 1999, p. 43 at <www.fbi.gov/publications/terror/terror99.pdf>.

7. Alan Sipress, "FBI Agents' Return to Yemen Mission at Issue: State Department Says U.S. Ambassador Willing to Allow Bombing Probe to Resume," *Washington Post*, July 7, 2001, p. A07.

cruise missile attacks against alleged terrorist sites in Afghanistan and Sudan in response to the 1998 U.S. embassy bombings in Kenya and Tanzania, other countries condemned the mission for being either inaccurate (the bombs likely hit the wrong targets) or unjustified (neither the Afghan nor Sudanese government was accused of sponsoring the attacks).[8]

Second, seeking to punish individuals rather than states or their leaders allowed the United States to promote the values of fair criminal justice and to send the message that terrorists were criminals, not powerful belligerents or, worse, martyrs. Even those who despised the United States got defense lawyers and a trial in civilian court with all of the U.S. Constitution's procedural guarantees. At the same time, U.S. courts had a perfect conviction rate, giving life sentences to terrorists involved in the 1993 World Trade Center bombing and the African embassy bombings.[9] International tribunals, however, were not so successful; for example, in the Pan Am 103 trial held in the Netherlands, one of two Libyan intelligence agents accused of planning and aiding in the terrorist attacks was acquitted.

Third, and most significantly, the soldiers, lawyers, diplomats, and spies complimented each other to wage an overall effort against terrorism, a phenomenon somewhat lacking in today's war efforts. Looking back to before 9/11, no agency had an "overriding impetus" to focus on terrorism, and the docket suffered from "rival conceptions of the national interest."[10] These rival conceptions were a natural product of a new terrorist threat. The enemy, in this case, was different, and it was known then, as it should be known now, that military action is just one of several ways to fight terrorists.

Today, lawyers, diplomats, and spies—along with financial investigators and nation builders—are taking part in a war led by soldiers. Once bombs replaced indictments abroad, it was easy to see how some might have considered constitutional restraints to be less relevant in the fight against terrorism. At the same time, it seemed logical that law enforcement agencies would enjoy expanded powers at home. So it was no surprise that, in October 2001, President George W. Bush signed a comprehensive counterterrorism law, the U.S.A. Patriot Act, which reads like a

---

8. Bryon York, "Clinton Has No Clothes," *National Review*, December 17, 2001, at <www.nationalreview.com/york/york-issue112901.shtml>.

9. Bill Keller, "Trials and Tribulations," *New York Times*, December 15, 2001, p. A31.

10. Barton Gellman, "Terrorism Wasn't a Top Priority," *Washington Post National Weekly Edition*, January 14–20, 2002, p. 10.

wish list of the DOJ and the FBI with increased surveillance, longer detentions, and greater wiretapping powers. "This government," Bush said, "will enforce this law with all the urgency of a nation at war."[11] War also has justified the holding of close to 2,000 detainees without disclosing their names or the reasons for their detainment, the questioning of thousands of Arab-American and Muslim nationals, the listening in on conversations between suspects and their attorneys, and the signing of a presidential order allowing the establishment of secret military tribunals for those accused of terrorism.

Domestically, then, lawyers have simply been enlisted in the military cause. In November 2001, Attorney General John Ashcroft announced a "wartime reorganization" of the Justice Department. "We cannot do everything we once did because lives now depend on us doing a few things very well," Ashcroft said as justification for cutting $2.5 billion from law enforcement programs not focused on counterterrorism.[12] Potential infringements on individual rights have become the equivalent of collateral damage during combat. "We must not let foreign enemies use the forums of liberty to destroy liberty itself," President Bush said at a speech before the U.S. Attorneys explaining his decision to detain hundreds of immigrants without disclosing their identities.[13]

It is, of course, understandable that after 9/11, war talk would dominate government discourse. What is less understandable is the extent to which the Justice Department has contributed to its own demise, joining the Bush administration's "war" philosophy without so much as a critique, much to the surprise of other government entities that recognize that the long-term costs of promoting the misleading theory that relying primarily on law enforcement to fight terrorism was what had led to U.S. vulnerability. In the struggles that exist within government, as various agencies seek agenda support from the White House, the DOJ has found itself in the odd position of being reminded by other agencies about what good law enforcement—and good counterterrorism—actually are. For example, the administration's plan to interview more than 5,000 Arab immigrants sparked an outcry from civil libertarians and immigration lawyers who said that the interviews would be used as an excuse to sweep

---

11. "Bush Comments on Signing New Antiterrorism Law," *Washington File,* U.S. Department of State, October 26, 2001, at <www.usinfo.state.gov/topical/pol/terror/01102600.htm>.

12. Branch-Brioso, "Ashcroft orders redesign of FBI; Reorganization reflects hard focus on terrorism," p. A1.

13. James Gerstenzang, "Response to Terror; Military Tribunals: Bush Defends War Tribunals as Necessary," *Los Angeles Times,* November 30, 2001, p. A1.

Arab communities for potentially criminal but not terrorism-related conduct. They need not fear, however, as the interviews have been wholly unsuccessful. It was state police and former law enforcement officials around the country who reminded the DOJ that rounding up Arabs was simply bad law enforcement. "It's the Perry Mason school of law enforcement, where you get them in there and they confess. . . . It is ridiculous," said Kenneth Walton, the creator of the FBI's first Joint Terrorism Task Force in New York.[14]

Similarly, it was the Department of Defense (DOD) that forced the DOJ to backtrack from the broad terms of the administration's original order creating military courts, simply because the proposal threatened U.S. efforts to hold together a broad based international coalition against terrorism. This was best evidenced by Spain's reluctance to extradite al Qaeda members who could be tried without full and fair due process.[15] Eventually, the DOD regulations, amending the original DOJ-written order that limited the right of appeal and procedural protections, designated a process that more closely resembles (but not perfectly) the military courts in which U.S. soldiers are tried.[16]

In this same regard, it was the Department of State that ultimately convinced the Bush administration to ignore the Justice Department's advice that the prisoners being held at Guantanamo Bay should not be treated as "prisoners of war" and therefore not subject to all protections of the Geneva Conventions. Press reports suggest it was the State Department's concern that U.S. and allied soldiers would be subject to similar amendments to international agreements that ultimately caused the Attorney General to defer.[17]

Indeed, with minor exceptions, the law in place before 9/11 was perfectly adequate for U.S. security, and the post-9/11 legal activity has come up remarkably short. In the United States, the only 9/11-related suspect in custody, Zacarias Moussaoui, was caught in August 2001 on immigration violations and detained under then existing law. The civilian courts that sentenced the 1993 World Trade Center and U.S. embassy

---

14. Frank Rich, "Confessions of a Traitor," *New York Times,* December 8, 2001, p. A23.

15. White House Press Release, "President Issues Military Order: Detention, Treatment, and Trial of Certain Non-Citizens in the War Against Terrorism," November 13, 2001; "Ashcroft defends use of military tribunals to try terrorists," CNN, November 21, 2001, at <www.cnn.com/2001/LAW/11/20/ashcroft.terrorism/>.

16. Aryeh Neier, "The Military Tribunals on Trial," *New York Review of Books,* February 14, 2002, pp. 11–14.

17. "Rumsfeld, Senators: Detainees Treated Well," CNN, January 28, 2002, at <www.cnn.com/2002/WORLD/americas/01/27/rumsfeld.guantanamo/>.

bombers were empowered to hear classified information and to sentence the convicted defendants to death. Even the pressing need for military tribunals now seems suspect, as not a single person has been put before them, and the administration is at pains to find a legal theory that would convict the men now being held at Guantanamo Bay.[18] The government, indeed, has even started to release some of the detainees, recognizing that in the confusion of the Afghan war, many were captured that may have had little to do with the Taliban, let alone terrorism. While there have been a few post-9/11 arrests—of alleged terrorist cells in Buffalo and elsewhere—the strength of the evidence against the groups is still subject to some debate. Compared with the nearly three dozen arrests by the Europeans in their terrorism-related investigations, the United States is far behind.

Preventing terrorism does not simply require more surveillance or fewer restrictions on law enforcement. Terrorists, whether those who struck on 9/11 or Timothy McVeigh, the mastermind of the Oklahoma City bombing, tend to stay within the bounds of the law in the days, and even years, before they strike. This is, of course, a challenge, but not one that is cured by being impervious to legal restrictions. War is noisy and chaotic; hunting down terrorists will require more precision. Thus, transforming laws into weapons of war many not serve the long-term mission of making the United States safer from terrorism. "The qualities needed in a serious campaign against terrorists—secrecy, intelligence, political sagacity, quiet ruthlessness, covert actions that remain covert, above all infinite patience—all these are . . . overridden in a . . . frenzy for immediate results," writes Michael Howard, professor of the history of war at Oxford University.[19]

If the increased powers that DOJ has sought or invoked were actually doing something to counter terrorism, then there would be a legitimate debate about the proper balance of liberty versus security. Why the DOJ has given up on its historic role as law enforcer is somewhat puzzling; it may be the politics of those now serving as the chief lawyers or the politics of trying to appear effective (under tremendous pressure) since 9/11. The point is, however, that lawyers are most effective in the war against terrorism when they do what they are trained to do: painstaking, private investigation. The more they stray from that role, the more they threaten their own effectiveness and undermine overall strategy against terrorism

---

18. "Winging it at Guantanamo," *New York Times Editorial*, April 23, 2002, p. A28.

19. Michael Howard, "What's in a Name?: How to Fight Terrorism," *Foreign Affairs* (January/February 2002), p. 9.

(the cooperation of European, African, and moderate Arab allies is essential, and is undermined by some of DOJ's efforts).[20] Law enforcement is not war; it requires such things as better communication with local and state law enforcement, analysis of surveillance, patient waiting, and, ultimately, the goodwill of other nations who are essential partners in these efforts. It was the Jordanians, after all, who discovered terrorists plotting attacks during the celebrations of the new millennium. The United States undermines both its internal efforts and international efforts when it strays from solid, historic practices of countering terror.

The soldier-lawyer-diplomat-spy model involved a series of checks and balances not unlike those between the three branches of the federal government. Relations between them have not always been smooth. None of them viewed terrorism as the grave, difficult-to-combat reality that it turned out to be on 9/11. Tension existed because there was not, nor is there now, a perfect strategy to stop terrorism. To prevent terror takes more than smoking out terrorists with U.S. force. A broad coalition of nations, rigorous diplomacy, an effective intelligence agency, political determination, better domestic preparedness, vigorous law enforcement, and a greater effort to understand the root causes of terrorism will together provide better security.

There is no particular necessity to pose the rule of law as inconsistent with military strikes. When the United States finds that military action is no longer the best solution to ending the terrorist threat, then other responses will need to come forward, and painstaking, not belligerent, lawyering will find its place again: equal, different, and often successful.

---

20.   Charles W. Corey, "U.S.-African Law Enforcement Cooperation Praised: First suspect in embassy bombings arrested," USIS at <www.usinfo.state.gov/regional/af/usafr/e8082701.htm>.

Chapter 4

Turning a Popular War into a Populist War: Preparing the American Public for Terrorism

Clarence Harmon

The horrific events of September 11, 2001, and the subsequent deaths from anthrax-contaminated mail have left an indelible mark upon the U.S. psyche. Americans are fearful, angry, and committed to bringing to justice the perpetrators of the terrorist attacks, especially members of the al Qaeda terrorist organization. Thus far, government efforts have focused on identifying, locating, and apprehending suspected terrorists; strengthening borders; funding security planning and first responder training at the state and local levels; protecting critical infrastructure; prosecuting the war against al Qaeda; and gathering intelligence worldwide in support of all these efforts. What has not yet happened, or at least has not been publicly discussed at any length, is the creation of a comprehensive, *localized* program that seeks to engage one of the nation's most valuable counterterrorism resources—the American people.

The federal government's rapid response to 9/11 reassured many Americans that the government could respond effectively in a crisis. President George W. Bush's initial creation of the Office of Homeland Security and his appointment of former Pennsylvania Governor Thomas Ridge as its head further helped to allay people's concerns. Increasingly, however, local officials are beginning to ask: how can public officials prepare states, cities, and neighborhoods against another attack? Despite the president's pledge to support local efforts through planning and funding, this question implicitly recognizes the limitations of the federal government's ability to protect Americans from weapons of mass destruction.

One recent federal effort to engage private citizens in homeland security is the creation of the Citizen Corps, a volunteer-based program with a budget of $230 million for fiscal year 2003. The primary intent of the

Citizen Corps is to involve Americans in community safety, emergency preparation, and emergency response activities. Since the program was launched, more than 53,000 Americans have signed up as volunteers. Its five national programs—Community Emergency Response Team Training, Medical Reserve Corps, Neighborhood Watch, Operation TIPS (Terrorism Information and Prevention System), and Volunteers in Police Service—may be utilized at the local level by Citizen Corps Councils. Citizen Corps attracts a diverse volunteer base, from health professionals to local government officials to community members. Currently, all state and territorial governors have appointed a Citizen Corps point of contact, and all states and territories will be receiving grants from the Federal Emergency Management Agency (FEMA) to support the development of local Citizen Corps activities.

Although the federal government has worked on engaging the public in preventing attacks through volunteer opportunities, Americans need a program that is built at the local level and prepares all citizens—through education, training, and the provision of resources—for a terrorist attack. In short, what is needed is not just an opportunity for citizens to volunteer in prevention efforts but an initiative like the civil defense program involving all community members.

This chapter begins by outlining civil defense programs from 1947 to the present. It then turns to a discussion about why a program of citizen mobilization based on the civil defense model is perhaps best suited to meet the biological weapons threat. Finally, it draws conclusions on how to adapt a civil defense model to meet the threat of biological weapons and offers recommendations to implement citizen participation programs at the local level.

U.S. Civil Defense Programs

The Civil Defense Program is more than 50 years old. Over the years since its inception, there has been steady erosion in the program as threats—primarily from the communist world—seemed to ease. This has occurred despite the fact that presidents, political advisors, and members of Congress have repeatedly recognized the need to reorganize civil defense policy and to support those reorganizations with funding, and, still, little has been done. The United States is now in a dangerous situation where threats against the nation are increasing while large gaps remain in its homeland defense strategy.

The concept of civil defense was first developed in the late 1940s. It comprised an extensive system aimed primarily at involving local communities in efforts, down to the neighborhood level, to plan for self-protection and survival in the event of nuclear war. The program was motivated by the fear that the Soviet Union might attack the United States with nuclear, biological, or chemical weapons. Mayors, local legislators, and other appointed and elected officials played major roles in the establishment and implementation of this system.

The stage for a civil defense program was set several years before President Harry Truman initiated the program. After the Japanese attacked Pearl Harbor on December 7, 1941, President Franklin D. Roosevelt called upon the nation to unite in winning the war. The president's call was answered by people across the country. Young women and men joined the armed forces. Others took jobs in the defense industry—in factories manufacturing airplanes, bombs, tanks, ships, and other military hardware. American resolve was further evidenced by a willingness to do without milk, meat, and fresh produce; luxury items were rationed. Citizen action gave a tremendous amount of support to the war effort.

President Truman, in establishing the first Civil Defense Program in 1949, recognized the potential of having Americans assist in protecting the nation. The federal government's initial effort in the program was to ensure the safety and ability of the people to survive an attack using nuclear, biological, or chemical bombs or agents. Civil defense sought specifically to achieve three goals: protect the population, protect industry, and improve post-attack life. Protecting the populace received greatest priority.[1]

Population protection entailed adequate warning, shelter, supplies, life-support equipment, instruction, public health measures, and provision for rescue operations.[2] Early civil defense programs organized units as small as single blocks, under the guidance of the Office of Defense Mobilization, and later, under the Federal Civil Defense Administration, created by President Truman in January 1951. Included among the "essential survival items" necessary for surviving a biological attack were blood-collecting and dispensing supplies, vaccines, antitoxins, medical instruments, and medical supplies.[3]

The first iteration of the Civil Defense Program provided guidance, training, coordination and technical assistance, and matching grants to procure supplies and equipment. Most importantly, it established a na-

---

1. The Office of Technology Assessment, "Civil Defense," in *The Effects of Nuclear War* (Washington, D.C.: Office of Technology Assessment, 1979) at <www.wws.princeton.edu/~ota/disk3/1979/7906_n.html>

2. Ibid.

3. "Essential Survival Items," Office of Civil Defense and Defense Mobilization, Appendix One (NP-35–1), February 1960.

tionwide shelter system.[4] The Federal Civil Defense Act of 1950 inaugurated the plans and federal funding for states and localities for these programs.

Attempts to institutionalize citizen participation were formalized in the early 1950s. A government publication released in 1951 outlined some of the concerns that drove the formation of the earliest civil defense efforts:

1. The enemy can produce a variety of effective biological weapons and chemical weapons and can deliver them against the civilian population and agricultural and water resources of the U.S. by a number of means, overt or covert.

2. Individuals are responsible for learning the techniques necessary to minimize the casualty-producing effects of biological and chemical weapons, such as training programs and information that are made available to them.

Another section of this same publication continued the theme of personal responsibility by urging individuals to buy their own protective equipment, such as masks and protective clothing. The report also stressed the importance of establishing procedures and providing supplies for mass citizen immunization.[5]

Civil Defense Programs were able to mobilize public support. For example, in locally based organizations, Americans volunteered to serve as Civil Defense block wardens and members of the Civilian Air Patrol. Yet from the beginning, there were difficulties such as disagreement over which branch and level of government should be responsible for civil defense. The program also suffered from weak leadership during this period, which persisted into the Eisenhower administration. Poor leadership, coupled with frequent policy changes, undermined the program. Competing defense priorities also diverted valuable resources and attention away from civil defense. Meanwhile, U.S. intelligence agencies learned that the Soviet Union was also engaged in a massive civil defense effort. Domestically, national policy continued to reflect an interest in civil defense, although funding did not match this expressed concern.

Civil defense received its greatest support during the Kennedy administration. During this period, President John F. Kennedy pledged a

---

4. "The National Plan for Civil Defense and Defense Mobilization, Annex, Number 24," Office of Defense and Defense Mobilization, October 1959.

5. "U.S. Civil Defense—The Warden Service," Federal Civil Defense Administration, August 1951.

"new start on Civil Defense" and requested congressional funding "to identify and mark space in existing structures public and private that could be used as fallout shelters in case of attack; to stock those shelters with food, water, first-aid kits, and other minimum essentials for survival; to increase their capacity; to improve our air-raid warning and fallout detection systems, including a new household warning system . . . and to take other measures that will be effective at an early date to save millions of lives if needed."[6]

The Johnson administration focused on antiballistic missiles and mutually assured destruction at the expense of civil defense. President Richard Nixon professed an interest in civil defense, but budget requests reached an all-time low during his administration. The "dual-use" policy—combining attack planning with disaster planning—was implemented during this time, and federal funding was allocated to state and local agencies.

Crisis planning, including evacuation and relocation, characterized the Ford administration. Under the Carter administration, the Defense Civil Preparedness Agency became a part of the newly established Federal Emergency Management Agency (FEMA) in 1979. President Ronald Reagan's civil defense budget request explicitly authorized the use of civil defense funds for peacetime disasters for the first time in U.S. history.[7]

Under President George H.W. Bush, new emphasis was given to FEMA's role in dealing with natural disasters, reducing the civil defense mission. This occurred despite evidence collected during the first Gulf War that Iraq, under President Saddam Hussein, had developed biological weapons.

President William Clinton gave strong verbal support to FEMA's civil defense role during the early days of his first administration (1992–1996). The Senate Armed Services Committee determined after a review of military intelligence data that the United States needed to remain vigilant against the increased threat posed by Iran, Iraq, and North Korea. Their findings emphasized the roles of the Departments of Defense and Justice, especially the Federal Bureau of Investigation (FBI), in counterterrorism efforts. This focus, however, had the unintended effect of further deemphasizing FEMA's civil defense role.

---

6. President Kennedy, Speech on the Berlin Crisis, July 25, 1961, at <http://www.cnn.com/SPECIALS/cold.war/episodes/09/documents/kennedy/>

7. The Integrated Emergency Management System (IEMS) was a response to those criticisms. B.W. Blanchard, "American Civil Defense, 1945–1984: The Evolution of Programs and Policies," FEMA Monograph Series, Vol. 2, No. 2 (1985).

Since the George W. Bush administration has had to contend with terrorism on a larger and more immediate scale than any of its predecessors, the focus on homeland security has now intensified. Under the President's 2003 Budget, $37.7 billion will be dedicated to homeland security, an increase of $19.5 billion from 2002.[8] Of this amount, the Office of Homeland Security will distribute $1.1 billion to states (and $5.9 billion, overall, for defense against biological weapons) to strengthen their capacity to respond to biological terrorism and other public health emergencies resulting from terrorism.[9] Like previous civil defense programs, this policy initiative provides funds for planning, equipment, training, and exercises to improve response capabilities. It does not address the growing national need for a program that seeks to ensure that a vast number of Americans can survive a biological attack.

THE THREAT OF BIOLOGICAL WEAPONS

Perhaps the threat for which civil defense is best suited today is biological terrorism. Biological weapons are at the forefront of the list of weapons that experts fear may be used against the United States.

Biological weapons typically have a very high casualty-to-quantity ratio. As little as 30 kilograms of anthrax spores with a density of 0.1 milligram per cubic meter in an area of ten square kilometers could kill between 30,000–100,000 people, depending on the population density and method of dispersal used to distribute the biological agent. The anthrax letter attacks perpetrated in the fall of 2001 indicated that a smaller concentration of spores than previously thought could be fatal to humans. Indeed, it appears that cross-contaminated mail containing as few as 10–100 spores caused the death of Ottilie Lundgren, a 94-year-old woman from Oxford, Connecticut.[10]

The casualty-to-quantity ratio described above is clearly greater than that which can be achieved with other classes of weapons of mass destruction. Nuclear weapons, for example, have the potential to inflict very high casualties, but they are bulky and difficult to build and detonate. It is estimated that one 12.5 kiloton nuclear device achieving five pounds per cubic inch of over-pressure in an area of 7.8 square kilometers could cause up to 80,000 deaths. A third class of weapons of mass de-

---

8.   White House Report, "Securing the Homeland, Strengthening the Nation," p. 7, at <www.whitehouse.gov/homeland/homeland_security_book.html>.

9.   As of November 2002, only two of the thirteen appropriations bills for fiscal year 2003 have been completed.

10.   Guy Gugliotta, "Study: Anthrax Tainted Up to 5,000 Letters; Cross-Contamination Blamed for the Deaths of Two Women," *Washington Post,* May 14, 2002.

struction, chemical weapons, tend to be less lethal than biological weapons. For example, 300 kilograms of sarin nerve gas with a density of 70 milligrams per cubic meter in an area of 0.22 square kilometers would produce up to 200 deaths, assuming that there are 3,000–10,000 people per square kilometer.[11] Moreover, chemical weapons tend to be sensitive to environmental factors that may cause the agents to degrade or be blown off course, rendering them less effective.

Not only do biological weapons cause potentially lethal diseases in exposed individuals, they can, depending on the biological agent used, infect individuals far from the epicenter of the outbreak. A troubling example is the prospect of dealing with an outbreak of a communicable disease such as smallpox, which was widely eradicated in the late 1970s.[12] According to the *Journal of the American Medical Association*, "Within th[e] group, [of transmissible disease agents], smallpox stands out because of its ease of transmissibility to ravage populations. There is a relative lack of immunity against smallpox in the population, and the thought of a smallpox epidemic instills terror in nearly everyone."[13]

The threat of a smallpox outbreak is also troubling because the vast majority of people living in the United States have no immunity to the disease. Routine vaccination ended in 1972, and only a few born after 1972 were ever vaccinated. Moreover, without boosters, immunity may fade over time, leaving many Americans who were vaccinated against smallpox before 1972 with only limited (if any) protection from the disease.

Despite the dangers of biological weapons, relatively little is known about them within policy circles, the medical arena, and among citizens. The United States ended its offensive biological weapons program in 1969, thus data on biological weapons are limited. Several factors convinced President Richard Nixon to end the program. First were the ethical concerns about intentionally spreading disease. These same concerns persist today and rightly limit research activities. Second were the political concerns at a time when the United States faced severe criticism at home and abroad for its combat use of toxic herbicide (Agent Orange) and tear gas during the Vietnam War. Third were the concerns about the

---

11.   Anthony H. Cordesman, "Weapons of Mass Destruction and the Global Nuclear Balance: A Quantitative and Arms Control Analysis," rev. ed., Center for Strategic and International Studies, December 4, 2001, at <www.csis.org/burke/mb/nuclear.pdf>.

12.   This was due in major part to a vigorous worldwide vaccination program.

13.   Donald A. Henderson, Thomas V. Inglesby, John G. Bartlett, et al., "Smallpox as a Biological Weapon: Medical and Public Health Management," *Journal of the American Medical Association*, Vol. 281, No. 22 (June 9, 1999), pp. 2127–2137.

efficacy and ease of employing biological agents as tactical weapons. Last, certainly, was the hope that by ending U.S. offensive biological weapons programs, the United States would establish a norm that would compel more states to follow suit.

Many states did renounce their offensive biological weapons programs and sign international agreements disavowing their use. As time progressed, however, not all states signed on, and even those that did—such as the Soviet Union—occasionally violated the ban. As a result, there are currently stockpiles of biological weapons, scientists with the knowledge to produce and weaponize biological agents, and state and non-state actors eager to obtain and possibly use these weapons against the United States.

In part because of both ethical boundaries that preclude research on certain biological agents and a general lack of understanding about weapons of mass destruction and their capabilities, the United States is ill-prepared to handle the growing threat from biological weapons.

Given this pessimistic scenario, what can be done to protect Americans? Unlike the case with nuclear and chemical weapons that offers only limited opportunities for mitigation once an individual has been exposed, the effects of biological weapons can often be substantially reduced. Additionally, contagious diseases can be contained if quarantine or evacuation mandates are appropriately implemented, and prophylaxis is rapidly distributed. Therefore, if the public is familiar with the signs of biological weapons exposure and educated regarding the appropriate response, available resources can be deployed to reduce the effects of a biological attack.

Those resources, however, are not yet in place. In late 2001, the federal government had only 15.4 million doses of smallpox vaccine stockpiled but more than 280,000 million people to protect.[14] Although Secretary of Health and Human Services Tommy Thompson estimated that the 15.4 million doses could be diluted up to five times and still retain its potency, covering a potential smallpox outbreak remains a significant challenge to the government.[15] To deal with this problem, the Department of Health and Human Services contracted with a private company for an-

---

14. It is believed that this vaccine can be diluted, creating up to 77 million additional doses, while maintaining immunity against smallpox. Another 70 million doses were discovered by the drug manufacturer Aventis Pasteur. With dilution and combined with the other available vaccines, this could potentially create enough doses to vaccinate 240 million people.

15. Laurie K. Doepel, "NIAID Study Results Support Diluting Smallpox Vaccine

other 155 million doses of smallpox vaccine. The combined solution of diluting and adding to the current vaccine supply promises to bring the total number of doses in the smallpox vaccine stockpile to at least 286 million.[16]

However, once these resources are in place, other issues will need to be addressed in the event of a smallpox outbreak. These include the "roles and missions of federal and state governments, civil liberties associated with quarantine and isolation, the role of Department of Defense, and potential military responses to the anonymous attack."[17] DARK WINTER, an exercise designed to simulate possible U.S. response to the introduction of smallpox in three states during the winter of 2002, highlighted some of the ethical, political, cultural, operational, and legal challenges involved in the containment of smallpox. These included stockpiled vaccines that would be difficult to distribute and disseminate; protective gear that would not be available to the entire population; the possible necessity of quarantine; and the launching of a public education and media campaign to eliminate the fear of biological weapons.

The myriad threats Americans are now confronted with require responses at every level. While the federal government debates a vaccine stockpiling and administration strategy, and state and local medical and public health communities plan and train to respond to an attack, Americans need to know what they can do to protect themselves. A review of the considerations that drove the decision to create the former civil defense system is thus a good place to begin a serious national discourse about this issue.

Moving Forward: A Modern Civil Defense Program

The most important battlefront in the war against terrorism may well be the U.S. homeland. There needs to be a thorough review of the nation's civil defense options as related to the ability to survive a biological weapons attack. The former shelter and neighborhood program may not be the only answer to this dilemma: it is however, a good place to begin the dis-

---

Stockpile to Stretch Supply," National Institute of Allergy and Infectious Diseases, March 28, 2002, at <www.niaid.nih.gov/newsroom/releases/smallpox.htm>.

16. "HHS Awards $428 Million Contract to Produce Smallpox Vaccine," U.S. Department of Health and Human Services, November 28, 2001 at <www.hhs.gov/news/press/2001pres/20011128.html>.

17. "Dark Winter," ANSER Institute for Homeland Security at <www.homelandsecurity.org/darkwinter/index.cfm>.

cussion. The federal government has war contingency plans that provide for the relocation of the president, cabinet officers, members of Congress, and other key government officials to secure, fortified shelters in the event of an attack. Local officials and others need to be reassured that the government also considers the safety of the populace to be its first priority: citizens deserve nothing less.

The United States needs a new kind of civil defense program—one that has the capacity to reach into cities, towns, individual neighborhoods, and rural communities and to provide the necessary education and resources to protect Americans from biological terrorism. This program would be equipped with warning systems against biological agents, would designate safe zones where supplies and equipment would be stored, and train citizens to guide their communities after an attack.

Elements of the shelter concept are particularly well designed to meet the demands of a biological attack. First, prepared locations for citizens to report to would be stocked with some measure of basic medical prophylaxis. Trained volunteers would report to these locations prepared to assist victims and concerned citizens. This would help to provide immediate care to untold numbers of citizens. Moreover, the predetermined locations would help supplement the nation's formal medical delivery system, alleviating bed shortages and the lack of trained medical personnel that would likely occur in a mass-casualty trauma.

Second, predetermined locations would represent one element of a public education campaign. These locations would have informational material about possible weapons, their effects, and response options. They would also house communications equipment to keep citizens informed. Education and training of the public would save lives, reduce the disruption and adverse psychological effects of a biological attack, and aid efforts by emergency workers.

Third, the system would provide a sense of unified effort through mobilization. As in any disaster, self-help will largely be the rule for many citizens during the first few minutes or even hours of a large-scale attack. Individual and collective measures taken before an attack may give citizens a sense of purpose and direction during and after the attack, increasing their chances of survival.

In order to make such a community-based response system work, mayors, local officials, and emergency management staff need to be integrated into national planning so that the programs can be appropriately augmented to match evolving threats. Civil defense programs are also more effective when they are developed at the top echelons of government in a "top down" manner and implemented in a "bottom up" process to include local leaders, particularly mayors.

Conclusion

Today, the fear of another attack on U.S. soil is as palpable as it was in 1941. The public wants—and needs—more and better information about what to expect in the way of further terrorist attacks. As they anxiously await the next alert from federal authorities, Americans grow increasingly perplexed over warnings that range from an "an attack is likely" to "an attack is imminent." Americans need better, more specific information on how to prepare themselves and their communities for a terrorist attack.

If citizens are involved in the process of defending the nation and themselves, they will be empowered to prepare for and manage an array of scenarios. The development of a model based on the old civil defense shelter system may be best suited to the protection of Americans, particularly against biological terrorism.

The goals of protecting Americans and maximizing their potential survival after an attack, while difficult, are not out of reach. Mankind has dealt with plagues, natural disasters, wars, and recurring large-scale disasters for centuries and has survived. Although resources are finite, U.S. resolve is great, and ingenuity and technological capabilities are enormous. By addressing this issue now, the federal government can turn a popular war against terrorism into a populist war on behalf of the American people.

Chapter 5

Telling It Like It Is: The Role of the Media in Terrorism Response and Recovery

Frances Edwards-Winslow

An important role of emergency management is the dissemination of warnings and instructions during a crisis. Community members need to learn of approaching hurricanes and floods, and of evacuation plans. In the United States, the most effective means at their disposal is the media. With 24-hour news, it is possible to provide life-saving information to many community members in a short period of time, often in multiple languages.

A principal role of the media is covering breaking stories in their community, especially those with safety implications. There is an adage in journalism: "If it bleeds, it leads." Therefore, many members of the media monitor police and fire scanners to ensure early coverage of breaking news events.

To succeed in their respective roles, emergency managers and the media must form a partnership based on their mutual interest in serving the community, although for different reasons. For emergency managers, the media are often the only effective way to reach the community with critical messages during a disaster. Emergency management staff must therefore study the media and practice interacting effectively with them. Most professional emergency managers take from 40 to 160 hours of classroom training in giving an interview, writing a media release, and setting up media interviews. Emergency managers invest time in preparing carefully worded messages that can be quickly customized for immediate release during an emergency or disaster. Teams of marketing personnel in public agencies develop a media plan, create a media center, and practice their skills to meet community needs for information during an emergency.

The media should and usually do take an equal interest in preparing themselves to work effectively with public agencies and in becoming familiar with the basics of emergency response. First, reporters should try to understand the story's context. What is the disaster history of the community? What risks have government agencies identified? Reporters should develop reference folders for the most likely disaster scenarios, including the websites of agencies that will have rapid and accurate information on a disaster, such as the U.S. Geological Survey, the National Oceanic and Atmospheric Administration (NOAA), and university research centers. Reporters should make a contact list for key people in public agencies and private organizations that will manage the response to and recovery from emergencies and disasters. The reporter will then be able to quickly collect accurate background information during an unfolding event and prepare meaningful questions for public officials.

Reporters and editors should become familiar with the governmental structure of the community that they are covering, if they are not already. As James Lee Witt, former director of the Federal Emergency Management Agency (FEMA), is famous for saying, "All disasters are local." Reporters need to know how the local community will organize to combat an unfolding disaster and who its partners will be. Having done research in advance, when disaster occurs, reporters can quickly develop educated stories.

Why Should the Media Take Advice?

Good journalism contributes to community recovery after any disaster. In the aftermath of a terrorist attack, the need for intelligent, balanced reporting is even greater. Since "the purpose of terrorism is to terrify,"[1] journalists have the choice of hyping the horrors and furthering the terrorist cause or of providing balanced, safety-oriented stories to calm the community. Such a choice can be the key to community recovery.

To prepare to cover a disaster, reporters can develop relationships with staff members of public agencies who will help them get stories during the disaster period. A trust relationship developed before the crisis will enable both a reporter and a public employee to work together in a more collegial fashion, especially under stress. Together they can determine the audience for a story, craft it to be most useful, and answer crucial questions: who needs the information? Why should they care?

---

1. Brian Jenkins, speech to the American Transportation Association, Washington, D.C., October 30, 2001.

Why Should Public Officials Talk?

There are two sides to a partnership. If reporters are to interview officials properly, officials in turn must prepare to participate actively. Most public agencies have a cadre of media-relations specialists whose role is to develop relationships with the journalists. These professionals create the basis for media interviews. Public officials must be prepared to accept guidance from their public information specialists and remain open to requests for media contact.

Because most reporters want to speak with first-line responders, public employees need to accept interaction with the media as an important part of their jobs. They need to take advantage of media-relations training available through government, educational, and consultant sources. They need to practice being interviewed while being videotaped and review the tapes to critique and improve their performance.

Public officials and employees must acknowledge that the media have an important role to play in disaster response and recovery. Electronic media outlets can disseminate information quickly, while the print media can provide detailed response information. For this information sharing to be effective, the media's representatives must have access to knowledgeable staff members of local agencies so that they can craft their stories based on the most current facts and most accurate advice.

A willingness to be truthful with a reporter is key to a successful interview. Staff members of public agencies must become comfortable speaking on the record. They will develop the confidence required by preparing well. Before an interview, agency representatives need to be briefed on the progress of an event, the expected actions or changes within the next few hours, and the anticipated point when recovery will begin. Officials should attend the briefing with a fact sheet that will guide the answers that they provide to reporters. While officials should do their best to prepare to answer questions after delivering a prepared statement, they should also be willing to say, "I don't know that right now, but I'll have an answer for you" in a specified period of time.

If a disaster is unfolding, the community has the right to understand its extent and the likelihood that it will worsen. The public needs to know how to respond and whether to prepare for even worse things to come. An honest interview by a knowledgeable public official, along with balanced and factual coverage by a reporter, can aid residents' search for emergency information. [2]

---

2. For a more complete discussion on preparing representatives of public agencies to effectively meet the media, please see Frances Edwards-Winslow, "Media Relations in the Midst of Disaster," unpublished manuscript, May 2000.

What Is Happening Now? A Local Perspective

In 1997, Congress launched the domestic preparedness program,[3] which was an amendment to the National Defense Authorization Act. Under this program, 120 of the largest cities in the United States, including two of the most isolated cities—Anchorage and Honolulu—began a partnership with federal agencies[4] to enhance the capabilities of state and local agencies to respond to potential terrorist attacks involving weapons of mass destruction.[5] San Jose, California, the eleventh-largest city in the United States, was one of those first cities.

In undertaking domestic preparedness, the city built on its history of civil defense and disaster preparedness. The media-relations plans drafted for use during natural disasters provided the basis for media relations during human-caused events, including terrorism. While most members of the media have a general knowledge of the mechanisms of natural disaster, few are experts on the threats motivating the domestic preparedness program, the many potential motivations of terrorists, and the likely weapons that terrorists might employ. Media relations in the midst of a terrorist event can therefore be extraordinarily difficult.[6] While the media and public agencies often have an adversarial relationship during the course of normal business, both parties need to develop a collaborative approach to covering a disaster, especially during a terrorist event.

Community members are, in a sense, public agencies' "customers."

---

3. The domestic preparedness program was initially mandated and funded through the Nunn-Lugar-Domenici Act.

4. These agencies included the Department of Defense for training, the Department of Health and Human Services for writing plans and developing stockpiles of equipment and pharmaceuticals, and the Department of Justice for crisis management. The Federal Emergency Management Agency, the Environmental Protection Agency, and the Department of Energy provide consequence management planning. For a more detailed description of the Domestic Preparedness Program, see Frances E. Winslow, "Metropolitan Medical Task Force," *The Handbook of Crisis and Emergency Management* (New York: Marcel Dekker, 2001).

5. Initially the focus was on battlefield weapons used in the Persian Gulf War and suspected of being deployed by countries unfriendly to the United States. In this amendment, weapons of mass destruction include radiological, biological, and chemical weapons. "Radiological," encompasses the use of low-yield radiological materials with conventional explosives to create "dirty bombs." "Biological" refers to diseases known to have been weaponized by nations before the Chemical and Biological Warfare Convention outlawed their use, such as anthrax and smallpox. "Chemical" refers to the human toxins deployed during World War I and in the war between Iran and Iraq, such as sarin.

6. Winslow, "Media Relations in the Midst of Disaster."

While people may not have much choice about who provides their public services, they do cast their votes for the officials who allocate tax dollars among competing public programs. Local government leaders have become sensitive to this role of residents as "customers" for public services. Many local governments have followed the philosophy of "entrepreneurial government" and placed customer service and satisfaction as top priorities.[7]

To the media, community members are also "customers." People can choose among many news outlets. Viewers will select the channels and programs that best meet their need for useful information. Newspapers are competing with news radio, 24-hour television news, and each other. The number of viewers, listeners, and readers directly affects the advertising revenues of media outlets, and building an audience base is critical. Therefore, expressed customer interest in specified topics will influence the shape of a station's or newspaper's content.

Thus, both governmental entities and media outlets view the community residents as customers. If they serve their common customers well, both media outlets and public agencies will benefit.

The Business of the Media Is News

News in the United States is big business. Since the advent of 24-hour television news, editors and reporters must fill airtime with updates and fresh stories. Most print journalists have daily deadlines that allow them to research their stories more thoroughly and to take a longer view than electronic journalists when crafting new coverage of an event. In addition, while most electronic journalists are generalists, print media often have the luxury of developing staff specialists on topics such as medicine, science, and local government. Public officials can therefore expect the print media to provide more accurate and in-depth information during a disaster. However, the need to compete with electronic media and with newspapers from all over the world that are available on the Internet often compels local print editors to adopt the same journalistic philosophy as their electronic counterparts.

News Is Not "Happy Talk"

In an era of "hard-hitting journalism," newspapers often prefer investigative, cutting-edge reporting. They also cover "hard news"—the tradi-

---

7. For more information, see the work of David Osbourne, Ted Gaebler, and the CAP program of the American Society for Public Administration at <www.aspanet.org>.

tional police beat and city hall stories of crime and corruption. The old "society page" that provided space for civic betterment activities and volunteerism has generally given way to a broader "living" section that encompasses topical features about parenting and household management.

Several years ago, San Jose launched a new program called "San Jose *Prepared!*," a local version of the national community emergency response team (CERT) program sponsored by FEMA.[8] At the end of the first year, the city's Office of Emergency Services (OES) sponsored a graduation for residents who had completed the 16 hours of training required for membership on a neighborhood response team. Over 100 San Jose residents gathered at a community center to receive thanks from Mayor Susan Hammer, graduation certificates, and San Jose *Prepared!* uniforms from several members of the city council.

The city's public information officer prepared a press release noting this outstanding response to the need for heightened community emergency preparedness. He noted the participation by elected officials and an anticipated audience of 400 people at the event, including family and friends of the graduates. He described the exhibits that would be part of the event. When OES staff members called the *Mercury News*, the local daily newspaper, to determine when reporters would arrive and whether they wanted to set up interviews with some of the graduates, they were rebuffed. The local section editor said, "We don't do 'happy talk' news at the *Mercury!*" and hung up. Staff, residents, and elected officials were disappointed, but two weekly neighborhood papers did cover the event.

On the following Sunday, OES staff eagerly sought to find out what local news took precedence over the story that 100 volunteers had each given 16 hours to learn skills to help their community. The banner headline on the local section was about a gang shooting involving three juveniles. There was definitely nothing happy about that headline, but why did the community need to see banner coverage of three lawless teens while making no mention of 100 caring residents?

---

8. The CERT program is now part of the Citizen Corps effort launched by President George W. Bush in his 2002 State of the Union message. It was begun in California after the Loma Prieta earthquake to train residents to provide immediate life-saving services in their own neighborhoods. Earthquake epidemiology shows that the most effective rescue occurs within the first few hours after a disaster. Most such rescue efforts are undertaken by victims' family and friends, often at their own peril. In the Mexico City earthquake of the mid-1980s, many would-be rescuers became additional victims through ill-considered efforts. The goal of the national CERT program is to teach search and rescue, disaster firefighting, disaster medicine, and psychology skills so neighbors can save lives within their community.

This type of coverage is damaging because the media can be partners in community betterment, whether in fighting against blight, boosting local sports teams, or encouraging safe behavior among readers or viewers. The editors of a local newspaper help create a community's image. Regardless of actual crime statistics, constant coverage of gang violence, break-ins, and drug arrests gives residents a sense that their community is dangerous. Coverage of community anti-litter campaigns and school sports successes creates an image of a functional community.

Educating: Preparing to Tell the Whole Truth

Reporters who work with local emergency managers in advance and develop their own resources will be able to cover a tragic story more effectively. When a disaster occurs, the reporter should take a few minutes to review the collected data, access a few disaster websites, and use this (public administration, geology, and disaster mechanism) information to develop a story outline and interview questions for public officials, first responders, and victims. This will result in a better story, as sensible questions will elicit interesting responses from people being interviewed.

Media conferences provide an opportunity for astute reporters to obtain useful information and unique details for their stories. In this interactive setting, a reporter who has laid the groundwork can ask questions that the public would ask, going beyond prepared press releases and remarks to the heart of the community's concerns. A collaborative approach with officials is most likely to engender rapport and responsive answers.

The anthrax attacks and hoaxes in the fall of 2001 demonstrated the success of this approach. Because the story unfolded relatively slowly, reporters were able to research some of the public health issues before interviewing representatives of local agencies. The reporters had enough background on the general mechanism underlying anthrax illness and the probable outcomes to elicit intelligent comments from interviews on specific plans and local concerns. The reporters came to their interviews prepared and left with material that was both useful to their communities and complimentary to reporters and agency representatives. They looked like partners in community safety, which itself proved reassuring to viewers and readers.

The Role of the Foreign Language Press

During a disaster, officials will provide specific guidance to enhance the safety of residents. For example, during a spill of hazardous materials, it may be prudent for residents to stay at home and seal off the house from outside air. Since many people would not know how to respond correctly, the media can provide step-by-step instruction.

Because they see U.S. troops distributing relief supplies in foreign nations, many Americans incorrectly assume that the federal government will provide material and financial help to residents of a disaster area. This is generally not the case. People must phone a toll-free number to register for federal assistance, which usually takes the form of long-term, low-interest loans. After the California floods of 1997, the media played a critical role in explaining the purpose of the toll-free number and encouraging people to register for assistance. The public service announcements and interviews with residents of flooded areas who had successfully registered helped motivate residents to get assistance with economic recovery.

Foreign language media are equal partners in outreach to English-as-a-second-language communities. The television media serve an especially critical role for both non-English-speaking members of the community and those with hearing impairments. Captioning in other languages and closed captioning enables these populations to gain access to information that they need. It is especially important for reporters who may be new to a community and perhaps unfamiliar with U.S. governance to lay a strong groundwork before participating in a rapid-fire media conference. A one-on-one meeting with an agency's public education specialists could provide such a foundation. Because listeners and readers may be unsure of the lines of authority during a disaster, the media member's role as educator is especially critical to the non-English-speaking community.

Following the Northridge earthquake of 1994, many residents of the Los Angeles area who were originally from Central America moved out of their undamaged homes and into city parks, living in their cars and makeshift lean-tos. In their nations of origin, these residents had experienced earthquakes that caused buildings to fall, killing their occupants. However, Los Angeles has strictly enforced building codes and no history of catastrophic residential collapse, apart from one "soft story" apartment building, has been recorded.[9] Still, many families with small children preferred to live outdoors, during the rainy month of January, resulting in many sick children, lack of proper public health and sanitation measures, and general discomfort.

---

9. In the Northridge earthquake, 17 first-floor residents of the Northridge Meadows Apartments were crushed in their beds when inadequate sheer walls in parking bays failed.

The Spanish-language media played a vital role in educating people in the parks on the safety of residential buildings in California. The media carried reassuring stories regarding the ability of families to reoccupy their homes. The city developed Reassurance Teams composed of building officials, clergy, and social workers who visited people in the parks to answer their questions and allay their fears, encouraging them to return to the comfort of their homes. Because the Spanish-language media covered the work of these teams, they expanded their influence while convincing people to leave the parks and go home.

Framing: Taking the Sensational Out of the Truth

The framing of a story influences how the audience perceives an event. A reporter who is educated about the unfolding disaster is able to present an intelligent story using the background material that he or she has amassed in advance. This is important in helping the community to see the event in its proper context. For example, if an area has flooded ten times in the last 100 years, government and community members will respond significantly differently than if the area has no prior history of flooding. The event will lack the element of surprise, and the residents are likely to have some notion about how to remain safe. A terrorist act perpetrated by a foreign group affects people differently than an act of domestic terrorism. Oklahoma City's Alfred P. Murrah Building bombing in April 1995 was the work of an angry U.S. citizen. The attack on the World Trade Center in 1993 was the work of a band of Islamic fundamentalists. The damage done in each case was stunning, but the framing of each story helped communities understand its meaning and future implications. In Oklahoma City, people anticipated a domestic search, while in New York City, the search was both domestic and international. The way the story is framed by the media influences the way the community sees the event.

Developing adequate background information on the risks from a disaster also enables the reporter to evaluate the emergency response realistically. It is appropriate for the media to criticize the official response if it falls short, but it is pointless to demoralize the responders and the community by creating unrealistic expectations. Some people think government should stay out of their lives until a disaster comes but expect the government to assume total responsibility for all the consequences when disaster strikes. In fact, individuals have great latitude in the mitigation steps that they choose to take, and the degree of risk often relates directly to those steps. A balanced story would present the range of options.

During the 1997 floods in San Jose, one reporter repeatedly featured a community member who thought that the city should have individually notified each resident along the reach of a creek that flooding was imminent. Instead of pointing out that flood warning is a NOAA obligation and that, in fact, authorities had issued urban and small-stream flash-flood advisories throughout the weekend, the reporter kept reiterating the resident's complaint. By law, the city has no duty to issue warnings, and no technical basis on which to issue them. The resident living next to a creek for more than 20 years was in a better position to evaluate the likelihood of flooding on his property. The reporter would have performed a better community service by reminding residents to heed the flash-flood warnings that stations had carried throughout the weekend. Instead, he chose to use the resident's complaint as a segue into a story on the failure of the city to protect this person's property.

Reporters should also be sensitive to the "outrage" factor associated with a particular event. "Outrage", in this context, has been defined as, "what the public sees as the risk and their related fears often have no correlation to the technical issues. In risk management and communication circles, these non-technical factors are often referred to as the 'outrage' dimension of risk."[10] The media are always tempted by a man-on-the-street interview that makes for good theater but not very good news.

Researchers have noted that the public is more willing to accept some events than others. People accept voluntary risks more readily than those that are imposed.[11] For example, people know that automobile fatalities occur frequently, but they choose to drive their cars on crowded freeways during rush hour knowing the risks. Natural risks seem more acceptable than artificial risks. "Natural disasters provide no focus for anger because there is no one to blame, whereas man-made disasters can usually be attributed to human error and thus become a focal point for public anger."[12] "Exotic risks" seem more dangerous than familiar risks.[13] For example, sarin is much more frightening than chlorine to most people, even though the mechanism of harm is similar. Although the amount of sarin needed to cause death is very small, inhalation of chlorine, which is readily available, can also cause death. Yet people willingly use chlorine as a disinfectant in their homes and accept its use in community swimming pools and at sewage treatment plants. "The person who communi-

---

10. California Governor's Office of Emergency Services, *Risk Communication Guide for State and Local Agencies,* Sacramento, 2001, p. 10.

11. Ibid.

12. Ibid.

13. Ibid., p. 11.

cates with the public must be aware that the public is usually more concerned with the outrage issues than the technical aspects."[14]

Furthermore, the audience encompasses at least four groups within the community. Researchers have named them activists, attentives, browsers, and inattentives.

Activists, highly concerned people, [are] a subset of extremely involved individuals and groups that dominate the risk controversy. Attentives [are] individuals who follow the issue closely. Browsers [are] individuals following the issue casually. Inattentives [are] the largest number of individuals who are paying little or no attention to the issue.[15]

Analysts advise professional emergency managers to leave the "inattentives" alone. The "browsers" will rely on the media for information. Emergency managers can interact with "activists" while allowing the "attentives" to watch.[16] However, in high-hazard situations when "attention is desired, the key challenge is getting the uninvolved to pay attention in order to protect themselves."[17]

It is at the nexus of information and the inattentives that the media's framing of an event can play a safety role during the response. A good story would explain risk in clear and simple terms and provide simple safety directions with a minimum of sensationalism. Such stories, carried in a variety of print and electronic outlets, will impress the browsers and ultimately reach even the inattentives.

The Year 2000 turnover, or Y2K, provided many examples of the importance of framing an issue to obtain action from the browsers and inattentives. Although the core concern was the change from two-digit year numbering to four-digit year numbering in computer programs, the risks from this change varied. Payroll systems, billing systems, and electricity systems were just a few of the large-scale systems that could have been affected. Media outlets covered the Y2K transition in stories ranging from the simplest to the most complex explanations. Yet because the message was consistent—the year change could affect you—the general public caught on.

Once the audience understood the potential problem, the media switched to advice from banks, utility companies, the American Red Cross, and FEMA on what to do. People understood that they needed a

14. Ibid., p. 10.

15. Ibid., p. 17.

16. Ibid.

17. Ibid.

supply of cash in small bills in case automated cash dispensing machines and computerized cash registers failed when the date changed. People understood the need for government agencies to invest scarce resources in converting to modern software and new computer hardware. Utility companies upgraded their systems, aircraft managers altered their operations, and emergency operations centers were opened in most large communities to see the new millennium in safely. The media communicated both the personal and the social dimension of change. As a result of the mitigation steps taken throughout the economy, very few Y2K impacts ensued.

Framing is especially important during the recovery phase of a disaster. When a community is damaged and the local economy looks bleak, the way a story is presented can determine the outcome of the disaster. Residents abandoned many areas of Los Angeles after the Northridge earthquake.[18] Even a single damaged building was seen to adversely impact the civic life and possibility of recovery for an entire neighborhood. Renters moved from yellow-tagged buildings, often finding new, permanent homes in other parts of the city. (A yellow tag, as designated by the Applied Technology Council of California means that the building has some damage that might worsen in aftershocks and should only be entered with caution and for brief periods to retrieve essential items).[19]

Ghost towns developed around even undamaged buildings, as tenants recognized that services had deteriorated and crime rates had risen. Los Angeles media coverage of the gang and drug activities in some of the yellow-tagged buildings contributed to abandonment of areas by frightened residents. During the one to two years while landlords waited for the Small Business Administration to approve their loans and contrac-

---

18. At the time of the Northridge earthquake, Los Angeles had an 18 percent vacancy rate, enabling displaced tenants to relocate to undamaged parts of the city. This process of abandonment came to be known as "ghost towning." The loss of these resident customers drove out small businesses. Tenants of undamaged buildings found the area less convenient and also moved to where small business services were still available. The result was the depopulation of whole neighborhoods, or a shift to residents whose income levels did not draw services back.

19. In an effort to make the safety of buildings after an earthquake easy for the public to understand, the Applied Technology Council of California created a post-earthquake posting scheme (ATC-20) for buildings. This system uses colored placards, generally printed in several languages appropriate to the community. A red tag means that the building is dangerous in aftershocks and may no longer be occupied until it is repaired. A yellow tag, as stated previously, means that the building has some damage that might worsen in aftershocks, and that it should only be entered with caution and for brief periods to retrieve essential items. A green tag means that any damage is superficial and the building may be inhabited.

tors waited to repair buildings, the tenant market shifted, often making it unlikely that the buildings would become economically viable again.

The municipal government of Los Angeles responded by creating media materials showing the new investment the city was making in ghost town areas. City officials promoted a city loan program that often included grants. As media outlets began to report these promotions, landlords looked toward recovery and refurbished their buildings in the hope of attracting new tenants. When the media initially framed the story as the degradation of the city's working-class neighborhoods, the community acted on that belief. When the media began to frame the story as "phoenix neighborhoods" that would arise from the earthquake better than ever, residents began to pursue recovery in those areas.

Careful framing of a story makes the media look evenhanded and thoughtful, enhancing their image with their customers. Careful framing gives government the chance to provide useful information to its constituents. The customers of both entities are able to understand the risks and mitigate them without letting outrage issues cloud their judgment.

Reporting: Best Practices in Covering the News

A disaster or emergency is always a gripping story. The popularity of television shows based on police, fire, and medical responses to crises is proof of the public fascination with life and death moments. But every emergency or disaster offers enough good material to make telling the truth profitable. A good story is based on the "Seven Cs" of good communication.[20]

First, the reporter should consider the makeup of the **community** and residents' preexisting knowledge of the risk. An earthquake in California is a surprise but not unprecedented or completely unexpected. An earthquake in New York, such as the one that occurred in April 2002, is unexpected by most people. One state has strict seismic resistance requirements in its buildings codes to limit the damage. The other has limited earthquake mitigation on any level, so damage levels and community concerns will differ. People in California are frequently exposed to information about how to prepare for and respond to an earthquake. People in New York State are less likely to have received pre-earthquake education. Thus, the starting place for the two stories should be quite different.

Second, stories about emergencies and disasters need to include

---

20. Frances Edwards-Winslow, "Nuclear Risk Communication and the First Responder," presentation at Nuclear Risk Communication Roundtable, Stanford University, May 20, 2002.

clear, simple safety information. Listeners may be unsure about the appropriate next steps. Electronic media coverage can provide life-saving information in the midst of an event. Reporters must be careful to find a credible spokesperson and maintain a clear and simple safety message.

Public information officers for emergency response agencies develop safety information for likely emergency scenarios in advance. These officers could share some of this information with news bureaus and science writers ahead of time to give them instant access to critical information. This would ensure that the safety message reporters first broadcast will be the most specific and useful safety message for the community. For example, information specifically on bioterrorism hazards is available at the Johns Hopkins University website and the Centers for Disease Control (CDC) website. Reporters and specialty writers could download this information in advance, since access to critical websites is often slowed by heavy use immediately after an event.

Third, reporters should be careful to outline the **consequences** honestly but without hype. Observed consequences and condition reports from credible sources, such as public agencies and nongovernmental agencies, should prove adequate for meaningful stories. Seeking out sensational comments on observed disaster consequences from scare mongers and ill-informed, self-appointed experts may make for a momentary sensation, but does not serve the community well.

Fourth, reporters should report a **consistent** safety message. Reporters should rely on the public agency dealing with the disaster or emergency to provide information on safe conduct for residents of the disaster area. It does the community no good for reporters to shop around for more sensational information. There are always alarmists who will denigrate the safety message provided by the government.

For example, after the 1989 Loma Prieta, California, earthquake a man captured attention by saying that the "drop, cover, and hold" message would kill schoolchildren. Local talk shows offered this man considerable airtime for his misguided viewpoint, even though public spokespersons stated that the data on which he based his point of view were incorrect. The man insisted that he had been in "dozens of earthquakes" where he had seen "hundreds of children" who stayed in their schools and were injured and killed. Since dozens of damaging earthquakes have not occurred in his lifetime in the United States, and children have never been in school during a twentieth-century earthquake in the United States, his comments were puzzling. When one alert reporter pointed this out and asked him where these school-hours earthquakes had occurred, he was forced to admit that he had, in fact, experienced only one, the Mexico City earthquake of the mid-1980s. Building codes for California schools are extremely strict,[21] making it unlikely that any school would either collapse or suffer significant structural damage during an earthquake. In fact, after the Northridge earthquake, even the red-tagged schools (not safe to inhabit) would not have posed an immediate life or safety threat to the students, had they been present.[22] On the other hand, epidemiological studies conducted by Eric Noji of the Centers for Disease Control and reported to the California Seismic Safety Commission show that people who ran outdoors were injured by roof tiles that slid off their homes and by bricks shaken from their chimneys. Thus, reporters must present accurate information on consequences.

Fifth, public agencies and nongovernmental organizations (NGOs) will strive to provide **coordinated** information about an event. A reporter should not be offended if every agency gives the same safety message and the same disaster response directions. If the reporter is seeking something to make the story unique, an interview with a community member acting on the coordinated message might be interesting.

Sixth, only facts obtained from **credible** spokespersons should be reported. Public agencies and NGOs will provide media releases and media conferences with community leaders and subject matter experts. They will issue confirmed statements regarding the disaster. While person-in-the-street interviews can be useful for "color," they should not be presented as factual information. A member of the public standing in one place is seeing only one small aspect of an event. That person's "truth" may be badly skewed and presenting it as fact will degrade the quality of the story.

Finally, **calming** messages are more constructive than scary reports. Unless Godzilla is really rising from the bay, it is probably fair to assume that local government agencies have plans in place to deal with the emer-

---

21. The California Legislature passed the Field Act after the Long Beach Earthquake of 1933. At that time most schools were made of brick for fire resistance. The earthquake occurred around 5:00 pm, so schools were unoccupied. However, experts calculated that if the earthquake had occurred during school hours, hundreds of children could have been killed by the failure of unreinforced masonry. The resulting new elements to the building code forbid the use of unreinforced masonry for school buildings and incorporated numerous structural safety elements into future school buildings. This code has been continuously upgraded, making schools the safest buildings in California.

22. Because the earthquake occurred before 5:00 am on the Martin Luther King, Jr. holiday, no one was present in school buildings when the earthquake occurred.

gency or disaster. In any case, adding to the public's fright will not produce good community outcomes. Calm people are more likely to think clearly and obey simple safety rules. People confronted by a terrorist event in their community do not need a reporter dwelling on how frightened residents are. The focus should be on steps being taken to mitigate the damage and preserve the safety of the community.

Mayor Rudolph Giuliani of New York City remained a calm figure in the midst of 9/11, steadfastly reassuring the public that emergency workers were managing the scene. Lives were lost and property was destroyed, but the community as a whole was able to assist its members and recover, largely because it heard calm and reassuring words reminding them that they could.

Partnership to Success

Reporters and public officials must lay the groundwork for successful partnerships in advance of a disaster. Regular interaction between members of the media and local emergency managers can build trust and partnership, ultimately benefiting the community.

In 2002, the San Jose metropolitan area experienced a 4.9 earthquake that caused only minor damage but upset residents. The *Mercury News* used this opportunity to run a full-page feature on earthquake preparedness that included large graphics and accompanying text. This rapid response was possible because of information provided by state and local emergency response agencies during Earthquake Preparedness Month each year. A file of useful information enabled the graphic artist to create an eye-catching page on short notice.

A full-page advertisement in the *Mercury News* costs $10,000 for one day, far beyond the reach of a local emergency management program. Because of a preexisting relationship, the newspaper's news coverage of the earthquake included a valuable public education piece.

Conclusion

No one ever handles a disaster perfectly. The pressure on local officials to make decisions rapidly and without all of the facts will inevitably lead to missteps. In retrospect, the responders will recognize areas where they can improve. The media members can honestly examine lessons learned from any tragedy by the public agencies. But the emphasis should be on the future and continuous improvement, not on the mistakes that cannot be remedied.

The media outlets that win the prizes for their coverage of the 9/11 attacks will surely be those that also served their community. Telling it like it is can be community building, lifesaving, and honest. A partnership between the media and local public agencies can benefit both entities, thereby serving the community.

Chapter 6

Is Density Dangerous? The Architects' Obligations after the Towers Fell

David Dixon

The war against terrorism threatens to become a war against the livability of U.S. cities. In the rush to respond to the threat of terrorism, a loose network of public officials, architects, developers, engineers, lawyers, planners, security consultants, and others who influence building codes are creating a new generation of planning and design regulations. Their purpose is to make terrorism more difficult and to reduce its human and material toll. Unfortunately, the broader, indirect impact of these regulations, with their focus on isolating people from buildings and shutting buildings off from streets, could undermine the vitality, sense of community, and civic quality of much of the urban United States.

In fact, the economic, social, and design dimensions of urban communities have been largely ignored in most of the approaches to fighting terrorism that have emerged since 9/11. The vitality of many U.S. cities hinges on public investment in areas that have been abandoned by the private sector—the very areas that will bear the brunt of new regulations that focus on decentralizing potential targets, such as court houses and other public buildings. Measures like these threaten efforts to revitalize older downtowns and reverse sprawl. A strong sense of community in urban areas—seen in revived streets and squares that are again drawing people together in cities—plays a critical role in building vitality and reversing economic and social fragmentation. The life of streets and squares depends on a lively interplay between buildings and the public realm, one that is undermined by closing entries to major buildings and surrounding them with security perimeters. Civic buildings and spaces shaped in the interests of security become bunkers, not the symbols of a democratic and open society that ennoble and enrich cities.

To understand better the trade-offs involved in fighting terrorism and maintaining the health of cities, it is critical to examine four core questions: what issues does the fight against terrorism raise? What new approaches to enhanced security are emerging? How can steps to fight terrorism affect cities? Are there better approaches to achieving a balance between protecting Americans against terrorism and promoting the livability of U.S. cities?

Issues Raised by the Fight Against Terrorism

The 1973 oil embargo led to a profound sense of vulnerability in the United States. A colleague of mine recalls, without fondness, her quaint Connecticut community's response to the embargo: joining many other communities in banishing windows from new schools. To a society single-mindedly focused on conserving energy, that windowless-school plan symbolized patriotism and civic responsibility. In retrospect, it also symbolized an aberration, a sense that energy conservation requiring the abolition of one of the qualities that make a school a nurturing place for learning. As with any issue, measures that make sense from one perspective can be disastrous from another.

The response to 9/11 by the American Institute of Architects (AIA) provides an informative glimpse into how security approaches are being shaped and by whom. In the wake of tragedy, the AIA made a fundamental commitment in taking a leadership role in shaping the U.S. response to terrorism. AIA has also committed the profession to respond quickly through a series of publications and conferences, which have focused on three areas: increasing architects' awareness of security issues and related planning and design tools; increasing awareness within the larger community of the profession's role in enhancing security; and participating with other disciplines in defining new planning and design standards to create more secure buildings and environments.

The AIA moved quickly to organize meetings between leading design and building professionals and public officials in Washington, D.C., in December 2001 and also organized a national conference on "Building Security through Design," co-sponsored by Sandia Laboratories in Albuquerque, New Mexico.[1] The AIA produced a pamphlet, "Building Security by Design," to suggest how the architectural profession could contribute to fighting terrorism. Discussion at both the Washington, D.C.

---

1. The "Building Security Through Design" Conference, Albuquerque, New Mexico, January 10–13, 2002. For a summary of the keynote session and additional information, see <www.aia.org/security/>.

meeting and Albuquerque conference was lively and conveyed the AIA's deep commitment to the quality and character of U.S. cities. However, professionals who showed the most interest in this topic—for example, by preparing the AIA's pamphlet—and who over the course of 2001 and 2002 have shaped emergent policy recommendations, have largely consisted of the architects, engineers, security consultants, and others whose primary concern has been finding ways to make embassies and courthouses safer. These practitioners, many of whom had become deeply concerned about security following the 1995 Oklahoma City bombing, brought to the discussion a heightened commitment to enhancing security but very little focus on the impact their recommendations could have on larger issues of urban development.

No one within the AIA and allied organizations (nor for that matter, our larger society) consciously sought to address the threats associated with terrorism from a narrow perspective. A constricted viewpoint, however, naturally emerged from the resulting dialogue, which was largely confined to like-minded architects, engineers, and security consultants with a shared history of dealing with the impacts of terrorist acts.

The potential regulations under discussion at local, state, and federal levels threaten to endow the United States with a new generation of buildings like the windowless school in Connecticut: civic structures hidden behind blank, blast-resistant walls; important public buildings quarantined inside lifeless zones free of vehicles or people; public employees scattered to greenfield sites; downtowns in need of revitalization but deprived of new courthouses or federal office buildings; and city streets rendered more dangerous by the elimination of the windows and doorways that promote interaction between people in the buildings and on the streets. It is perhaps the greatest irony that in recent decades much of our urban environment was rescued from fear—and cities and society were made far safer—by the conscious creation of more open buildings, the blurring of the separation of public and private space, promotion of community, and drawing of people back to our streets and squares. A single-minded focus on defending against terrorism threatens all of these hard-won gains.

Forging approaches that better balance the response to terrorism with the equally essential need for buildings and public spaces that promote vitality, community, and a civic spirit will require new participants in the dialogue. A broad range of people for whom this is not a familiar issue must step forward to participate, including architects, planners, community leaders, elected officials, real estate professionals, and others with a direct stake in the character and quality of cities.

Concerns about terrorism are here to stay, and they have raised a heightened awareness about security in the national psyche. The odds of being harmed by terrorism may be dwarfed by the odds of suffering from conventional hazards like fires, sick building syndrome, and workplace accidents. Nevertheless, the new focus on terrorism means that unions will press for safer workplaces, insurers and lenders will lobby to reduce risks, air travelers will demand greater security, and a long list of others will continue to call for tangible responses to terrorism threats.

A very large part of our built environment will be shaped by concerns about terrorism. This is true particularly in urban environments, where the kinds of deep perimeter setbacks and windowless ground floors that characterize the counterterrorism approaches most often discussed, are the most difficult to accommodate. All symbolic buildings and spaces can be perceived as potential targets. No one can predict where terrorists will strike because no one can determine precisely which structures have the desired symbolic value to a terrorist. The long list of targets begins with emblems of economic and military power, such as the office towers and government buildings attacked on 9/11. From there, the list expands to include: symbols of government—courthouses, embassies, federal office buildings, state houses, city halls, and other public facilities; infrastructure—airports, utilities, hospitals, power grids, water systems, and highways; reminders of the national educational and cultural influence—universities, research facilities, and museums; symbols of U.S. history and values—historic monuments and houses of worship; and places where people gather in large numbers, including theme parks, athletic events, festivals, and concerts. Because the list is endless, the impact of new regulations can be limitless.

Post-9/11 Approaches to Enhanced Security

The new sense of vulnerability fostered by 9/11 is leading to the creation of a web of planning and design regulations intended to help defend against terrorism. The potential regulations themselves appear relatively straightforward. The following list—not exhaustive—includes the planning and design tools most often recommended by architects, engineers, and security consultants for enhancing security (the tools are described in order of decreasing impact on civic quality, sense of community, and vitality of cities).

PROTECT BUILDING PERIMETERS

Initially conceived to protect buildings against vehicle-borne bombs, this concept has grown to account for pedestrian- and boat-borne bombs. Protecting building perimeters is primarily associated with significant public buildings, but the proliferation of Jersey barriers and bollards around office buildings and other potential targets after the 9/11 attacks suggests potential wider applications. Proposed measures for protecting perimeters have taken three principal forms.

The most pervasive measure, already implemented by the federal government following the Oklahoma City bombing, has been to remove parking and servicing lots from beneath buildings, where possible, and require that all new parking facilities be located in surface parking lots or in freestanding parking garages. While federal agencies had already begun to focus on creating deep setbacks to protect buildings from bomb blasts following that bombing, this measure has received far more focus following 9/11. A distance of 100 feet has generally been suggested as the minimum setback to protect a building from a blast associated with a car or small truck, but hardened walls can reduce the distance. While security professionals initially recommended vehicle-free setbacks, there have also been increasing calls for pedestrian- or boat-free zones. Barriers, ranging from relatively unobtrusive installations (for example, well-designed bollards, streetscape elements, or even parked cars if by permit—all used in the Federal Triangle in Washington, D.C.) to far more intrusive installations such as the Jersey barriers placed in front of the Sears Tower in Chicago following 9/11, can be used to create deep setbacks or to transform sidewalks or small landscaped areas into shallow setbacks. In some cases, public streets have been closed to protect buildings, the most notable example being Pennsylvania Avenue at the White House. The third measure focuses on "crime prevention through environmental design," which focuses on observation zones, free of plantings or other obstacles to surveillance, increased lighting for surveillance cameras, increased security staff, and similar steps to monitor activity around a building perimeter.

HARDEN BUILDINGS

The most dramatic example of a "hardened" building is probably the J. Edgar Hoover Federal Bureau of Investigation building in Washington, D.C. The federal government became far more interested in hardening courthouses and other potential federal targets after the Oklahoma City bombing. The initial focus, which was on land-based bombings, has since been expanded to include air-borne threats. The focus on resisting the impact of bomb blasts has expanded from a building's exterior walls to include its internal structural system and finishes.

Proposed measures for hardening buildings primarily fall into two broad areas. The most visible measure involves strengthening street-level walls to the point at which they can sustain bomb blasts for defined levels—a standard that has risen as the perceived power of potential bombs has increased—or at least reduce internal damage and harm to inhabitants. Eliminating or severely reducing the amount of glass and the number of entryways at street level represents an important aspect in strengthening street levels.

A less visible, but just as important, measure is strengthening structural systems to limit loss of life and property for defined blast levels, particularly by greatly increasing blast and fire resistance and incorporating emergency stairs and exits capable of withstanding blast and fire damage. Closely related steps include increasing fire suppression systems, employing films and other technologies designed to strengthen glass and minimize shattering, and installing stronger window frames and other structural elements intended to reduce the risk of window systems' detachment from building walls in the event of an explosion.

CONTROL ACCESS

The most visible response to 9/11 for most people has been the introduction of airport-like security measures at entrances to city halls, major office buildings, and other important buildings and spaces. Perhaps less obvious has been the closing of many entry points to create single points of entry and exit that can be monitored efficiently. Major sporting events, theme parks, and other places where people gather in large numbers have also greatly increased their control at entry points. In addition, the many other points at which a bomb could be introduced into a building—mail systems, utility corridors, and other less obvious points of entry—have become subject to much greater control. Proposed measures for controlling access fall into three broad areas.

A sharp increase in the number of buildings that limit entry points and monitor all entrants has been the most visible change in access control since 9/11. (A single entry is usually suggested as a way of maximizing the ability to monitor while minimizing related labor and other costs). Monitoring usually consists of computerized identity checks and can also include scanning people's bodies and personal effects, combined with occasional searches. Efforts to increase control of entry points have also extended to locking manholes and other potential entries to underground access points and to controlling and monitoring non-"front door" entries, such as loading docks, utility corridors, and other potential points of entry. (This monitoring can require additional staff for buildings that receive frequent deliveries).

The second, less visible, but also widespread measure involves collecting more complete information about all employees—permanent as well as temporary (including construction and maintenance work-

ers)—who regularly staff a building. The proliferation of photo identification cards worn by employees is the most evident sign of this trend.
The third measure involves greatly increased monitoring of mailrooms
using observation cameras and similar devices. These mail rooms may
also need to be hardened to protect adjacent building areas from potential
blasts associated with mail bombs.

STRENGTHEN HEATING VENTILATING AND AIR CONDITIONING (HVAC) SYSTEMS

Perhaps the most difficult task ahead is to prevent biological and chemical hazards from being introduced into the air supply, drinking water, or
other systems within buildings or within larger communities. A closely
related and equally difficult challenge involves limiting the damage to
human life once these hazards have been introduced. Proposed measures
to strengthen heating, ventilating, and air conditioning (HVAC) systems
primarily fall into two broad areas.

The less expensive measures focus on: locating air intakes where they
are not readily accessible from the street, adjacent roofs, or by construction or similar workers; controlling access to utility rooms and monitoring them; and providing triggers that immediately shut down or in other
ways shift operation of air-handling systems once a threat has been detected. To avoid significant loss of life, it is important to shut down ventilation systems or, in some cases, greatly increase air changes within a
minute or less. Far more expensive measures involve providing High
Efficiency Particulate Air (HEPA) filters or irradiated air for buildings.
Though highly effective, such measures can add 20–40 percent or more to
the cost of operating a typical office building, taking into account full
maintenance and regular replacement of worn-out and costly filters. The
chief problem to date with these measures has been inadequate maintenance and replacement—which greatly diminishes effectiveness—due to
high costs.

ENHANCE EMERGENCY CAPABILITIES

The emergency preparedness protocols introduced for the World Trade
Center Towers following the 1993 bombing, which included emergency
drills, have been credited with saving many lives on 9/11. Proposed measures to further enhance emergency capabilities primarily fall into three
broad areas.

The first set of measures includes: separating access stairways and
emergency exits to enable fire department and other emergency personnel to enter a building without interference from building inhabitants
who are exiting; providing intermittent "safe" floors—hardened and provided with enhanced fire and smoke suppression—for tall buildings; and

enhancing emergency preparedness for individual buildings and public spaces with regular safety drills. The second set of measures, which has received particular attention following analysis of the structural failures that led to the towers' collapse focuses on strengthening structural systems' protection from blast and heat, preventing collapse altogether or delaying collapse long enough to prolong the period during which people can be evacuated. The third set of measures focuses on increased maintenance budgets to allow frequent replacement of air filters, cameras, and other equipment.

CREATE "DESIGNATED SECURITY ZONES"

These zones, which normally include buildings and public spaces adjacent to potential targets, such as the blocks immediately surrounding courthouses, require increased investment to harden buildings or undertake other measures to limit damage and loss of life that might result from an attack on a nearby target. Proposed measures to create designated security zones involve extending the protective measures applied to potential target buildings to nearby buildings as well. Proposals for security zones focus on combining perimeter protection and hardening efforts to buildings located close to courthouses, federal office buildings, or other potential targets, generally within 100 feet. These measures could significantly increase the construction and operating costs for buildings that are not themselves considered likely targets. Buildings in these zones would also be heavily impacted by street closures or other measures to keep vehicles and pedestrians away from potential target buildings.

The measures taken to fight terrorism will not be static. One of the most significant challenges will be to create regulations for protecting buildings and public spaces that will reflect changing technology and increased experience. A number of measures that could significantly reshape approaches to enhanced security are on the horizon.

PROTECT BUILDING PERIMETERS

New technologies are becoming available to scan vehicles or people and to detect bombs, possibly reducing the need to set back or harden buildings. Increased surveillance capabilities, related to on-site cameras and even to satellite photography, can provide increased protection around high-profile buildings.

HARDEN BUILDINGS

New materials and construction practices are emerging that significantly enhance fire protection and suppression for structural systems. New glass coatings and strengthened window frames reduce the dangers of shattered and flying glass associated with bomb blasts.

CONTROL ACCESS

One of the most controversial and far-reaching changes in technology is the increased ability to verify personal identities—and associated personal histories—using analysis of facial images, identity cards, and related techniques. These techniques could greatly diminish the need for time-consuming monitoring of building entries—and even the need to reduce the number of entries—but they also raise significant privacy and civil rights issues.

STRENGTHEN HVAC SYSTEMS

New technologies are becoming available to detect hazards in air and water systems more rapidly.

How Can Steps to Fight Terrorism Affect Cities?

Approaches to fighting terrorism are already beginning to affect the vitality, sense of community, and civic quality of the urban United States. The impacts threaten to become visible in every major city.

VITALITY

Much of the economic strength has been drained from U.S. cities over the past several decades because of the transition from an industrial economy to one based on service delivery and technology. Closely related—in fact, almost a ghostly twin—is the problem of sprawl. Many older cities lost their economic base with the departure of industrial jobs and the emergence of new economic activity in suburbs. For example, the value of Detroit's tax base, in constant dollars, shrank by more than 75 percent between 1950 and 1990 as the city's economy, based on manufacturing, deteriorated. At the same time, sprawl continues to claim open space (Massachusetts has lost half its farmland since 1950); boost congestion (total miles driven in the greater Boston area have increased roughly 15 times faster than population since 1970); and increase social fragmentation (80 percent of children living in poverty are concentrated in a few older urban areas in the Boston metropolitan area and cut off from their middle-class peers). How do regulations to fight terrorism make it more difficult to revitalize older cities and fight sprawl?

REVITALIZING OLDER COMMUNITIES

For years, the General Services Administration (GSA) brought the only significant new investment to many older communities by locating post offices on older main streets, courthouses and federal office buildings in older downtowns, and federal office buildings in high-unemployment communities. In Boston, the creation of Government Center, which houses federal, state, and city employees, sparked revitalization of Boston's nearby Financial District; 20 years later, the O'Neill Federal Office Building led to a revitalization of the city's Bulfinch Triangle area. Two decades after that, a new federal courthouse has opened the door to redevelopment of Boston's Seaport District. This pattern is repeated around the country. For many older downtowns, new public buildings represent the only hope for new investment.

The GSA's federal courthouse program is the source of significant new investment in many older cities. The most striking new building of the past decade in Cleveland is its new federal courthouse. In Wheeling, West Virginia, a new federal courthouse is helping to galvanize downtown revitalization efforts. The largest office development anticipated for central Birmingham, Alabama, is a new Federal Bureau of Investigation building. This pattern is even more critical for smaller cities across the country.

Much of the private investment in older cities is subsidized to reduce the risk of entry into questionable markets, particularly in the first round of new private investment. Projects like Quincy Hall Marketplace in Boston, new sports stadiums in Cleveland and Baltimore, and other nationally recognized projects that have led the way in bringing private investment back to older downtowns were heavily subsidized. The costs of fighting terrorism threaten to do just the reverse—increase rather than subsidize the cost of these investments. In January 2002, *Newsweek* quoted billionaire businessman Warren Buffett as saying that the costs of development associated with terrorism " . . . could slowly but surely lead to the de-urbanization of America and the closing of any iconic buildings."[2] He was particularly concerned with spiraling insurance costs associated with terrorism.

FIGHTING SPRAWL

In December 2001, Steven Johnson, writing in *Wired* magazine, suggested that "if there are to be new rules for the new warfare, one of the first is surely this: Density kills."[3] A few months later, in an issue of *Architectural Record*, noted architect Leon Krier suggested that the high death toll asso-

---

2. Steven Brill, "Osama's Hidden Tax," *Newsweek*, Vol. 138, No. 2 (January 14, 2002), pp. 50–51.

3. Steven Johnson, "Blueprint for a Better City," *Wired Archive*, Issue 9.12 (December 2001) at <www.wired.com/wired/archive/9.12/mustread_pr.html>.

ciated with the attack on the World Trade Center argues for lower buildings. There appeared to be a strong sentiment against building towers in city centers.

Yet, high-rise buildings represent an important alternative to sprawl because they help achieve urban densities. The choice between creating density versus sprawl is a difficult one. In most regions, sprawl is the real enemy. Suburban shopping centers continue to drain life from older main streets, and sprawl has reinforced racial and economic segregation. Security-driven steps, such as decentralizing public employees, isolating major buildings within large, empty setbacks, and avoiding height when land is scarce all undermine essential tools for fighting sprawl: focusing growth toward developed areas and reestablishing densities traditionally needed to support urban main streets and public transit.

The Bureau of Alcohol, Tobacco, and Firearms (ATF) decided to locate a new office building to help revitalize a part of downtown Washington, D.C. The building is proceeding, but the ATF has asked for a 100-foot setback that is free of vehicles *and* pedestrians. No matter how attractively designed, such pedestrian-free zones are a serious threat to pedestrian-oriented downtowns. In April 2000, the Federal Reserve Bank announced plans to begin moving employees out of denser urban centers to limit the damage that would be caused by an attack on a single major facility. This decentralization will export jobs, disposable income, demand for housing, indirect tax revenue, and many other benefits out of urban cores.

COMMUNITY

The 2000 census reported the stark reality of a country in which the gap between rich and poor has grown dramatically, and patterns of racial and economic fragmentation have increased just as dramatically. Despite a widely reported influx of young professionals and older empty nesters into urban neighborhoods, core communities emerged with family income levels that dropped to less than half the levels found in outer suburbs. In region after region, a growing majority of suburban residents rarely go into downtown to live, work, or shop, with few exceptions: cities as diverse as Denver, Albuquerque, Cleveland, and other urban centers report sustained increases in people from across their regions bucking the suburban trend and rediscovering the city as a place of entertainment, arts, and culture. Every city in this country is heavily invested in efforts to draw larger numbers of people to reacquaint themselves with its streets and squares—mixed-use environments where they can rediscover the forgotten pleasures of urban life. As a society, Americans are heavily invested in rediscovering the common ground that these streets and squares provide in an era dominated by economic and social fragmentation. The alternative is even greater isolation between city and suburb, poor and rich.

There are several key strategies for making city streets and squares vibrant: promoting "eyes on the street"—fostering a sense of safety by lining streets and squares with buildings that have extensive windows; concentrating as much employment as possible along and near these streets and squares to create the economic critical mass needed to support shops and restaurants (in reviving cities, the only option is often public employment); and opening streets and buildings onto each other in ways that promote interaction, dissolving the boundary between buildings and the public realm with shops, multiple entries, and other methods that encourage interaction.

Regulations intended to fight terrorism threaten to stifle rather than promote community in urban zones. The architect of Boston's new federal courthouse, which occupies a magnificent waterfront site at Fan Pier, designed a winter garden overlooking the harbor and downtown to house public events. At a conference of architects, the following question arose: whether the events of 9/11 had diminished public use of this space. The immediate answer was yes. The more important answer, however, was that the courthouse already represented ways that security concerns can diminish a lively public realm. Sitting on the principal pedestrian route between the Financial District and the new Seaport District, the courthouse turns a blank wall to the street for an entire block, placing the building in splendid isolation, dampening nearby public life and severing the two districts it was meant to connect. During planning sessions for the courthouse, the city and many others had asked the GSA to incorporate shops and galleries into this blank wall to enliven the street and reflect the area's character as an arts district. The GSA responded that security concerns precluded these uses.

In sharp contrast, Boston's State Transportation Building, which opened in 1984, embodies community-friendly design: a mix of uses, including shops, services, and restaurants to revitalize Boston's Park Square; parking hidden below the building; and a fully public interior "square," enlivened by cafés, entertainment, and steady pass-through traffic from multiple entrances.[4] These qualities also happen to be the hallmarks of "defensible space," which promote safety by fostering a vital, people-filled public realm.

---

4. Paul McGinn and Theresa A. Mitton, *10 Massachusetts State Transportation Building*, Boston: Massachusetts Port Authority, 1990.

Eli Naor, a California architect who grew up in Israel, has remarked that throughout its years of crisis, Israel has remained committed to buildings and public spaces that promote community. Faced with terrorist bombings, the great public buildings of cities like Madrid and Paris have not closed important public buildings off from streets and squares. The United States should consider these approaches.

CIVIC QUALITY

In the wake of the Oklahoma City bombing, Senator Daniel Patrick Moynihan urged Americans to commit themselves to continuing to create buildings and public spaces that convey our values as an open and democratic society. His words resonate more strongly today. U.S. civic values are at stake as new regulations to fight terrorism are pondered.

The U.S. State Department and architects designing embassies and other federal buildings abroad have long wrestled with the apparent contradictions between a society that prides itself on openness and freedom and the bunker-like architectural qualities that most readily meet security concerns. While both the State Department and these architects deserve significant credit for keeping the debate alive and for continuing to seek a balance between security and the expression of an open society, the results hold little promise as a model for U.S. cities. Although the State Department has worked hard to enhance the architectural quality of its facilities abroad and to minimize the intrusiveness of measures intended to promote security, the deep setbacks, hardened street levels with visibly heavy walls and few windows, fences, heavy security at limited entry points, and security measures represent disturbing models for the courthouses, city halls, and other public buildings that constitute civic architecture in the United States. Yet these are the approaches being promoted to enhance security after 9/11. Within the dense confines of many cities, architects will be challenged to create symbolic buildings that, despite their reliance on obvious security measures, do not communicate a sense of fear, isolation, discrimination among different groups of people, or other messages inappropriate to a democratic society.

This concern extends to a broad range of values that shape the civic quality of our cities. To the extent that concerns about security supersede other values—commitment to historic preservation, meeting the needs of people with disabilities, energy conservation, preserving the environment, and public safety—these other values become more difficult to maintain. Creating barriers around historic buildings alters their character and diminishes a sense of connection to both historic values and traditions. Reconfiguring air handling to protect internal air supplies can significantly increase energy use. Encouraging large zones of quarantine around buildings may lead to the establishment of more greenfield sites. Isolating buildings from parking forces people with disabilities to walk much longer distances. While a single point of entry can still allow multiple points of exit for fire safety, there is the danger of complicating fire safety. The list of potential contradictions is very long.

Avenues to Resolution: Next Steps

There are no easy ways to balance security and the livability of cities. The United States cannot afford to ignore the threats of terrorism but can even less afford to undermine its cities at a time when they already face many critical economic and social challenges. Five important questions emerge as starting points for further dialogue.

DESIGN: ARE THERE GOOD URBAN DESIGN MODELS?

Following the Oklahoma City bombing, the GSA organized a panel of architects, planners, and others to devise an approach to protect federal buildings in Washington, D.C., that remained sensitive to Senator Moynihan's admonition about creating buildings worthy of a democratic and open society. The panel suggested approaches based largely on protecting buildings with street furniture. Subsequently, architects designed artful "hardened streetscapes" for the Federal Triangle in Washington, D.C., that made innovative use of benches, bollards, and streetlights, together with more street trees to protect civic buildings and enhance the public realm, preempting far more drastic proposals to ban vehicles and people and erect walls around public buildings. It is worth noting that without the added rationale of security, these streetscapes would never have benefited from the more generous budget, with accompanying increases in quality of materials and design, which became available when enhanced security became part of the program.

RISK MANAGEMENT: ARE THERE WAYS TO INSURE INVESTORS AGAINST THE CATASTROPHIC COSTS OF TERRORISM?

Unlike "conventional" disasters like fires or earthquakes, the potential costs associated with terrorism cannot be quantified because the threat cannot be defined. This uncertainty is translating into extraordinary insurance premiums. Randall J. Larsen, director of the ANSER Institute for Homeland Security, a government-funded think tank, was quoted by *BusinessWeek* in June 2002, as saying "The problem with security spending is, how do you define 'enough'?"[5] In his January 2002 interview with *Newsweek*, Buffett argued for government-sponsored insurance programs for terrorism that would enable the federal government to mediate between the unknowable risks associated with terrorism and the need to establish insurance protection for those who would become liable following acts of terrorism. The alternative is insurance so expensive that it becomes a brake on development, buying or selling, refinancing, or even continued occupancy of buildings perceived as possible targets.

PRIORITIES: HOW SHOULD ONE BALANCE COSTS AND BENEFITS?

Buffett's concern needs to be broadened to address the challenge of creating new tools to balance the costs and benefits of responding to the risks of terrorism. The costs of prevention are sometimes hard to see as well. Several commentators have noted, for instance, that by choosing to drive over the Thanksgiving holiday in 2001, large numbers of Americans actually placed themselves in greater danger than they would have faced in an airplane, given the far lower mortality rate associated with flying (even with terrorism factored in). It is clear that our society cannot afford to "harden" every potential target—and, far short of this goal, in a world of finite resources, how much of our building dollars does society really want to dedicate to security at the expense of design, sustainability, durability, and other essential qualities? *BusinessWeek* reported in June 2002 that the Brookings Institute has projected that "improved major building security" will cost $2.5 billion per year. Those dollars would be sufficient to build enough homes to house 50,000 Americans every year.[6] Worse, the historic interplay between offensive and defensive strategies suggests that the very steps taken to counter terrorism will simply lead terrorists to search for new targets or new means to threaten current targets. Architects and planners can play a leadership role in assessing the real costs and benefits of fighting terrorism, given competing values and claims on resources.

TECHNOLOGY: HOW CAN FINDING NEW TOOLS HELP PROTECT AGAINST TERRORISM?

Technology can play a larger role in enhancing security. The first step is to establish a performance-based approach to regulations intended to re-

---

5. Lee Walczak et al., "America's Biggest Job: Is the U.S. any less vulnerable to terror these days? Here's the good news—and the bad," *BusinessWeek*, June 10, 2002, pp. 34–36.

6. Ibid.

duce the threat of terrorism and its impacts. Performance-based regulations would, for example, specify the blast level that a building must withstand, rather than setting the thickness of its walls, amount of glass, or other structural characteristics. In turn, the entity charged with administering building regulations would need to certify that a proposed design meets the appropriate standards. Traditional building codes are not performance-based. A new generation of codes, shaped to counter terrorism, can now be crafted to take advantage of rapid technological progress. New technologies will likely reduce the negative impacts on cities of many of the planning, design, and engineering-driven approaches to enhancing security discussed above.

The tools becoming available through advancing technology are already making a difference. In some cases, new technologies obviate undesirable physical design measures. For example, the widely reported photographing and scanning of faces of those attending the 2002 Super Bowl, while raising significant privacy concerns, eliminated the need for highly visible barriers and elaborate checkpoints that, from a design perspective, would have been far more drastic and would also have conveyed a sense of fear. The extent to which security officials can use technology to know who is entering a building or space can make it much easier to open buildings onto public spaces and in other ways to enliven the public realm.

Technology and design can also advance in tandem. Films and other techniques for strengthening glass and minimizing the hazards of shattering represent a far more benign way to "harden" the edges of buildings facing streets than eliminating all windows. Similarly, hardening parking structures to resist an explosion has already reduced the post-9/11 separation required between parking facilities and airport terminals and offers flexibility in locating parking for potential target buildings in urban settings. The principles of good urban design call for parking to be located below public buildings rather than in freestanding structures. Similarly, hardening structural systems and improving emergency-exit and life-protection systems offer distinct advantages over a moratorium on future towers.

VALUES: SHOULD PRIVACY BE SACRIFICED TO PRESERVE COMMUNITY?
Woven into every aspect of the above discussion is the direct or indirect need to find the right balance between values. Enhancing security can diminish privacy, community, freedom of access, convenience, and other values. However, in many cases, if Americans are willing to sacrifice privacy, the nation can preserve other values and address security concerns. At the heart of this discussion lies this trade-off: if authorities know the

identity of people entering a building or public space and can quickly gain sufficient information about their histories, the public can operate with much freer and more convenient access to buildings and spaces—and much greater openness between symbolic buildings, spaces, and the adjacent public environment.

U.S. society is already choosing to make these trade-offs. People tolerate the fact that airlines make it quicker and easier for passengers they know—through frequent flyer programs in most cases—to board airplanes. Most people tolerate "cookies" from Internet sites that provide information about which sites they visit in return for greater convenience in gaining access to those sites. While many commentators expressed concern at the photographing of mass numbers of spectators at the Super Bowl to identify any known terrorists via computer checks, the practice was largely accepted with the understanding that this allowed much more convenient and open access to the stadium. There is no need to keep pedestrians 100 feet from a high-security office building if it is possible to know who those pedestrians are. Architects can locate shops and cafés in public buildings facing public sidewalks if it is possible to know who is entering those shops and cafés. There are privacy tradeoffs that Americans should and would never make—for example, those that sacrifice freedom. It very well may be, however, that gaining a new understanding of the balance between privacy and other values may unlock the ability to promote security without sacrificing those values.

Conclusion

No U.S. city is faced more directly with the dilemma of enhancing security while also promoting urban values than New York City. As Mayor Michael Bloomberg stated in his January 2002 inaugural address, "We will rebuild, renew and remain the capital of the free world . . . New York is safe, strong, open for business and ready to lead the world in the 21st century. We will continue to improve our quality of life and attract visitors, tourists and businesses in record numbers. We will focus on public safety. We will work tirelessly to provide safe streets and homes for all New Yorkers. We will go forward. We will never go back."[7] In this address and in subsequent statements, Mayor Bloomberg stressed that the rebuilding of the devastated World Trade Center site and of lower Manhattan should be focused on people, not fear, honoring the memory of the victims by creating a plan that unites people and fosters renewed

---

7. Inaugural Address of Mayor Michael R. Bloomberg, January 1, 2002. For the complete transcript, see <www.studentvoices.org/news/index.php3?NewsID=2220>.

urban vitality. Echoing his call, a lead editorial in the *New York Times* urged that proposals to rebuild the World Trade Center site incorporate " . . . features, which make an urban area live and breathe."[8]

Terrorism and enhanced security are concerns now firmly planted in the national psyche. It is difficult for most Americans to accept the need to balance the risks associated with terrorism against the costs and benefits of responding to these risks. In the absence of quantitative measures for most risk assessments, Americans will need to establish qualitative measures for deciding where and how to respond to terrorism. Architects, planners, and others who deal daily with the qualitative issues of city building can play an important leadership role in this effort, in part because the people who traditionally make risk assessments cannot. This qualitative assessment will need to address such issues as competing claims for scarce dollars in building projects, finding a balance between enhanced security and lively public realm—a balance that will probably be different in every case, depending on the security and urban context—and even determining which buildings and spaces should be viewed as potential targets in the planning and design process.

As with the response to any crisis, a thoughtful response will leave our society stronger and our public realm more vital. Just as the initial narrow responses to the energy crisis matured into much more complex thinking about sustainability, which in turn has enriched large aspects of our built environment, a fully nuanced response to concerns about terror can provide new understanding and resources to enrich our ability to foster community. To date, the debate about new policies and regulations to shape our fight against terrorism has been dominated by professionals with backgrounds in designing buildings where security is the paramount concern. We need participation by a far wider array of practitioners who are focused on the quality, character, and vitality of cities. In this way, through a broad based national dialogue, we can ensure that there is a commitment to building livable communities and can avoid the kind of single-minded responses that brought a small Connecticut town its windowless school.

---

8. "The Downtown We Don't Want," *New York Times*, July 17, 2002, p. A18.

Chapter 7

Beyond Business Continuity: The Role of the Private Sector in Preparedness Planning

Juliette N. Kayyem and Patricia E. Chang

When a hijacked jet—American Airlines Flight 77—crashed into the Pentagon on September 11, 2001, executives of Science Applications International Corporation[1] had 14,000 workers in offices around the Washington area, but received no guidance from government authorities as to whether it would be safe to release them. That same day, Washington Hospital Center canceled all elective surgery, cleared out beds and operating rooms, and prepared to receive victims, but failed to receive word from local officials that there were few injured victims to treat.[2]

Earlier that morning in New York, after American Airlines Flight 11 and United Airlines Flight 175 hit the north and south towers of the World Trade Center, nearly everyone who could evacuate did so promptly. Their escape was facilitated by revisions made in the evacuation plan by the Port Authority after a terrorist bomb exploded in the World Trade Center in 1993. In addition, the structurally sound buildings, which were equipped with stairwells larger than building codes require,

The authors thank Robyn Pangi for her substantive and editorial comments, Robert Peck, George Vradenburg, Judith Russell, Ernest Tollerson, and Ira Jackson for their insights on public-private partnerships, Marshall Carter for engaging in peer review, and editor John Gravois for his attention to detail.

1. SAIC is the nation's largest employee-owned research and engineering firm.

2. Neil Irwin, "Area's Private Sector Weighs Role in Emergency Plan," *Washington Post*, November 29, 2001, p. E01.

stood long enough to give potential survivors a chance to escape.[3] These factors helped save hundreds, and possibly thousands, of lives.[4]

These accounts illustrate the range of private sector responses on that day and also demonstrate the vital role that the private sector plays in ensuring the safety and well-being of its employees. Some entities in the private sector, which had not previously worked on contingency planning or had depended on inadequate contingency plans, were forced to improvise hasty patchwork measures on 9/11. On the other hand, those private sector entities that already had adequate disaster plans in place prior to that day were able to recover much more quickly and maintain a critical level of functionality. Perhaps one of the most important lessons learned by the private sector was how foresight, prompt intervention, and emergency planning can save lives and greatly aid business recovery and continuity at the same time. Conversely, a sobering look at 9/11 shows that a lack of preparation for disasters may complicate consequence management, halt business activity, and endanger lives. One lesson is clear: emergency planning needs to take place before a crisis occurs, and the private sector is an essential actor in that process.

When the nation's domestic preparedness program began in the 1990s, the focus was primarily to ensure that the federal, state, and local governments were well equipped to deal with any potential terrorist attack. A similarly limited view has also been adopted by the private sector. Since 9/11, the issue of business continuity—the idea that planning is needed for businesses to operate and deliver uninterrupted services to customers during natural and man-made disruptions—has been the focus of much discussion within the business community. While business continuity is essential, there is an even greater need for an integrated public and private domestic preparedness strategy—one that views the private sector not merely as a profit making entity but as an entity responsible (as the government is) for protecting life and ensuring security.

The first part of this chapter argues that the private sector's current lack of integration into domestic preparedness programs is dangerous

---

3. Dennis Couchon, "For Many on Sept. 11, Survival was No Accident," *USA Today*, December 20, 2001, at <www.usatoday.com/news/attack/2001/12/19/usatcovwtcsurvival.html>. The Port Authority also made other crucial improvements prompted by the 1993 attacks: placing reflective paint on stairs, railings, and stairwell doors; adding arrows to guide people along corridors to stairway connections; installing loudspeakers so that building managers could speak to people in their offices and hallways; and adding a second source of power for safety equipment.

4. Ibid.

and explains the need for public-private emergency planning. The second part provides models and recommendations that would facilitate private sector involvement in public safety and security planning.

Lack of Attention Given to the Private Sector Role

Since 9/11, the government has focused much time, energy, attention, and money on fighting the "war against terrorism." Some of the changes include increased federal attention to counterterrorism measures; the creation of new entities to fight terrorism, including the Office of Homeland Security and the Department of Homeland Security; and sweeping changes in legislation to empower law enforcement and intelligence communities with new tools, such as expanded wiretapping and surveillance capabilities.[5] These changes operate with budgetary funding. A total, so far, of $37.7 billion has been allocated for the homeland security program, which provides support for first responders, defense against bioterrorism, security for U.S. borders, and investment in technology that facilitates information and intelligence sharing.[6] The federal government, however, has focused primarily on coordinating ways in which federal, state, and local government agencies will respond to a mass casualty event; it has paid too little attention to integrating the private sector into nationwide counterterrorism efforts.

By neglecting the private sector in its emergency planning, the government limits the number of potential needs that its homeland defense initiatives can address. Historically, the private sector has not been a part of disaster planning. The responsibility has been given primarily to first responders at the state and local level, to the Federal Emergency Management Agency (FEMA) for "consequence management," and to the Department of Justice for "crisis management" at the federal level.[7] Assigning an emergency management role in crises to the public but not to the private sector has contributed to an oversight of private sector involvement in domestic preparedness.

Bob Peck, president of the Greater Washington Board of Trade, illustrates this point:

---

5. Adam Cohen, "Fighting Terror at Home: Rough Justice," *Time*, December 2, 2001, at <*www.time.com/time/nation/article/0,8599,186603,00.html*>.

6. White House Report, "Securing the Homeland, Strengthening the Nation," p. 8, at <www.whitehouse.gov/homeland/homeland_security_book.html>.

7. Richard Falkenrath, "The Problems of Preparedness: Challenges Facing the U.S. Domestic Preparedness Program," Belfer Center for Science and International Affairs Discussion Paper 2000-28, December 2000, pp. 4–5.

"On September 11, I looked out of my window; the federal government did a chaotic job of evacuation; there was gridlock on the streets and we [Washington Board of Trade] started getting all these phone calls from businesses wanting to know if they should evacuate and how to secure their buildings. . . . There were also rumors that the Metro was closed down, that were not true. . . . They [government officials] are used to planning their part of the deal [after a terrorist attack]. They [government officials] will tell the public to clear the area, so that they may do their job. But the private sector is not integrated."[8]

In other words, there is a disconnect between the government and the private sector during and after a crisis situation.

Paralleling this disconnect is the way that businesses have reacted in the aftermath of 9/11. Many businesses, while concerned with revamping their disaster-preparedness plans, have merely been focused on recovering and maintaining their own operations and systems after the attacks. The disorder created in New York City's financial district, for example, was especially difficult to resolve. Approximately 20 percent of the downtown Manhattan office market—or 15.5 million square feet of office space—was destroyed in the attack. An additional 12 million square feet of office space was damaged as a result of falling debris, building collapse, and fires.[9] Corporations near Ground Zero (such as Merrill Lynch, American Express, Morgan Stanley Dean Witter, and Lehman Brothers) worked frantically in the first few hours after the attack to locate their dispersed employees. These corporations also attempted to return to business by relocating to their satellite office spaces, pulling up backup files, and trying to stem the loss of revenues.[10]

Some companies that were affected by the attacks did an extensive revision of their employee safety, facilities, communication, information technology, and insurance coverage strategies in the following weeks.[11] Such changes in emergency response and incident management procedures have been highlighted in Figure 1.

These efforts to alter business continuity plans were mostly, if not completely, focused internally, neglecting how the government may guide or assist in contingency planning. Instead of collaborating with the

---

8.   President Bob Peck, telephone interview, February 28, 2002.

9.   "After September 11, 2001: The Impact of Terrorism on Corporate America," *Business Facilities,* October 2001, at <www.facilitycity.com/busfac/bf_01_10_cover.asp>.

10.   Ibid.

11.   Deloitte & Touche Report, "Business Continuity Management: Unique Perspectives from Ground Zero," October 12, 2001, p. 3, at <http://www.deloitte.com/vc/0,1639,sid%253D2330%2526cid%253D3444,00.html>.

government to assess risks, determine protection needs, select and implement cost-effective policies and controls, and initiate program tests, businesses made their security and emergency preparedness decisions individually. In other words, businesses concentrated solely on improving their own particular response when addressing safety concerns, mirroring how the government focuses on its own agenda for homeland security.

Peck characterizes the private sector response as follows: "The private sector people dealt like the government people, for instance, [by] putting more security in their lobbies. . . . But more needs to be done on the front of preparedness . . . and with coordinating with the government."[12] George Vradenburg, the strategic adviser to AOL/Time Warner and a co-chair of the Potomac Regional Preparedness and Recovery Task Force, agrees: "What is needed is a clear shared vision in regional private-public partnerships and a coherence to how government works with businesses and task forces."[13] As the events of 9/11 have shown, the risks are too great and the costs are too high for a lack of preparation and coordination between the public and private sectors to persist.

LIMITED PROGRESS

To a certain extent, some recognition has been given to this lack of preparation and coordination. The terrorist attacks have ratcheted up the stakes, giving new impetus for the government and private industry to plan safe communities. For example, federal, state, and local government agencies have made some progress working with private sector entities in the areas of aviation security and cyber security. Even before 9/11, Presidential Decision Directive (PDD) 63 on critical infrastructure protection was issued in May 1998 with the intention of "improv[ing] federal agency security programs, establish[ing] a partnership between the government and the private sector, and improv[ing] the nation's ability to detect and respond to serious computer-based attacks."[14] After 9/11, the Aviation Security Act of 2001 put forth that, "The existing fragmentation of responsibility for that safety and security among government agencies and between government and nongovernmental entities is inefficient and unacceptable in light of the hijackings and crashes on September 11,

---

12.   President Bob Peck, telephone interview, February 28, 2002.

13.   George Vradenburg, telephone interview, February 19, 2002.

14.   GAO Report to the Subcommittee on Technology, Terrorism, and Government Information, Committee on the Judiciary, "Critical Infrastructure Protection: Significant Challenges in Developing National Capabilities," GAO-01-323, April 2001, p. 9.

Figure 1. Changes in Business Continuity Planning.

Area Impacted	Revisions Considered or Made
Communications	Communications plans should be in place in order to reassure, give instructions, and share information. Good communication is needed to prevent rumors and misinformation. New technology has made it possible for telecommunications to be an alternative for conducting business, bypassing the necessity of face-to-face interaction.[a]
Leadership	Management needs to review its emergency planning and practice executing decisions before a crisis occurs. Learning how to effectively handle a disaster is a management responsibility; consequently, leadership should familiarize itself with how to declare a disaster and how to appropriate necessary resources in response.
Transportation	Many employees were stranded or unable to work after 9/11. Businesses relying on transportation for critical functions were paralyzed: overnight shipping was postponed, and paychecks went undelivered.[b] Commuting to recovery sites was in some cases, difficult or impossible.
Geographic Location	Many companies affected by 9/11 have chosen to diversify their geographic locations. According to Tenantwise.com, an online real estate broker, only 17 percent of the 137, 919 employees displaced by the attacks have returned as of March 2002.[c] Some Wall Street firms—Lehman Brothers Holdings Inc., Cantor Fitzgerald, and Fiduciary Trust—have relocated to midtown Manhattan.[d] In all, firms based in downtown New York have moved 30 percent of their employees outside the city, many of them permanently.[e]
Personnel Backup	Few companies have thought about succession planning, and those that have focused primarily on the potential replacement of top executives.[f] Cantor Fitzgerald experienced one of the worst losses, with 700 employees killed as a result of the terrorist attacks.[g]
Database Backup	Companies have learned that some redundancy in operations and processing is helpful. With the destruction of desktop and laptop computers, local area networks (LAN)s, and other technology and data support systems on 9/11, managers realized that paper files still remain an important means of information storage and maintenance for work in progress.[h]

Figure 1. *Continued.*

Area Impacted	Revisions Considered or Made
Key Dependencies	Companies should understand dependencies on key vendors; the reliance on extended enterprises such as suppliers and service providers became a problem especially when the shipment of supplies was delayed and manufacturing cycles were disrupted. Understanding dependencies will help to minimize the risk of a supply chain or service breakdown.[i]
Security	Both physical and logical security efforts should be reviewed, and the right amount of preparedness should be chosen. This includes, but is not limited to, the physical security of buildings as well as the security of IT systems.[j]
Insurance	Companies should review insurance coverage to capture the required information for preparing a claim. The ability of carriers and reinsurers to assume resulting liabilities should be verified in advance.[k]

[a] Ibid., p. 6.

[b] Ibid., p. 5.

[c] Special Report: Overview of Current Situation, March 21, 2002, Tenantwise.com at www.tenantwise.com/032002wtc.asp.

[d] "Moving Back Downtown?" *Wall Street Journal Online,* March 15, 2002, at www.online.wsj.com/public/resources/documents/MovingBack-2002–03–15.htm.

[e] Michael Siconolfi, "Wall Street Firms Rebuild," *Wall Street Journal,* March 11, 2002, p. M1.

[f] Neil Kaufman, Jack Pullara, Mary Grace Davenport, and Chris Thompson, "Insights from the Events of September 11: Is your organization prepared?" PriceWaterHouseCoopers Global, at <www.pwcglobal.com/images/gx/eng/fs/bcm/0911insightsv2.pdf>.

[g] "Solemn Tribute for Cantor Fitzgerald," MSNBC, October 1, 2001, at www.msnbc.com/news/636359.asp.

[h] Neil Kaufman et al., "Insights from the Events of September 11th: Is your organization prepared?"

[i] Ibid.

[j] Ibid.

[k] Deloitte & Touche Report, "Business Continuity Management: Unique Perspectives from Ground Zero," p. 7.

2001."[15] It also placed more responsibility on the federal government for overseeing private security functions and security personnel at U.S. airports.[16]

There has also been more vocal attention given to private sector security. For instance, public officials are more frequently issuing statements that stress the importance of consistent communication from the government to the private sector. "A lot of businesses . . . are getting different messages from different levels of government . . . " regarding emergency procedures. "We have to go seek out private sector entities to make sure we're helping them prepare for [an economic] recovery. There has to be a meshing of public and private sector operations," states one local official.[17]

This sentiment is echoed in the White House Report, "Securing the Homeland, Strengthening the Nation." The report tasked then OHS Director Office of Homeland Security Director Tom Ridge with creating a national strategy for homeland security that will be based "on the principle of partnership with state and local governments, the private sector, and citizens."[18] In a briefing with members of the National Association of Manufacturers (NAM), the nation's largest industrial trade association, Governor Ridge said:

"But, in fact, for it [national counterterrorism strategy] to be a successful national strategy, the federal government, the state and local governments, have to be involved; the public sector certainly has to be involved. But very much at the heart of a successful strategy will be the involvement of the private sector. And to date, that involvement has been substantial and specific, and in the months and the years ahead we will continue to build on really the foundation that the private sector has laid, [and that] the public sector has been working on over the past couple of months as well."[19]

---

15. Public Law 107-71, 107th Congress, 1st sess., (November 19, 2001), Aviation Security Act of 2001. The Aviation Security Act, S. 1447, became Public Law No. 107-71 on November 19, 2001.

16. Ibid.

17. Neil Adler, "Officials preach regional response to emergencies," *Gazette*, December 7, 2001, at <www.gazette.net/200149/business/news/83117-1.html> The local official quoted is Gene Lynch, deputy chief of staff to Governor Parris N. Glendening of Maryland.

18. White House Report, "Securing the Homeland, Strengthening the Nation," p. 6 at <www.whitehouse.gov/homeland/homeland_security_book.html>.

19. Transcript of Governor Tom Ridge, "Issues Briefing" with National Manufacturers Association, February 13, 2002, p. 5 at <www.nam.org/tertiary.asp_TrackID_ &CategoryID_513&Document>.

Accordingly, federal, state, and local officials have noted that rethinking the role of the private sector in disaster planning is essential for many reasons.

REASONS FOR GOVERNMENT TO INVEST

There are many reasons why the government should be invested in engaging the private sector in its strategy for homeland security. First, more than 80 percent of information systems are owned by the private sector.[20] Approximately 90 percent of critical infrastructure is owned by the private sector, including banking, finance, transportation, and intelligence systems, utilities and water supplies, and communication networks.[21] Some of the most valuable institutions, and therefore the most desirable targets, are owned by the private sector.

Second, 9/11 made evident the fact that the private sector has a crucial role to play in emergency planning and response. Many essential services used in an emergency—communications, power, water, food, and medical services—are owned or operated by private businesses.[22] Should a weapon of mass destruction (WMD) attack occur, private doctors, hospitals, and emergency technicians would treat most of the victims. Likewise, in a crisis situation, pharmaceutical companies would supply stockpiles of the critical medicines and vaccines; manufacturers would supply the necessary protective equipment and gear; banks and financial institutions would provide monetary support to the disaster site; privately owned communications systems would provide equipment and repairing services; and privately owned universities, schools, hospitals, or other buildings might contribute space for triage and other support activities.[23]

Third, most Americans spend a majority of their time away from home, inside of private institutions that have their own regulatory proce-

20. Gilmore Commission, *Third Annual Report to the President and the Congress of the Advisory Panel to Assess Domestic Response Capabilities for Terrorism Involving Weapons of Mass Destruction,* December 15, 2001, p. 41.

21. Sandra Swanson, "National Security Council Contemplates Computer Security Issues," InformationWeek.com, October 31, 2001, at <www.informationweek.com/story/IWK20011031S0008>.

22. The private sector also is a producer of innovative technology, medicines, services, and products that help combat terrorism. Many private companies, for instance, work as subcontractors to government agencies or as outsourcers of critical functions in an emergency.

23. Potomac Conference White Paper, "Regional Preparedness and Recovery," November 29, 2001, pp. 3–4, provided by Karen Roberts, Director of the Potomac Conference, via email, February 11, 2002.

dures. These institutions have significant influence over people's actions. Employers of the private sector are often responsible for planning emergency communications and evacuation efforts, including school closures, the provision of shelter, blood drives, vaccination programs, and other functions.[24] The decisions made by these private institutions affect the conduct and welfare of employees as well as the surrounding community. The government should factor this reality into their emergency and crisis planning.

Fourth, incorporating the voice of the private sector into the national homeland security strategy would also help stave off inefficiency in the war against terrorism. Without the input of the private sector, counterterrorism efforts may be fragmented and critical information may remain stove-piped. A fragmented strategy may consequently cause confusion, duplicative efforts, and an ineffective alignment of resources with strategic goals.[25] On the other hand, once the roles and responsibilities of the government and private sector are clarified and delineated, the burden of counterterrorism is shared—to the benefit of both.

Fifth, the U.S. Constitution and our legal regulatory system view the private sector, for the most part, as an entity that is not easily controlled. The Fifth Amendment to the Constitution states explicitly that there shall be no government taking of private property without just compensation. President Harry S. Truman's attempts to control the steel mills during the Korean War, which was fought by the United States without a declaration of war, were invalidated by the Supreme Court in 1952.[26] Without congressional authorization, the Court said, the President of the United States could not simply take control of industry, regardless of the need during a war. Thus, in the event of an emergency, the government may not have the legal authority to force private entities to act in certain ways—for example, to provide transportation or safe havens for the population.[27] A domestic preparedness strategy that integrates the private sector will help ensure, first, that there is a working cooperation between government and business so that expectations and demands can be dis-

---

24. Ibid.

25. Statement of David M. Walker, GAO Testimony before the Senate Committee on Governmental Affairs, "Homeland Security: A Framework for Addressing the Nation's Efforts," GAO-01-1158T, September 21, 2001, p. 4.

26. *Youngstown Sheet & Tube Co. v. Sawyer*, 343 U.S. 579 (1952) (Steel Seizure Case).

27. Juliette N. Kayyem, "U.S. Preparations for Biological Terrorism: Legal Limitations and the Need for Planning," Belfer Center for Science and International Affairs Discussion Paper 2001-4, March 2001, pp. 12–13.

cussed, and second, that any legal impediments can be determined before an event, and legislation may be sought to remedy any deficiencies.

Finally, joining private and public efforts to homeland security may also help the government sustain an appropriate level of responsiveness and readiness for future disasters. Involvement of both the private and the public sectors in emergency planning will assist in sustainability and in the maintenance of focus and political support for emergency preparedness planning, even when the attention given to terrorist threats has waned. Understanding and appreciating the value of preparedness by both the private and public sectors will ensure the longevity, if not the success, of emergency planning.

REASONS WHY THE PRIVATE SECTOR SHOULD INVEST

The private sector should be invested and engaged in domestic preparedness programs for reasons ranging from obligation to self-interest. First, the clearest reason for private sector involvement in emergency preparedness is to ensure employee safety. After 9/11, senior executives and boards recognized a "heightened sense of responsibility" for the safety of their people and consequently addressed the "human factor" of business.[28] Many businesses realized that their greatest asset was their people, and that the greatest loss to the company was not the loss of revenues but the loss of human life.

Second, the failure to provide for planning may have unintended consequences for the private sector. For instance, the events of 9/11 should change the way businesses think about their people and the way that they provide for their needs, particularly for their mental health needs. Greg Farris, executive director of business continuity planning at Morgan Stanley Dean Witter, noted that people were so deeply influenced by the World Trade Center attacks that they required assistance from crisis counselors in "getting back to normal and being productive again."[29] A well-developed and robust emergency response plan, under the guidance of an incident commander, can provide for the safety of employees as well as for necessary mental health resources.

Third, as discussed earlier, the private sector needs to be invested in emergency preparedness because business continuity plans are a corporate necessity. Corporations that engage in business continuity planning recognize that the risks leading to business process failure, asset loss, reg-

---

28. Deloitte & Touche Report, "Business Continuity Management: Unique Perspectives from Ground Zero," p. 4.

29. Stan Gibson, "Reporter's Notebook: Disaster Recovery," eWEEK, October 22, 2001, at <www.eweek.com/article/0,3658,s%253D704%2526a%253D15168,00.asp>.

ulatory liability, customer service failure, or reputation damage may be mitigated.[30] Adequate business continuity planning may also ensure the safety of one's staff, preserve valuable information, minimize service interruptions, and help resume normal services.[31] Yet focusing solely on business continuity is a far too limited approach. With government assistance and guidance, businesses may be better assured that their safety efforts and continuity plans are as comprehensive and realistic as possible.

Fourth, having public-private preparedness plans in place may help maintain consumer and shareholder confidence. For example, the knowledge that the government and the private sector are working on safety precautions has helped reassure some air flight passengers hesitant to fly after 9/11. Confidence in the safety of a region may help recover losses (as in the case with aviation security), as well as help attract new jobs and economic growth to that area.[32]

Finally, the private sector should be engaged in preparedness planning with the government because there are needs that the private sector alone cannot meet when disaster strikes. One such need is government guidance that provides accurate and timely information during an emergency, guidance that allows the private sector to craft an appropriate response and execute its role in emergency preparedness. Other private sector needs include the protection of vital records and the maintenance of open communication lines. Lastly, the government plays a part in stimulating economic recovery after disasters, e.g., President Bush's renewal of his pledge of at least $20 billion in monetary assistance to New York.[33] (All in all, 9/11 created a $54 billion loss in the Lower Manhattan economy, displacing more than 100,000 jobs.)[34] Integrating the private sector during emergency planning can help ensure that all vital services, including those outside the government, will continue.[35]

·

---

30. Deloitte & Touche Report, "Business Continuity Management: Unique Perspectives from Ground Zero," p. 11.

31. A.T. Kearney Pamphlet, "Business Continuity and Corporate Security: A Timely Solution for Today's Challenges," on file with the author. For more information, please access <www.atkearney.com>.

32. Potomac Conference White Paper, "Regional Preparedness and Recovery," p. 12.

33. Raymond Hernandez, "Bush Offers Details of Aid to New York Topping $20 Billion," *New York Times*, March 8, 2002, p. A1.

34. Kathryn S. Wylde, "The Old Downtown Economy Won't Return," *New York Times*, March 29, 2002.

35. Potomac Conference White Paper, "Regional Preparedness and Recovery," p. 8.

BARRIERS TO PRIVATE SECTOR INVESTMENT. Despite the many compelling reasons for private sector integration, numerous private-public collaborations have not yet occurred. This is partly because of historical precedent—there has been a traditional lack of government attention given to private sector involvement. The stronger and more troublesome reason is that there are significant barriers and obstacles hindering security investment. Investing in security may, in fact, be to many companies' disadvantage. "Security is not an income generator, it's a cost generator. . . . People want to spend as little as possible," states Kevin Surette, a security consultant in Litchfield, Maine.[36] "Security is not going to add to your bottom line. It's a necessary evil," adds Joe Grillo, a chief operating officer at HID Corp.[37] Consequently, even if standards for preparedness are the responsibility of the government and are federally mandated and developed, the costs for implementing or evaluating these practices still fall mainly on the private sector. Security is often viewed as a huge cost, instead of an investment with a sizable return in the form of preventing losses.

Exacerbating this problem are substantial legal concerns—concerns that organizations could face antitrust violations for sharing information with industry partners, that their information could be subjected to Freedom of Information Act disclosures, or that they could face liability concerns. These, along with cost concerns, currently limit private sector involvement.[38] Whereas more rhetorical attention is being paid to the lack of private sector involvement in preparedness, substantial initiatives to address this problem are either lacking or are still burgeoning.

How to Engage the Private Sector: Models

The work that remains to be done is daunting but nevertheless achievable. In a practical sense, private and public partnerships will need to foster effective communication to and from the private sector and the government. "We need those in positions of authority to communicate clearly and calmly. Unless public officials and private sector leaders coor-

---

36. Rachel Zimmerman, "Workplace Security (A Special Report): Tools to Protect Mail," *Wall Street Journal*, March 11, 2002, p. R7.

37. Maureen Tkacik, "Workplace Security (A Special Report): Ready Response: Plenty of companies are aiming to cash in on the security business, but so far it's no bonanza," *Wall Street Journal*, March 11, 2002, p. R12.

38. A Report of the Heritage Foundation Homeland Security Task Force, "Defending the American Homeland," The Heritage Foundation, 2002, p. 22–23.

dinate in advance, mixed messages will complicate the job of surviving, recovering, and putting communities back together. That's why advance planning is so critical."[39] states Mike McCurry, founder of Grassroots Enterprise and co-chair of the Potomac Task Force.

Advance planning entails developing public and private dialogues on issues of common concern, understanding differing motivations and perspectives, cooperatively defining roles and responsibilities, and addressing burden sharing issues.[40] As private and public entities learn to work together, they will be better able to discover the gaps in domestic preparedness, identify and share some of their best security, safety, and recovery practices, and work to standardize their emergency planning with government guidance.

Perhaps the most difficult question to answer is how the private sector should be integrated into domestic preparedness programs. One model of how public and private sectors have worked together effectively on a transnational problem emerged during the Year 2000 turnover (Y2K). During the 1990s, many feared that computer systems, software applications, and embedded microprocessors would crash or malfunction on January 1, 2000. Because they were programmed with date fields using just two digits for the year, people were concerned that they would simply return to 1900, instead of 2000, at the start of the new millennium.[41]

According to the Office of Management and Budget, the federal government spent an estimated $8.34 billion to prevent the Y2K problem; the Commerce Department estimated that U.S. government and businesses combined spent roughly $100 billion.[42] With roughly 180 billion lines of software code to be rewritten and millions of embedded chips that needed to be replaced or destroyed, the magnitude of the technological and managerial challenge was brought to international attention as a *bona fide* emergency.[43] The attention resulted in massive mobilization with a

---

39. Email correspondence from Potomac Director of Communications relaying quote, March 5, 2002.

40. Executive Summary, "Bioterrorism in the United States: Threat, Preparedness, and Response," Chemical and Biological Arms Control Institute, November 2000, p. 27.

41. Y2K Risk Assessment Task Force, "Y2K: A Global Ticking Time Bomb?," CSIS at <www.csis.org/html/y2k.html>.

42. Final Committee Report, "Y2K Aftermath—Crisis Averted," The United States Senate Special Committee on the Year 2000 Technology Problem, February 29, 2000, p. 11 at <www.senate.gov/_bennett/y2k.html>.

43. Y2K Risk Assessment Task Force, "Y2K: A Global Ticking Time Bomb?"

leadership role for the federal government and partnerships with the private sector and international governments.

The federal approach to the Y2K situation may be organized into the following five categories:

- Congressional oversight of agencies to hold them accountable for demonstrating progress to heighten public awareness of the problem.
- Central leadership and coordination to ensure that federal systems were ready for the date change, to coordinate efforts primarily with the states, and to promote private sector and foreign government action.
- Partnerships within the intergovernmental system and with the private entities, divided into key economic sectors to address such issues as contingency planning.
- Communications to share information on the status of systems, products, and services, and to share recommended solutions.
- Human capital and budget initiatives to help ensure that the government could recruit and retain the technical expertise needed to convert systems and communicate with the other partners and to fund conversion operations.[44]

A homeland security plan may demand a level of leadership, oversight, and partnership similar to the Y2K model.[45] However, Homeland Security Director Ridge realizes its distinct challenges: "You may say homeland security is a Y2K problem that doesn't end January 1st of any given year," he has said, alluding to the fact that unlike the relative success of initiatives and partnerships formed to face the Y2K situation, initiatives and partnerships addressing counterterrorism need to be sustained over time.[46]

Since 9/11, two of the most visible prototypes that have addressed the needs of private industry in crisis situations are: the Potomac Confer-

---

44. Statement of Henry L. Hinton, Jr., GAO Testimony before the Subcommittee on National Security, Veterans Affairs, and International Relations House Committee on Government Reform, "Homeland Security: Progress Made; More Direction and Partnership Sought," GAO-02-490T, March 12, 2002, p. 12. The five categories are taken verbatim from this statement.

45. Statement of David Walker, "Homeland Security: A Framework for Addressing the Nation's Efforts," p. 6.

46. Liza Porteus, "Ridge calls homeland security a Y2K problem with no deadline," GovExec.com, February 28, 2002, at <www.govexec.com/dailyfed/0202/022802td1.htm>.

ence Regional Task Force on Preparedness and Recovery, working in collaboration with the Washington Council of Governments' (WASHCOG) Task Force on Homeland Security and Emergency Preparedness; and the New York City Partnership (NYCP).[47] In response to 9/11, the Potomac Conference Regional Task Force on Preparedness and Recovery (the Potomac Conference Task Force) was launched in Washington, D.C., on November 29, 2001, to promote regional collaboration and to spur businesses, nonprofit organizations, and public officials in all levels of government to prepare for future crises. More specifically, its goal is to work with public sector leadership to "develop and implement a comprehensive, integrated plan for prevention, response, and recovery from any potential crisis in the Greater Washington region."[48] The Potomac Conference Task Force, comprised of 160 individuals from businesses, nonprofit organizations, and the government, was divided into four break-out groups that would address emergency preparedness, business and nonprofit continuity, economic recovery, and communications.[49]

Similarly, the NYCP is comprised of 200 "partners"—leaders from the business, real estate, and investment communities. Founded in 1979, the NYCP is a nonprofit organization that works on legislation, regulation, and public issues impacting businesses and the economy.[50] Since 9/11, it has engaged in studies and actions devoted to rebuilding the Lower Manhattan business community. The NYCP, however, is still in the preliminary stages of addressing public-private collaboration and is currently working on designating a safety and security task force dedicated

---

47. There are other regional organizations that work on emergency preparedness activities, such as various regional councils of governments, regional chambers of commerce (such as in Florida or South Carolina, where chambers of commerce concentrate on preparedness and recovery from hurricanes), and regional civic organizations, such as the Orange County Business Council and the South Bay Economic Development Partnership in California, and the Regional Plan Association's "Civic Alliance to Rebuild Downtown New York," in New York.

48. Regional Task Force on Preparedness and Recovery Status Update, The Potomac Conference, January 10, 2002, at <www.bot.org/html/news/News-TPC011802.asp>.

49. The four groups have various responsibilities, including: identifying common terminology to convey threats and emergency procedures in order to minimize confusion; developing a "best practices" tool kit along with a resource bank of mentors and coaches that may be used for continuity planning; integrating their work with regional tourism and economic development initiatives in order to encourage regional economic growth; and developing methods of informing the public during an emergency so that they may decide what actions to take within their households.

50. For more information, please access <www.nycp.org>.

to this issue.[51] Promoting partnerships such as the Potomac Conference Task Force or the NYCP may maximize resources and foster useful regional relationships.

HOW TO ENGAGE THE PRIVATE SECTOR: RECOMMENDATIONS AND TOOLS

While the government is relying on the private sector for greater support in protecting critical infrastructure and the nation, many in the private sector are looking to the government to encourage safer networking and information sharing in nonlegislative and nonregulatory ways. The government should take active steps to foster a private-public approach to homeland security and to encourage private sector participation in domestic preparedness. There are three steps involved in the process: researching the problem, providing risk and threat assessments to the private sector, and, finally, implementing policy tools that encourage private sector integration into homeland security.

The first step is to understand the problem fully before making recommendations and taking action. A public-private commission comprising people who have worked on critical infrastructure protection, health officials from the private and public areas, businesses leaders, and government officials should examine the lack of private sector integration into homeland security. Any recommendations made by this proposed public-private commission should be framed in terms of establishing and maintaining private sector involvement in domestic preparedness programs.

Second, after understanding the problem and focusing on what needs must be met, the government should offer assistance with risk and threat assessments. Risk assessments are "decision-making support tools that are used to establish requirements and prioritize program investments."[52] Risk assessments form a "deliberate, analytical approach that results in a prioritized list of risks"; this list may be used to select countermeasures to create a certain level of preparedness for an area.[53] Threat assessments are tools that "identify and evaluate each threat on the basis of factors such as capability and intent to attack an asset, the likelihood and severity of the consequences of a successful attack."[54]

---

51. NYCP's Senior Vice President Ernest Tollerson and Vice President of Research and Policy Judith Russell, telephone interview, March 10, 2002.

52. GAO Report to Congressional Requesters, "Combating Terrorism: Need for Comprehensive Threat and Risk Assessments of Chemical and Biological Attacks," GAO/NSIAD-99-163, September 1999, p. 5–6.

53. Ibid.

54. Ibid.

Without the benefits of a threat and risk assessment, many companies rely on worst-case chemical, biological, radiological, or nuclear scenarios to generate countermeasures for prevention. This means that the company, working from a worst-case scenario, focuses on vulnerabilities (which are unlimited) rather than credible threats (which are limited).[55] Compared to worst-case scenarios, targeted threat and risk assessments give better guidance as to how to address threats and allocate resources, taking into account how much preparedness is necessary.[56]

Since 9/11, many in the private sector have taken security matters into their own hands. This is evident from the rise of security spending and technological security devices: private security guards, metal detectors, digital cameras, electronic photo identification cards used to track employees, facial recognition systems, and fingerprint readers.[57] Other companies have chosen to irradiate mail and check ventilation systems in anticipation of a bioterror event.[58] Still others have decided to strengthen the structure of their buildings,[59] or even to relocate.

Risk and threat assessments, however, will help companies decide what level of preparedness and action is appropriate, while factoring the context of the business operation together with the likelihood of an attack. Thus, a small company in Iowa will not necessarily face the same safety concerns or the same safety requirements as a large investment bank in downtown New York. A company's level of preparedness needs will differ by location, density of personnel, industry, and a range of other factors.

Lead federal agencies should develop a best-practices model for the private sector that enables them to conduct more accurate risk, vulnerability, and survivability assessments.[60] Such a model would allow indus-

---

55. GAO Report to Congressional Committees, "Combating Terrorism: Selected Challenges and Related Recommendations," GAO-01-822, September 2001, p. 45.

56. Ibid.

57. Kris Maher, "Workplace Security (A Special Report)—Life Goes on . . . but Differently: For many workers, day-to-day life has changed, in ways both small and large," *Wall Street Journal*, March 11, 2002, p. R14; and Dennis K. Berman, "Workplace Security (A Special Report)—Tools to Protect Against Future Threats," *Wall Street Journal*, March 11, 2002, p. R10.

58. Rachel Zimmerman, "Workplace Security (A Special Report): Tools to Protect Mail," *Wall Street Journal*, March 11, 2002, p. R7.

59. Susan Warren, "Workplace Security (A Special Report): Tools to Protect Buildings," *Wall Street Journal*, March 11, 2002, p. R6.

60. "Defending the American Homeland," The Heritage Foundation, p. 24.

try to address its security needs according to its own defined set of performance standards, as opposed to a set of government specifications, which may be less flexible, and therefore more difficult to meet. The Defense Department's internal assessment program may serve as a guide in developing best practices.[61] In addition, the Department of Justice Office for Domestic Preparedness and the Federal Bureau of Investigation (FBI) have worked together to provide state and local governments with a risk and threat assessment tool.[62] This tool includes a step-by-step methodology for assessing threats, risks, and requirements, which could likely be put to use by the private sector.

Third, the federal government possesses a variety of policy instruments (such as regulations, tax incentives, and regional coordination and partnerships) that could be used to encourage or mandate that private sector entities take actions addressing security concerns. The methods for engaging the private sector may rest on frameworks ranging from the regulatory to the rewarding, to the simple removal of barriers to security investment.

Figure 2 details some methods of engaging the private sector, as categorized by the three frameworks mentioned above:

The *regulatory* framework operates under the assumption that the government must take more active measures in setting standards for infrastructure and programs vital to preparedness. In the most stringent regulatory framework, federal agencies would support standards adopted by the private sector, and these standards would be placed under federal oversight. A less stringent regulatory framework would present alternatives to federal preemption and operate on a more voluntary basis. The five regulatory models in Figure 2 were referenced in a Government Accounting Office report.[63] These models represent the spectrum of shared regulatory authority.

Enforcing these standards is a separate issue, which can be addressed in a regulatory framework. Depending on how stringent the chosen regu-

---

61. Ibid.

62. Statement of Raymond J. Decker, GAO Testimony before the Senate Committee on Governmental Affairs, "Homeland Security: A Risk Management Approach Can Guide Preparedness Efforts," GAO-02-208T, October 31, 2001, p. 6.

63. Statement of Patricia A. Dalton, GAO Testimony before the Subcommittee on Government Efficiency, Financial Management, and Intergovernmental Relations, Committee on Government Reform, House of Representatives, "Combating Terrorism: Intergovernmental Cooperation in the Development of a National Strategy to Enhance State and Local Preparedness," GAO-02-550T, April 2, 2002, p. 15.

Figure 2. Summary of Methods of Engaging the Private Sector.

Framework	Method
Regulatory	5 regulatory models:
	1) Fixed federal standards that override all state regulation.
	2) Federal minimum standards that override less stringent state laws but allow states to establish standards more stringent than the federal standards.
	3) Inclusion of federal regulatory provisions that states may choose to accept.
	4) Cooperative programs in which voluntary national standards are written and set by federal and state officials.
	5) Widespread state adoption of voluntary standards written and set by quasi-official entities.
	(These models may be enforced in a variety of ways—by audits, committees with federal oversight, or trade associations.)
Rewarding	• Tax Incentives
	• Honor Roll
Removing Barriers	• Freedom of Information Act (FOIA) Exemptions
	• Antitrust Exemptions
	• Tax Penalty Removals

---

latory framework may be, entities that enforce these security standards (or recommendations) may respond in kind.[64] A variety of entities may be "enforcers." For example, companies may undergo regular federal audits, engage in voluntary reporting to committees with federal oversight, or report to trade organizations which would oversee the enforcement of these standards. If standards or recommendations are not properly implemented, these entities may respond in a punitive fashion.

The methods used in a *rewarding* framework consist of incentives that encourage the private sector to increase its security precautions. Incentives would include measures such as tax incentives and designation on an honor role. Tax incentives may consist of special exclusions, exemptions, deductions, credits, deferrals, or tax rates in the federal tax laws.[65]

---

64. It should be noted that the first two models are more stringent than models numbered three through five.

65. States that have promoted commercial and industrial applications of renewable energy technologies, for example, have provided incentives such as income tax credits, property tax exemptions, state sales tax exemptions, loan programs, special grant programs, industry recruitment incentives, accelerated depreciation allowances, as well as project development grants.

Tax incentives do not generally permit the same degree of federal oversight and targeting as grants.[66] Similarly, a biannual "honor roll," a list used for comparing companies and noting exemplary performance, is suggested to highlight the top 100 companies that have adopted these security standards—to stimulate and encourage voluntary participation.[67] The honor roll would essentially create a competitive atmosphere in industry, in which the adoption of comprehensive security systems is rewarded with recognition. More importantly, it would likely be utilized by "potential customers, investors, and insurers" in their decisions choosing between potential providers.[68]

Finally, the methods used in the *removing barriers* framework simply entail doing that which is expedient to encourage private sector involvement in security. This includes providing Freedom of Information Act (FOIA) exemptions[69] to specific companies. FOIA exemptions limit certain business records from disclosure. Many companies fear that any information that they share about their vulnerability or risk of intrusion will become public knowledge and will therefore damage public and shareholder confidence. Companies hesitate to disclose that information, even if it is vital to the interest of national defense. Competitors may also use FOIA requests to gain information about a company's practices or systems—information that may include trade secrets.[70]

The damage done when confidential information is made public may be detrimental to businesses; "an inadvertent release of confidential business information, such as trade secrets or proprietary information, could damage reputations, lower consumer confidence, hurt competitiveness, and decrease market shares of firms."[71] Targeted FOIA exemptions, how-

---

66. Statement of Patricia A. Dalton, "Combating Terrorism: Intergovernmental Cooperation in the Development of a National Strategy to Enhance State and Local Preparedness," GAO-02-550T, p. 15.

67. "Defending the American Homeland," The Heritage Foundation, p. 24.

68. Ibid.

69. FOIA exemptions make the following records exempt from disclosure: information vital to national defense; information related to solely internal personnel rules and practices; information specifically exempted from disclosure by statute; information that is a trade secret; information contained in inter- or intra-agency memorandums or letters that would not be available by law; information that violates personnel and medical files; information compiled for law enforcement purposes. For more information please see <www.federalreserve.gov/generalinfo/foia/exemptions.cfm>.

70. "Defending the American Homeland," The Heritage Foundation, p. 22.

71. Statement of Joel C. Willemssen, GAO Testimony before the Subcommittee on Government Efficiency, Financial Management and Intergovernmental Relations, Committee on Government Reform, House of Representatives, "Critical Infrastructure

ever, would encourage some businesses (which would be identified beforehand by the government's commission) to share critical information with the government in the interests of protecting the nation and to cooperate with other related companies in making threat assessments of infrastructure without compromising business concerns. This is especially pertinent for critical infrastructure facilities such as nuclear power plants, chemical and electrical facilities, banking and financing institutions, water supply facilities, transportation systems, and the communication network.

The government should also provide narrow antitrust exemptions, such as the legislation passed by Congress, the Information and Readiness Disclosure Act,[72] which exempted any information sharing for the purposes of Y2K preparedness from antitrust laws. Antitrust laws are meant to prevent businesses from colluding and price-fixing, but they also inhibit companies from sharing information on infrastructure vulnerability or from working on the means to protect it.[73] When homeland security is threatened, however, any cooperation to protect critical infrastructure should be exempted from antitrust laws to protect cooperative companies from unjust lawsuits.

Finally, Congress should remove tax penalties that make it more difficult for the private sector to invest in security measures. Industry is only allowed to depreciate its spending for security-related purchases, often over an extended period. This creates a tax on investment spending, which, in turn, increases the effective cost while discouraging businesses from spending on security.[74] Removing tax penalties on companies that invest in security will encourage the private sector's participation in domestic preparedness. Congress should revise the tax code to permit infrastructure owners to deduct the full cost of security-related spending in the year that such expenses are incurred.[75]

These three frameworks (*regulatory*, *rewarding*, and *removing barriers*) and their methods are by no means comprehensive, yet this list may serve as a guide to government action. These policy tools, however, are most effective only after private sector and government needs have been

---

Protection: Significant Challenges in Safeguarding Government and Privately Controlled Systems from Computer Based Attacks," GAO-01-1168T, September 26, 2001, p. 28.

72. Previously the S. 2392, the Year 2000 Information and Readiness Disclosure Act became Public Law 105-271 on October 19, 1998.

73. "Defending the American Homeland," The Heritage Foundation, p. 23.

74. "Defending the American Homeland," The Heritage Foundation, p. 24.

75. Ibid.

researched properly through a private-public commission, and risk and threat assessments have been issued. There are both advantages and disadvantages to each framework as policy tools. For reasons detailed in the following paragraphs, a step in the right direction would favor the *removing barriers* framework, as opposed to the *regulatory* or *rewarding* frameworks. After the *removing barriers* framework has been successfully implemented and its shortfalls revealed, a mix of *regulatory* or *rewarding* factors may then be augmented, depending on need.

Figure 3 summarizes the advantages and disadvantages of each of the frameworks.

ADVANTAGES/DISADVANTAGES

Each of the frameworks has its merits and drawbacks. A benefit of the *regulatory* framework is that it would help standardize security efforts. On the other hand, regulatory models (especially on the more stringent side) may be politically difficult to maneuver, as most businesses balk at government regulation of their trade. Second, rigid standards enforced by a regulatory model often do not allow firms to adapt these standards according to their own organizational capacity and needs. Another disadvantage of the regulatory model is that it may discourage, or worse, stymie, any innovation of private sector solutions to security problems. When the private sector takes responsibility for security, the internal regulatory strategies may perhaps be less costly and more effective than they would be under government standards.[76] Finally, the enforcement of the regulatory model would be subject to constant or continual evaluations or measurements, checking if businesses are sufficiently prepared. This could be costly to both parties, without a distinct end point in the development of private sector preparedness.

The *rewarding* framework may encourage greater information sharing and investment in security in the private sector without incurring the political difficulties of the regulatory framework. A significant disadvantage to the rewarding framework, however, is that it may be costly in a period of economic decline. Using rewards and incentives may also give certain companies competitive advantages that they would not ordinarily possess unless the rewards were distributed to companies across the board. Economic policy might be skewed toward favoring larger corpora-

---

76. This idea originated from a working paper that focused on managing environmental improvement within organizations. Cary Coglianese and Jennifer Nash, "Bolstering Private Environmental Management," JRWP01-011, John F. Kennedy School of Government Faculty Research Working Paper Series, April 2001, p. 2. For more information, see <www.researchmatters.harvard.edu/story.php?article_id<290>.

Figure 3. Summary of Three Frameworks: Advantages and Disadvantages.

Framework	Method	Advantage + / Disadvantage −
Regulatory	• 5 regulatory models	− Politically difficult − Regulation is often rigid − Stymies innovation − Based on constant evaluations + Standardizes security efforts
Rewarding	• Tax Incentives • Honor Roll	− Potentially expensive − Skews economic policy toward corporations + Encourages greater information sharing and security investment
Removing Barriers	• Freedom of Information Act (FOIA) Exemptions • Antitrust Exemptions • Tax Penalty Removals	− May be seen as bolstering only corporate welfare + Encourages companies to share information + Encourages cooperation on efforts to protect critical infrastructure + Removes legal and financial obstacles to security investment

tions that the government has targeted as necessary information sources. It should be noted that there is a trade-off that occurs when governments target specific companies for rewards; the government may be compromising a bit of security standardization when targeting only a specific number of companies for rewards.

The *removing barriers* framework, although not a complete solution, poses the best point of entry for government to encourage private sector investment. However responsible and careful the use of exemptions and tax penalty removals may be, removing barriers may still be seen as solely promoting corporate welfare. It is beneficial to all, however, insofar as it encourages companies to share information crucial to national defense, encourages cooperation on efforts to protect critical infrastructure, and removes legal and financial obstacles to security investment.

STATE AND LOCAL

The above recommendations demonstrate options for federal activism. Initiatives that integrate the private sector on a state and local level are also important. Public-private partnerships cannot be built without the involvement of local governments. One means of encouraging local-level involvement would be to place business leaders on state counter-terrorism task forces.[77] Many of the already existing state task forces would likely benefit from the perspective of the private sector.

Regional coordination is another means of fostering private sector engagement at the state level. With regional coordination, mutual aid agreements, many of which are already in effect, provide a structure for resource-sharing and assistance among jurisdictions in response to an emergency.[78] Because individual jurisdictions may be short-handed in an emergency, these agreements allow resources to be deployed quickly across a region. In some cases, these agreements may provide a means for the state to share services, personnel, supplies, and equipment with counties, towns, and municipalities within the state and with neighboring states. Other agreements also provide cooperative planning, training, and exercises for private and public entities to prepare for emergencies.[79] The Emergency Management Assistance Compact (EMAC) is an example of an interstate mutual aid agreement that allows states to assist one another in responding to natural and man-made disasters. Currently, there are 42 states and two territories that are members of EMAC.[80]

Conclusion

Since 9/11, businesses have responded to the continuing threat of terrorism in a variety of ways. One rather dramatic means in the New York City area has been the relocation of businesses to areas less likely to be victimized, such as Connecticut and New Jersey. There is, however, a more measured, and more realistic, response. Instead of "running for the hills," a more collaborative approach toward integrating the private sector into domestic preparedness planning may go far in minimizing and mitigating the harm to property, commerce, and most importantly, people.

Homeland security is a task that involves not only public entities and officials but private entities and officials as well. Some attention has been

---

77. In a meeting with the National Association of Manufacturers (NAM), Governor Ridge requested that more private sector leaders be engaged in security initiatives on a local level. Transcript of Governor Tom Ridge, "Issues Briefing" with National Association of Manufacturers, February 13, 2002, p. 12–13.

78. Statement of Patricia A. Dalton, "Combating Terrorism: Intergovernmental Cooperation in the Development of a National Strategy to Enhance State and Local Preparedness," GAO-02-550T, p. 15.

79. Ibid.

80. For more information, see <www.nemaweb.org/emac/index.cfm>.

paid to private sector engagement in homeland security but mostly in the form of lip service versus action, while substantial initiatives to address this problem will likely not be implemented anytime in the near future. Currently, the private sector is not integrated into domestic preparedness programs because of historical reasons, cost concerns, and legal impediments. The need for public-private partnerships, however, is vital for many reasons. Research by a public-private commission, government assistance in issuing threat and risk assessments, and the utilization of policy instruments will likely benefit not only the private sector but the nation as a whole.

Chapter 8

Inside and Outside the Loop: Defining the Population at Risk in Bioterrorism

Robert F. Knouss

The term "weapons of mass destruction" refers to four principal classes of weapons that can have a significant impact on our environment and, more importantly, on the health of the people living there—chemical agents, biological agents, radiological weapons, and nuclear weapons.[1] Until now, public policy has concentrated on detecting and reducing the threat from these weapons and preventing their release. In the wake of the September 11, 2001, terrorist attacks, more attention in the health care sector is being focused on responding to their release.

To be successful, the health care response to the release of a weapon of mass destruction must have three important characteristics. Simply stated, but far more difficult to accomplish, they are: protection of those who are not initially exposed from eventually becoming affected; identification of those who have been exposed so that appropriate steps can be taken to prevent their exposure from progressing to clinical illness; and assurance that those who are symptomatic have timely access to appropriate health care.

In this chapter, the variety of effects that each type of weapon of mass destruction may produce is explored. After determining when, how, and where a weapon has been released, the first challenge for the public

Special appreciation is expressed to Colonel Robert Gum, U.S. Army Medical Corps, for his review of the text and his helpful suggestions.

1. Because of the potential consequences of these instruments of terror on so many people, some commentators prefer the term "weapons of mass effect" to reflect more adequately its characteristics.

health sector is to identify the affected population, to communicate the risk analysis to the public, and then to take the steps required to enhance their protection. To illustrate the variety of consequences that may affect those exposed, several examples are provided below from events that have occurred over the last three decades. Lessons are drawn from these examples, including some that may assist in determining which populations are most likely to be affected.

The Varied Effects of Weapons of Mass Destruction

Even though public policy tends to regard weapons of mass destruction generically, they vary substantially in their impacts on human health.

Large explosive devices produce physical injury from the blast or the heat that they generate. Crush injuries are common either directly from a blast or, secondarily, from the resulting structural collapse or projectiles that are produced. These weapons differ in their effects according to variation in the magnitude of a blast, the heat generated, and the structural damage created. Explosions are immediately evident, as are their effects. Occasionally, sequential detonations can produce additional consequences by exposing rescuers and other responders to injury.

Chemical devices act by interrupting essential physiologic functions. Nerve agents, such as sarin and VX, can produce a variety of symptoms, including dim or blurred vision, runny nose, increased salivation, nausea and vomiting, chest tightness, and shortness of breath. The effects of nerve agents vary according to the extent of the exposure and the agent's route of entry (the skin or the lungs). Very high exposures can result in rapid incapacitation with convulsions, loss of consciousness, and death ensuing within minutes. Cyanide may produce transient rapid breathing within seconds, followed very quickly by convulsions and death. These effects, especially where lethal doses are concerned, require extraordinarily rapid countermeasures.

Another category of chemical agents called vesicants, including mustard and lewisite, can produce skin, eye, and respiratory tract injury. Skin damage can be extensive, and respiratory damage can lead to pneumonia. Although a victim may be without significant symptoms for hours, the effects on the respiratory tract, blood-forming elements, and skin can lead to death for those with substantial exposure. Some blister-forming agents, such as phosgene oxime and lewisite, can produce immediate pain and can be life threatening, depending on the dose.

The third category of chemical agents is pulmonary irritants, such as phosgene and chlorine, which are widely used industrial chemicals. Phosgene is estimated to have produced 80 percent of the chemical fatalities in World War I.[2] Phosgene exposure produces only minor irritant effects initially but, four or five hours later, may result in fulminant pulmonary edema and death. Chlorine is also a very strong upper and lower respiratory tract irritant.

Radiation-producing weapons, unlike explosive and chemical devices that have observable characteristics at the time of exposure, can be used in ways that silently produce their effects long after exposure. A device can be positioned so as to expose unsuspecting victims to symptom-producing levels of radiation. More difficult to detect are those instances in which radioactive material is either ingested or inhaled as a result of a terrorist act. Symptoms, such as generalized weakness, loss of concentration, chills, headaches, and mood changes may not be readily recognized due to their lack of specificity and gradual progression.

Biological agents, likewise, can be released silently and may not produce clinically evident symptoms for days while the bacteria or viruses incubate. Early differentiation from the common cold or influenza may be impossible until further, characteristic symptoms develop. Some agents can be easily aerosolized and can produce inhalational, cutaneous, or gastrointestinal disease. While the bacterium that produces anthrax is not communicable from person to person, other diseases, such as smallpox, are highly contagious and, in a vulnerable population, can produce high rates of morbidity and mortality. Bubonic plague and tularemia, when released as bioweapons, can be spread within wild animal populations and then transmitted to humans. Some agents, for example bubonic plague, can also be transmitted by insect vectors.

A subset of biological agents known as toxins differ from chemical agents in that they are produced by living organisms and are much more toxic than their inorganic counterparts. Some toxins act very quickly. Botulinum toxin, for example, is far more toxic than the most potent nerve agent and can cause paralysis and death within hours. Ricin and T-2 mycotoxin are potent protein toxins that can cause death anywhere from days to months after exposure.

The point of these descriptions is to illustrate that the effects of mass casualty-producing weapons can vary considerably, depending on the type of weapon, how it is released, where it is released, how much is released, and the conditions when under which it is released. Additional variables include: whether it can be spread from human to human; whether it can be spread through an intermediary vector; what symptoms it produces; its potential to cause death; and the time between expo-

---

2. Brij B. Mathur and Gopal Krishna, "Toxicodynamics of Phosgene" in Satu M. Somani, ed., *Chemical Warfare Agents* (San Diego, Calif.: Academic Press, 1992), p. 237.

sure and effect. Finally, a profound variable is whether the nature, location, and timing of the threat is known in advance or is divulged after the fact by those responsible. In some cases, the release may be silent and engineered to strike terror through public attention to growing numbers of people becoming symptomatic and seeking help in the health care system.

Advance warning of an attack, particularly details concerning which agent may be used and when and where it may be released, has obvious benefits in determining the population at risk. The effect of large explosive devices, and even the release of chemical agents, will be quite obvious. Appropriate health information concerning the affected population, protective actions that can be taken, and sources of health care must be transmitted quickly and effectively. Even if this information is universally available, the task of ensuring that all potentially affected people have access to appropriate care may continue to be a challenge. At the same time, those who are unnecessarily worried must be reassured in order to reduce their potential demands on the health care system.

Biological and radiation devices may be used to expose human populations such that their effects are not noticed until victims begin presenting themselves to the health care system. The release of these weapons produces consequences that are complex and largely unpredictable, except in general terms. The immediate effects can create confusion, and the response may initially be chaotic rather than orderly and effective.

The First Responsibility—Caring for the Affected People

After an attack, the most urgent need is to protect those who have been exposed and provide care to those who have been injured. If the numbers are high, the health care system may be rapidly overwhelmed. Demand for attention from those who are worried, yet not directly affected, can further overload health care resources. For example, within the first few hours of the 1995 sarin attacks in the Tokyo subway system, an estimated five times the number of people that were exposed to the nerve agent sought health care from more than 60 hospitals in the greater metropolitan area.

Early detection systems, robust surveillance and health alert mechanisms, capable laboratory networks, and the capacity to expand to accommodate increased casualty care demands can improve the efficiency of the health care system and the ability to respond to a mass casualty event. Confidence in the health care system and the support of local, state, and federal governments are critical. However, in order to achieve the level of confidence necessary to avoid panic and civil unrest, those who are not ill must believe that they are being protected, and those who are at risk of becoming ill must feel confident they can rapidly obtain necessary services.

In order to properly reassure the public, public health authorities and community leaders must conduct rapid incident analysis and characterization. That critical information then must be widely transmitted, convincingly and reliably. In addition, simple, effective steps for the public to enhance its own protection must be clearly explained. Appropriate services, including vaccination or the dispensing of prophylactic drugs, must be made available rapidly. Clear identification of the populations at risk of being exposed, plus the groups that have already been exposed and may be at risk of becoming ill, must also be accomplished shortly after the event.

Making these determinations may not be easy. Public health officials and other responders must identify when and how exposures may have taken place and, in the case of communicable diseases, how the disease may spread. They must then track the pattern of transmission and inform the public about how to protect themselves. Unless the sources have been self-declared, drawing these conclusions from available information may be difficult, and judgments by public health authorities may have to be made quickly with less than complete information. Past experience shows that deliberative processes for drawing conclusions about population vulnerability have taken days, months, or even years. More rapid, almost immediate, decisions about affected groups may have to be made in the future, even in cases in which clandestine exposures may occur and evidence of release may be gained solely from otherwise unexplainable disease patterns or service demands.

LESSONS FROM PAST RELEASES OF BIOLOGICAL, RADIOLOGICAL, AND CHEMICAL AGENTS

Over the last 30 years, there have been several incidents involving the release of biological, radiological, or chemical agents that may help elaborate the challenges and complexities of determining what exactly has happened in an incident, what agent was used, and who might have been affected. The source of a clandestine release of biological agents may be difficult to characterize sufficiently to initiate the steps necessary to protect an unsuspecting population. Unexplained increases in the demand for services, particularly if they are for the treatment of similar symptoms, should prompt an investigation to discern the cause. Epidemiological investigation, however, may not provide answers as swiftly as desired, particularly if the full range of possible causes is not considered.

An outbreak of clinical salmonellosis in The Dalles, Oregon, in 1984 illustrates this point.[3] Over a period of 32 days, 731 people presented to the health care system with gastroenteritis caused by *Salmonella typhimurium*. Although at least 45 people were hospitalized, no one died. Investigation through passive surveillance by the Wasco-Sherman Public Health Department, the Oregon Health Division, and the Centers for Disease Control and Prevention (CDC) determined two weeks after the first case was diagnosed that the source of the salmonella was contaminated salad bars in local restaurants. As a result, all salad bars in The Dalles were closed. Although new cases continued to be reported for the next two weeks, the rate of new infections decreased rapidly. During the course of the investigation, common sources for this type of outbreak, such as the water supply, were investigated and eliminated. No common food distributors could be identified that would explain the pattern of exposure. Investigations of the hygienic conditions of the food service areas in the source restaurants were also unproductive, even when the outbreak seemed clearly linked to food consumption.

About one year after the initial outbreak, *S. typhimurium* isolates were found in cold storage areas on a ranch operated by a local religious commune led by Bhagwan Shree Rajneesh. Based on information from an informant, it was determined that members of the commune had intentionally contaminated the salad bars. The motivation was to sicken voters and render them unable to cast ballots against an upcoming referendum that the Rajneesh followers wanted approved.[4]

Originally, investigators had eliminated intentional contamination as a cause of the outbreak for a variety of reasons and had not suspected vote tampering because the incidents did not directly coincide with an election. Perhaps new sensitivities to the possibility of bioterrorism would change investigative practices if the event were to occur again. However, the amount of time required to determine potentially affected groups remains a challenge to the timely identification of populations at risk and the initiation of effective preventive measures. Distinguishing a terrorist-perpetrated food borne outbreak from a naturally occurring one is, at best, difficult, as the same organisms may be the cause of both.

Another example of a much delayed explanation of an epidemic caused by a bioterror agent is described by Jeanne Guillemin in her book

---

3. Thomas Torsk, Robert V. Tauxe, Robert P. Wise, John R. Livengood, Robert Sokolow, Steven Mauvais, Kristen A. Birkness, Michael K. Skeels, John M. Horan, and Laurence R. Foster, "A Large Community Outbreak of Salmonellosis Caused by Intentional Contamination of Restaurant Salad Bars," *Journal of the American Medical Association*, Vol. 278, No. 5 (August 6, 1997).

4. The attack was discontinued prior to Election Day.

Anthrax: The Investigation of a Deadly Outbreak.[5] In 1992, Guillemin, along with a research team, carefully investigated the outbreak of a disease that occurred in humans and animals in the Soviet Union around Sverdlovsk in April and May 1979. Evidence of the epidemic was first noted on April 8, when several human deaths were reported. The deaths were confirmed several days later as having been caused by inhaled *Bacillus anthracis*. Although an aggressive vaccination program was underway by mid-April, 62 people had died of the disease by May 16, with the onset of symptoms occurring as early as April 4.

For years, the official explanation was that the outbreak had been caused by the consumption of contaminated meat. Whether or not the true source was known by the responsible scientific community in the Soviet Union at the time of the incident remains unknown. Retrospective international investigation, however, produced some surprising results. Anthrax spores, in a quantity possibly as little as one gram, had been released from a government lab on the afternoon of April 2. Weather conditions carried the spores for at least five kilometers from their origin in concentrations high enough to result in human and animal disease.

The investigation of this anthrax epidemic led to several new insights into human anthrax outbreaks. The two most important insights were that inhalation anthrax can develop weeks after exposure, in this case up to six weeks later, and that only a fraction of those exposed will develop the disease, for whatever reason. (The value of the vaccination effort in preventing human disease was not determined.) Another important corollary is that animal disease outbreaks may be important indicators of potential threats to human health and may consequently help define the human populations at risk. Careful study of this outbreak may point to ways of improving the identification of populations requiring protective actions—from disease surveillance observations and epidemiological determinations—in such a way that others can, at the same time, be reassured about their negligible risks.

Assessment of the population at risk of exposure was difficult in the days following the still unexplained U.S. outbreaks of letter-disseminated *B. anthracis* that, in October and November 2001, exposed media employees and family members, congressional staffs, mail handlers, and even inadvertent recipients of passively contaminated mail to the disease. At first, it was unclear whether the first victim, a 63-year-old male photo editor in Florida, had been exposed to anthrax spores during a trip to Vir-

---

5. Jeanne Guillemin, *Anthrax: The Investigation of a Deadly Outbreak,* (Los Angeles, Calif.: University of California Press, 1999).

ginia and North Carolina several days before he become ill, or whether the infection was from some other source.

An investigation of the outbreak, which occurred in two distinct waves over the succeeding five weeks, revealed that the source had been contaminated mail processed through the Main Branch of the West Palm Beach Post Office in Florida, the Morgan Station Postal Facility in New York City, the Hamilton, New Jersey, Processing Facility, and the Brentwood Mail Facility in Washington, D.C. All were downstream mail-processing facilities from the Cataret Hub and Spoke facility in New Jersey. At least 32 facilities that received mail from the four major processing centers eventually produced positive environmental samples of B. anthracis. The originally tainted mail undoubtedly produced cross-contamination of mail handling equipment, workers, and facilities when the letters were cancelled and sorted for delivery.

Although the source of the letters has not been determined, tens of thousands of individuals who might have come in contact with contaminated mail were identified and were provided with prophylactic antibiotics. A few accepted vaccination toward the end of the first 60 days of their treatment. Determination of the affected population took time, and the full extent of the population at risk was deduced relatively slowly, over weeks. Occasionally, there was obvious physical evidence of contamination, as in the case of the letter opened in the Hart Senate Office Building, which released a cloud of suspicious powder. Otherwise, contamination was first detected by the onset of human illness. Although many were spared acute disease by steps taken to treat affected groups, by November 30, 18 people out of 22 suspected cases had been confirmed to have developed inhalational or cutaneous anthrax, and five of them had died.[6]

Biological weapons that cause communicable diseases pose even greater challenges. In addition to the difficulties involved in detecting their release and circulation, the containment of their spread requires a successful strategy directed at vulnerable but yet-to-be exposed groups. The use of smallpox as a biological weapon would be viewed by many as producing a "worst case" scenario.

The last naturally occurring case of smallpox was recognized in Somalia in 1977. (Later laboratory exposures have been documented.) Prior to that, since time immemorial, smallpox had been a frequently lethal (30 percent fatality rate), naturally occurring disease. Spread from person to person, smallpox is devastating to unprotected populations. There is his-

---

6. "Anthrax as a Biological Weapon, 2002: Updated Recommendations for Management" *Journal of the American Medical Association*, Vol. 287, No. 17 (May 1, 2002) at <http://jama.ama-assn.org/issues/v287n17/ffull/jst20007.html>.

torical precedent for its use as a bioweapon. For example, British forces used smallpox as a weapon against an unsuspecting Native American population that accepted infected blankets during the French and Indian War. After an aggressive worldwide twentieth-century vaccination campaign, smallpox was eradicated as a human disease with only two known reserves of the smallpox-producing virus, variola, still in existence, one in the United States and the other in Russia. Notwithstanding this achievement, it is the most ominous of the potential bioweapons. Large quantities of the virus are known to have been produced by adversaries of the United States during the Cold War. Health experts fear that some of these stocks may have been stolen before the remainder was destroyed.

Today, populations would be very vulnerable to the introduction of variola, as smallpox vaccination for the general population was discontinued in 1980 (1972 in the United States). This extreme vulnerability was demonstrated in one of the last smallpox outbreaks, which occurred in Yugoslavia in 1972, when an infected pilgrim returning from Mecca introduced the virus. Within days, 11 people who had come in contact with him developed the disease, constituting the first-generation cases. In the next round of transmission, over 100 second-generation cases were identified. By the time the epidemic was controlled, it had produced 124 cases of smallpox, 26 of which proved fatal. To stop the disease from spreading further, millions of residents were vaccinated, the country's borders were closed, internal travel was restricted, and more than 10,000 people were quarantined.[7] In the United States, the CDC has developed disease control recommendations, including vaccination strategies, to contain any terrorist release of smallpox. Identifying the source, characterizing the pattern of contacts, and controlling the spread through aggressive vaccination and quarantine will be essential.

Distinguishing smallpox from other illnesses, particularly chickenpox, is critical but far more difficult today, as few clinicians are old enough to have seen a case of smallpox during their professional careers. As a result, the smallpox rash may not be readily recognized before the disease spreads among close contacts, particularly in densely populated areas. In each succeeding wave of infection, the number of people who develop the disease might increase almost exponentially every two weeks.

If used as a weapon, smallpox could be disseminated as an aerosol, substantially increasing the number of people initially infected and increasing the likelihood that the many who are infected could not be

---

7. F. Fenner, D.A. Henderson, J. Arita, Z. Jezek, I.D. Ladnyi, *Smallpox and Its Eradication* (Geneva, Switzerland: World Health Organization, 1988).

identified early enough to vaccinate or quarantine them. With such a large population potentially exposed, determining the population at risk in order to contain the resulting epidemic might not be possible, and a global eradication effort would likely have to be reinitiated. Other moderately communicable diseases, such as bubonic plague, could be used effectively as a bioweapon and produce similar disease control challenges. Identification of the populations that are already exposed or are at high risk of exposure is critical for any containment strategy.

Radiation events require rapid risk assessment, rapid identification of those likely to be affected, and rapid recommendation of protective actions that the public should be taking. In recent years, there have been several accidents that have highlighted the need to define the population that may need to take quick action to protect itself from radiation injury. At Three Mile Island in Pennsylvania, sizable quantities of radioactive material could have been released into the atmosphere in 1979. Although raised as a possibility, meltdown of the reactor core never materialized. Should a release have occurred, however, the population at risk would have had to have been rapidly determined, so that public health officials could have provided directions for shelter-in-place or evacuation, food protection, distribution of potassium iodide, and other actions required to reduce the health effects on an exposed population.

Similar issues were raised in 1986 when, in the days after the Chernobyl nuclear power plant accident in the Soviet Union, Europeans monitored the atmosphere to determine where the cloud of radioactive material was traveling and which populations were at increased health risk. In the immediate vicinity of the reactor, radiation monitoring and disease surveillance identified those requiring preventive services.

A less well-known incident occurred in Goiania, Brazil, in 1987, when a cesium-137 core from a radiotherapy device that had been removed from an abandoned medical clinic and left in a junkyard was opened. The glowing substance from the radiotherapy device attracted children and workers alike, who not only contaminated their skin but passively spread the radioactive material to their eating utensils after they had handled it. Ingestion of the material made decontamination most difficult, because even with the best treatment, it is unlikely to remove the isotope completely from human tissue. About a week elapsed between the initial exposure and the time that the first symptomatic individuals presented themselves to the health care system. Almost immediately, the cause of their complaint was determined. However, days passed before all of the radiation "hot spots" were identified and 244 exposed individuals were brought to the attention of the health care system. In this case, authorities used aerial monitoring to track the spread of the isotope and target areas for decontamination, to identify locations where residents were likely to have been exposed, and to prevent further exposures.[8]

Each of these examples illustrates a different way in which a population may be affected by the release of a weapon of mass destruction. In the Oregon restaurant example, food was contaminated; only those who had eaten tainted salad bar ingredients were affected. Aside from the fact that this was a purposeful contamination, little distinguishes its effects from what might happen in a naturally occurring food borne disease outbreak. A large population could be and sometimes is made ill by the accidental contamination of mass-produced and distributed food products. In incidents with a widespread effect, assuring the safety of—and restoring confidence in—the food supply must be an important component of the response.

Chemical agents such as sarin produce their effects directly. Identifying the population at risk, therefore, involves determining who may have been immediately exposed to the agent, either directly or through inhalation of its vapors. Identifying the contaminated environment is essential to protect those who have not already entered it. These tasks may be easier in cases involving chemical agents than those involving other types of weapons or mechanisms of distribution.

Other types of weapons of mass destruction raise challenging but less difficult issues regarding the question of who is at risk of being directly affected. The passive release of sarin, an organophosphate chemical weapon, in the Tokyo subway system in 1995 resulted in the deaths of 12 people, mostly first responders who came into direct contact with the liquid. Others were overcome by the vapors that gradually evaporated from the containers. As mentioned previously, however, of the estimated 5,500 people who sought care from regional hospitals, more than 4,000 did not have even minimal physical signs of exposure.[9] To minimize the demand for health services by concentrating on those most in need of immediate services, the public must be clearly informed about who is most likely to be at risk of exposure. Over the long run, the psychological impact of this type of event may demand less distinct definitions of those in need of care, but, in the immediate aftermath, specific protective advice should be provided.

If an atmospheric release has been used to spread a biological, chemi-

---

8. Leslie Roberts, "Radiation Accident Grips Goiania," *Science,* Vol. 238 (November 20, 1987).

9. Richard J. Brennan, Joseph F. Waeckerle, Trueman W. Sharp, and Scott R. Lillibridge, "Chemical Warfare Agents: Emergency Medical and Emergency Public Health Issues," *Annals of Emergency Medicine,* Vol. 34, No. 2 (August 1999).

cal, or radiological agent, then wind direction, humidity, and temperature, as well as the conditions for diffusion and settling of the agent, will determine the area affected. Risk will vary according to the extent and duration of exposure, as well as the concentration, size, and electrostatic properties of the agent. Some models fail to take into account the length of time that the material may be able to be suspended in the atmosphere, variation in wind direction and velocity, the presence of obstructions such as ground features, and the physical properties of the material.

In the case of the *B. anthracis*-caused epidemic in Sverdlovsk, retrospective analysis years after the event arrived at an approximation of the amount and time of release of spores into the atmosphere. Prospective analysis might have permitted prophylaxis of the exposed population. Lessons learned from the Sverdlovsk analysis, however, were not wholly applicable to the recent anthrax attack in the United States. Each new event reveals additional information about the behavior of bioweapons in a civilian population and contributes to our understanding of how best to detect, characterize, and respond to them, should the challenge be repeated.

As difficult as it is to determine the population at risk for a noncommunicable disease such as inhalation anthrax, it is potentially even more difficult to make sound estimates of the population requiring protection from an intentionally introduced communicable disease. The route of transmission of bacteria or viruses from person to person, the level of virulence of the organism, the capability to transmit the disease before symptoms emerge, and the density and movement of the affected population are all factors. More difficult is the realization that, unlike physical determinants of dispersion, human behavior, as unpredictable as it is, may be the most significant determinant of who may ultimately be at risk of exposure. Furthermore, these diseases may be introduced into noncontiguous areas by human travelers, commercial transportation of agricultural products, dispersion of insect vectors, or migration of wild animal populations. Quarantine and isolation strategies may therefore be only partially effective in cases where the disease is not limited to human populations and human carriers.

ADDRESSING THE CHALLENGE

Scientific monitoring can provide essential data points in determining which population may be most affected by an attack. Much has been made, for example, of the military and civilian applications of environmental sensing devices that can analyze large volumes of air to determine whether they are contaminated and with what. The location of air monitors, collection time, and sample volume are all data that can help determine exposure risks, provided there is an adequate system to interpret and confirm the information collected. Surface sampling, although it provides less critical information, can help define the affected area without directly defining the risk of exposure. The collection of clinical samples from humans, including nasal swabs, that were collected in response to the aerosol anthrax exposures in Washington, D.C., can help identify the exposed population and approximate the area and time during which the risk of exposure was significant.

Veterinary surveillance among wild and domestic animal and bird populations may help to determine the extent of dispersion of chemical and biological agents. Passive surveillance of dead animals, for example, can assist in determining the extent of the release of chemical agents, particularly in sparsely populated, rural areas. Active surveillance of rodent populations in urban settings may provide additional information or even an early warning, regarding the release of biological agents. Sentinel poultry flocks and animal herds are already part of active surveillance efforts to detect various encephalitides as well as other diseases that can affect humans naturally.

In addition to environmental sampling, syndromic surveillance, a technique developed by the CDC for detecting unusual clusters of human signs and symptoms of illness, can be used to uncover a population-based health problem. For instance, continuous analysis of demand for services among ambulance companies, emergency rooms, and clinics may be an effective way to estimate the affected population quickly and is already being practiced by some emergency response communities. Data collection and analysis, as well as rapid laboratory investigations, are critical to making judgments about the nature of the threat and the population that may be vulnerable.

Clinical data and environmental samples, rather than being collected passively, can be actively sought in an investigation to characterize the population that needs protection or reassurance. Several strategic public health decisions may be dependent on the accuracy and scope of the interpretation of the data collected. They include decisions concerning what information should be provided to the public about the nature of the threat, decisions concerning who is vulnerable and how they may reduce their risk, decisions concerning the type of personal and community-based protections that should be implemented by the public health sector, including the initiation of vaccination or pharmaceutical prophylaxis of those affected, and decisions concerning the direction of those needing services to the most available resources that can provide them.

At the same time, the personal health care system must be alerted to expect an increase in demand in the affected and potentially affected areas, if that increase has not already materialized. Plans must be made ready to augment local capacity for health care, through expansion of existing institutional provider capacity and the activation of any auxiliary capacity that might be available for such emergencies. Other ways to expand the health care system, depending on the threat and the estimation of the ultimate scope of the demand, include: mobilization of reserve health professionals in the community; importation of health care personnel, equipment, and supplies from outside the local area; provision of services in adjacent or even distant communities; and support of expanded home-based care, through Internet communication of health information and community-based, mobile health care personnel.

In addition to the provision of health services, the identification and communication of the population at risk will determine who should be targeted for rapid distribution of prophylactic pharmaceuticals or biologicals.

Conclusion

Although public policy and public perception tend to aggregate all threats from weapons of mass destruction, the public health consequences differ substantially from one category of agent to another—and within each category, among the specific agents included. To limit their effect, one must understand the characteristics of each agent and how each agent may affect humans after release. From this knowledge, public health authorities must be able to make rapid judgments about the populations most likely to be affected in order to launch the resources that are necessary for their protection and to make essential services easily accessible. Meeting this challenge will require new systems for detection and characterization of such threats and, most importantly, new systems for accurately determining who among the public is at risk.

Chapter 9

After the Attack: The Psychological Consequences of Terrorism

Robyn L. Pangi

History suggests that there may be many more psychological victims than physical victims in a terrorist attack. This may be true for a conventional attack, such as the use of hijacked aircraft to destroy high-occupancy buildings. The attacks on the World Trade Center and the Pentagon resulted in thousands of deaths and physical injuries, and the psychological casualties numbered in the tens to hundreds of thousands. An attack using an unconventional weapon of mass destruction—a biological, chemical, nuclear, or radiological device—may produce even more extreme numbers. Psychological casualties easily outnumbered physical casualties in the anthrax attacks in the United States in 2001, which resulted in 22 confirmed or suspected illnesses and five fatalities, but affected millions. Likewise, the sarin attacks in the Tokyo subway system in 1995 engendered thousands of psychological casualties, compared to a dozen fatalities and several hundred injuries. Indeed, these psychological effects are integral to the "success" of the terrorist actions, which seek to destroy the fabric of U.S. democracy by inflicting death and terror. Hence, it is important to prepare the nation physically and psychologically for a possible attack. In this way, the populace can render an attack less effective and, perhaps, make the prospect of carrying out an attack less attractive to terrorists.

Consequence management is the term that describes all the opera-

The author wishes to thank the following people for providing information for and helpful comments on this paper: Juliette Kayyem, Patricia Chang, Nozomu Asukai, Tetsu Okumura, Susan Hamilton, and Anand Pandya. She also wishes to thank Miriam Avins for her editorial assistance.

tions undertaken after a disaster to mitigate its effects and facilitate the community's recovery. Fear management, a relatively new branch of consequence management, reduces the incidence of adverse psychological effects following a disaster. By definition, fear management is "the mitigation of panic and the management of public response following a weapons of mass destruction (WMD) or other mass casualty incident." [1]

Fear management is built upon an understanding of the potential psychological effects of a terrorist attack. It is critical to anticipate victims' reactions so that first responders can plan accordingly. In other words, panic and shock, if prevalent, will affect response operations and must be anticipated. On the other hand, if—as studies indicate—panic is relatively rare, first responders need to plan for more likely scenarios such as an influx of the "worried well" and a convergence of volunteers. Moreover, since early intervention can mitigate the short- and long-term psychological impact of trauma, response planning should include assistance for victims who are dealing with psychological effects of terrorism.

This chapter draws from the experience of Japanese officials, emergency response personnel, and physicians during and after the attack on the Tokyo subway system in 1995 with the nerve gas sarin. After the sarin attack, various Japanese organizations sought to record and study the short- and long-term psychological impact of terrorism on the victim population, so this terrorist attack provides helpful evidence as the United States begins to think about fear management as an integral part of disaster response. The paper first discusses the Tokyo attacks and reviews data on the mental health consequences it had for victims and first responders. It then discusses the factors that influence individuals' and communities' responses to a disaster, and explores the facets of response that are most relevant to a terrorist attack. Next, the chapter highlights several issues relevant to the potential reactions of first responders, the rescue and recovery workers who spend the most time at the site of the attack. Lastly, it identifies implications for emergency responders in the United States and makes concluding recommendations.

Aum Shinrikyo Attacks the Tokyo Subway System

The attacks that occurred in Tokyo on March 20, 1995, provide the most comprehensive and historically grounded set of facts regarding the short- and long-term effects of terrorism using weapons of mass destruction. On that day, just before 8:00 a.m., five members of the Aum Shinrikyo cult

---

1. Mark J. Morgan and Paul M. Camper, "Fear Management," April 1, 1998, unpublished manuscript, p. 1.

used sharpened umbrella tips to pierce bags of sarin that they had carried with them onto three different lines of the subway system. The cult members immediately exited the trains and fled to a safehouse; the trains they had been riding on converged on the Kasumigaseki station—home to most of Tokyo's government offices and the power center of the city.

Sarin is a nerve agent; in its pure form, as little as one drop on the skin can be fatal. Individuals who are exposed to sarin may suffer nausea, vomiting, eye irritation or temporary blindness, shortness of breath, and loss of muscle control. Not knowing the source of the problem, but aware of sick passengers and an unusual odor, subway workers evacuated passengers from the stations *en masse*, many choking, vomiting, and blinded by the chemical. The passengers fled up the stairways—often collapsing in the streets—while firefighters, police officers, and emergency medical technicians (EMTs), most of whom were unprotected, ran down the stairs to assist the victims. The scene was quickly broadcast over television and radio. Images of confusion and destruction dominated the morning news and provided Tokyo and the world with its first glimpse of terrorism with a weapon of mass destruction.

Approximately 5,500 people went to 280 medical facilities on the day of the attack and in the following days. In all, 1,046 patients were admitted to 98 hospitals. Twelve people died as a direct result of the sarin attack.[2] Fortunately, the enormous potential for catastrophic damage was not actually achieved. The more than 30 train lines of the public and private transit system in Tokyo sprawl through 400 miles of underground tunnels and above-ground tracks. More than nine million passengers ride the subway daily. A rush-hour attack could thus have caused chaos and massive numbers of casualties and fatalities.[3] However, the sarin used in the subway attack was only 30 percent pure and was simply poured into plastic bags that were then wrapped in paper, placed on the floors, and punctured—it caused far less devastation than pure sarin or an aerosol delivery vehicle would have.

Hard Data: The Psychological Response in Tokyo

The physical effects of the sarin attack were relatively contained. In all the hospitals that dealt with sarin victims, fewer than 20 patients were admit-

---

2. Nozomu Asukai, "Health Effects Following the Sarin Attack in the Tokyo Subway System" unpublished manuscript, p. 2.

3. Ian Reader, *Religious Violence in Contemporary Japan: The Case of Aum Shinrikyo*, Nordic Institute of Asian Studies Monograph Series, No. 82 (Great Britain: Curzon Press, 2000), p. 23.

ted and treated in intensive care units.[4] Among those seen only briefly by medical practitioners, headache and malaise were the most common persistent, generalized symptoms noted after discharge from the hospital. [5]

The more common response was psychological. A predominant psychological response in Tokyo was a phenomenon known as the "worried well"—uncontaminated and unexposed individuals who fear, despite evidence to the contrary, that they have been contaminated. Some of these unexposed individuals exhibited psychosomatic symptoms that led them to believe that they were in danger. Other people associated preexisting conditions with symptoms described by sarin victims, such as eye pain or nausea. Individuals who fell prey to these phenomena frequently went to medical facilities seeking treatment. In the sarin attack, the worried well outnumbered physically affected victims by a margin of five to one—adding a significant burden to an already stressed medical system.

As in most disasters, there is a range of responses any individual might experience after a terrorist attack. Experts define psychological effects of a trauma as "a wide range of negative feelings, somatic symptoms, upsetting thoughts, and dysfunctional behaviors that are precipitated by an unusual and compelling experience."[6] Many psychological symptoms experienced after a disaster are considered to be "normal reactions to abnormal circumstances,"[7] and patients typically reach a full recovery. The type of disaster, direct effect on the victim, and mental and physical health of the individual before the disaster all affect recovery.

Researchers in Tokyo attempted to record individuals' responses to the sarin attack. Most of the evidence from the immediate aftermath is anecdotal, but there is a more substantial body of recorded evidence about the long-term psychological effects. This paper focuses on panic, acute stress disorder, and post-traumatic stress disorder—the conditions that were recorded by mental health care professionals after the sarin attack—to illustrate the range and frequency of reactions to mass-casualty terrorist attack.

---

4.   Asukai, "Health Effects Following the Sarin Attack," p. 3.

5.   Patients were considered to be in "critical" condition if they had cardiac or respiratory arrest and in "moderate" condition if they exhibited signs and symptoms other than eye problems or mild headache after first six-hour observation. Those in "mild" condition mainly had eye problems; these patients were retained for six hours for observation and then released.

6.   Don M. Hartsough, "Measurement of the Psychological Effects of Disaster," in Jerri Laube and Shirley Murphy, eds., *Perspectives on Disaster Recovery* (Connecticut: Appleton-Century-Crofts, 1985), pp. 22–61, at p. 23.

7.   Ibid.

PANIC

In an attack, the greatest immediate mental health concern of first responders is mass panic. Such panic involves reactions that may run counter to the individuals' or the common good, such as refusing to evacuate a dangerous location, taking drugs for which there is no medical indication, or being unable to control emotions or actions. Panic may be loosely defined as irrational behavior in the face of extreme circumstances. While this sort of behavior is most often associated with traumatic events such as terrorist attacks, there is little evidence that people panic in the face of disaster.

Panic was a seldom seen response in Tokyo. The responses that were seen in Tokyo were similar to those seen in other disasters. What is often referred to as "panic" consisted of hasty mass evacuation of the subway cars and terminals.[8] This process was complicated by the number of individuals sickened or temporarily blinded by the chemical release; the influx of response personnel; and the lack of clear instructions. However, subway riders were effectively evacuated, and while many reported for medical care, most proceeded to work on foot or by taxi. Indeed, rather than being viewed as irrational actions evidencing mass "panic," rapid flight from the traumatic scene, intense emotions, the desire to assist others in need or to forge human contact, fear, or anger are actually rational responses to a disaster.

ACUTE STRESS DISORDER AND POST-TRAUMATIC STRESS DISORDER

Since panic does not appear to be imminent, are there critical longer-term psychological responses, of which first responders and mental health professionals should be aware? Acute Stress Disorder (ASD) and Post-traumatic Stress Disorder (PTSD) are perhaps the most widely documented adverse reactions experienced by disaster survivors.

Acute Stress Disorder is a mental condition that can occur following exposure to extreme stress or trauma but does not last longer than one month. St. Luke's hospital treated 641 individuals on the day of the sarin attack, the greatest number of victims seen at any single facility that day. The hospital conducted a follow-up survey of 610 patients one month after the attack (which falls into the timeframe for ASD); 408 patients responded. They reported the following symptoms:

---

8. "Where possible [evacuation] is the first line of action . . . it differs from panic in that there is control and a degree of rationality and in that it is still social, recognizing the needs of others as well as the self." Beverly Raphael, *When Disaster Strikes: How Individuals and Communities Cope with Catastrophe* (New York: Basic Books, 1986), p. 61.

- 32 percent feared the subway;
- 29 percent experienced sleep disturbances;
- 16 percent had flashbacks of event;
- 16 percent suffered depression;
- 11 percent were jumpy and easily frightened;
- 10 percent had nightmares; and
- 10 percent were irritable.[9]

According to the study, almost 60 percent of respondents still suffered from some symptoms one month after the incident; these symptoms can also be interpreted as an early indication of PTSD.

PTSD is similar to ASD: the main difference is that while ASD presents within one month of the traumatic event, PTSD usually does not present until six months after the event, and the symptoms last longer than one month.[10] One criterion for diagnosing PTSD is that the disturbance causes clinically significant distress or impairment in social, occupational, or other important areas of functioning.[11] People with PTSD may be more likely to neglect their health and thus deteriorate physically. Unabated stress also leads to physical disorders, including headaches, muscular pain, gastrointestinal distress, hypertension, lowered immunity, and other ailments.[12] Chronic PTSD sufferers can experience job

---

9. Asukai, "Health Effects Following the Sarin Attack." See also Sadayoshi Ohbu, Akira Yamashina, Nobukatsu Takasu, Tatsuo Yamaguchi, Tetsuo Murai, Kanzoh Nakano, Yukio Matsui, Ryuzo Mikami, Kenji Sakurai, and Shigeaki Hinohara, "Sarin Poisoning on Tokyo Subway," June 1997, <http://www.sma.org/smj/97june3.htm>.

10. "As indicated in DSM-IV, the diagnosis of posttraumatic stress disorder is made if the symptoms (such as recurrent and intrusive recollections of the event, flashbacks, avoidance, and increased arousal) continue for more than one month." Acute PTSD is diagnosed if symptoms last for less than three months, chronic PTSD if symptoms last for more than three months. Elizabeth K. Carll, "Workplace and Community Violence: Intervention and Prevention," in Elizabeth K. Carll, ed., *Violence in Our Lives: Impact of Workplace, Home and Community,* (Needham Heights, Mass.: Allyn and Bacon, 1999).

11. Brian W. Flynn, "Disaster Mental Health: The U.S. Experience and Beyond," in Jennifer Leaning, Susan M. Briggs, and Lincoln C. Chen, eds., *Humanitarian Crises: The Medical and Public Health Response* (Cambridge, Mass.: Harvard University Press, 1999), p. 148, pp. 4–23, pp. 15–16.

12. "PTSD is distinctive among psychiatric disorders in terms of its potential to promote poor health because of both the physiological and psychological abnormalities associated with this disorder." Asukai, "Health Effects Following the Sarin Attack," p. 9. See also E.E. Flynn, "Victims of Terrorism" in Paul Wilkinson and Alasdair Stewart, eds., *Contemporary Research on Terrorism* (Aberdeen, Scotland: Aberdeen University Press, 1987), pp. 337–356 at p. 349.

loss, marital problems, increased substance abuse, suicide attempts, ulcers, headaches, and hypertension.[13]

Statistics on PTSD among the victims of the sarin attack are available for the period from six months to six years after the attack. One study of 35 inpatients in a metropolitan hospital six months after the event found that 26 percent were at high risk for PTSD. Based on this data, the study concluded that overall, 20–25 percent of at least moderately poisoned victims suffered from PTSD or subthreshold PTSD symptoms.[14] The same hospital surveyed 20 patients who visited for a checkup two years after the event: 10 percent were identified as suffering from PTSD; 10 percent were identified as recovered from PTSD.

The Special Case of Rescue Workers

Perhaps no class of people on the scene of a disaster is as vulnerable to psychological stress as rescue workers. Rescue workers help victims physically and mentally cope with and recover from the disaster—but they, too, are vulnerable to psychological reactions when confronting traumatic events. "In the aftermath of . . . terrorist attacks, the intensity of responders' work, the long duration of the response campaigns, the multiplicity of risks, the horrifying outcomes of the attacks, and the lack of knowledge about hazards all contributed to stress."[15]

First responders are confronted with several stressors.[16] The largest is that they must choose between professional and familial responsibilities. Additionally, first responders who do participate in the response effort repeatedly confront horrifying scenes of death and destruction. The psychological consequences, particularly when the rescue worker may be putting his or her life at risk by entering a contaminated area, can be extreme.

There is limited data on how the sarin attacks affected first respond-

---

13.   Charles B. Wilkinson and Enrique Vera, "Clinical Responses to Disaster: Assessment, Management, and Treatment," in Richard Gist and Bernard Lubin, eds., *Psychosocial Aspects of Disaster* (New York: John Wiley and Sons, 1989), p. 243.

14.   Asukai, "Health Effects Following the Sarin Attack," p. 5.

15.   Brian A. Jackson, et al., *Protecting Emergency Responders* (California: RAND, 2002), p. 16.

16.   Psychological reactions to this type of stress are abundant. "Since September 11, at any given time there are 75 FDNY members 'off the line' for stress-related issues. Before the catastrophe, the average was 5–10." After the Oklahoma City bombing, studies found that "eight emergency workers and three police officers committed suicide, police divorce rates increased 300 percent and police disciplinary problems rose 45 percent." O'Shaughnessy Daily News online.

ers. Following the attack in Tokyo, 27 firefighters were interviewed by mental health care providers. Four exhibited PTSD: all four had been severely poisoned by the sarin.[17] This data, though incomplete, reinforces the notion that disaster plans must account for the needs of first responders and other rescue workers.

What Determines Rates of Post-Attack Stress or Anxiety Disorders?

The nature of an attack, individuals' proximity to the attack site, their previous exposures to trauma, their social network, and numerous other factors can influence the likelihood that victims will suffer psychological effects.

- *Trauma and Disaster:* a terrorist attack with weapons of mass destruction is a traumatic event, but it is unlike other traumatic events like street crime because it is also a disaster. While many traumas affect only one or a few people, a disaster "overwhelm[s] the available community resources, further threatening the individuals' and the community's ability to cope."[18] A terrorist attack, which might overwhelm both individual coping mechanisms and the community's response and recovery system, may have a greater effect than disasters or traumas experienced in isolation of one another.

- *Natural vs. Man-made Disaster:* part of what makes mass-destruction terrorism so frightening is the technological nature of the attack. Unlike an "act of God" such as a hurricane or flood, man-made disasters, such as chemical spills—even when accidental—have an element of blame. The many unknowns surrounding chemical, biological, nuclear, and radiological disasters, coupled with the threat of environmental degradation and long-term health consequences that they carry, make them more frightening to many people.

- *Intentional vs. Accidental Disaster:* when technology or nature is intentionally perverted by man in order to harm others, "studies suggest that the disaster take[s] a greater emotional toll" on the victims.[19] Ac-

---

17. Asukai, "Health Effects Following the Sarin Attack," p. 5.

18. Robert J. Ursano, Brian G. McCaughey, Carol S. Fullerton, "Trauma and Disaster,' in Robert J. Ursano, Brian G. McCaughey, Carol S. Fullerton, eds., *Individual and Community Responses to Trauma and Disaster: The Structure of Human Chaos,* (Cambridge: Cambridge University Press, 1994), p. 6.

19. "Coping with Disaster and Trauma," Mental Health Association in New York State, <http://www.mhanys.org/factsheet_trauma.htm>.

cording to a psychiatrist who follows sarin victims, trust in society tends to increase after accidental and natural disasters but tends to *decrease* after an intentional disaster.

- *Proximity:* those closest to the attack scene are most susceptible to psychological damage. However, as the effects ripple out from the epicenter of the attack, even those people not directly affected by the attack may require physical and mental health services.
- *Previous Exposure to Trauma or Stress:* those who have experienced previous trauma, are experiencing concurrent trauma, or already suffer from a psychological disorder may be at higher risk of adverse effects. This may be particularly important in planning for rescue workers, who frequently encounter catastrophic situations.
- *Social Network:* access to a strong social network can reduce the stress of a disaster. Isolation from other victims or counseling options, on the other hand, can heighten victims' stress.

Each of these factors was at play in the sarin attack. The attack was an intentional, man-made, traumatic disaster. The attack occurred in the center of a densely populated urban area during rush hour, resulting in thousands of physically and psychologically affected individuals. Moreover, because it primarily affected individuals during their workday commute, the victims did not have a preexisting social network at hand. Although it is impossible to speculate on the previous traumatic exposure of the victims, it is known that many of the response workers had confronted difficult scenes in the past and might therefore serve as an example of individuals who encountered repeated trauma.

Lessons Learned from Tokyo

Four factors specific to the Tokyo subway attack additionally affected the recovery of the victims. First, since the attack occurred in the transportation system of a major metropolitan area, all that the victims had in common was the time of their commute. They lived far apart, did not necessarily work together, and had no opportunity to interact with fellow victims after the attack—so there was none of the community building and identification that might have alleviated much of the stress for individual victims. Weak social networks hindered the natural course of psychological recovery through informal group debriefing and the formation of a sense of community.

Second, psychiatrists and public officials involved in consequence management following the subway attacks concede that the delay in providing psychiatric treatment adversely affected the emotional recovery of some victims and their families.[20] Dr. Nozomu Asukai studied 45 patients in one metropolitan hospital one month after the attacks. His team offered psychiatric intervention for high-risk patients, consisting of one or two interviews with a psychiatrist. Most of the patients reported a feeling of relief following psychiatric intervention. However, these feelings of reduced stress were not reflected in the patients' test results six months later: the follow-up study revealed no significant improvement in their test scores.[21] Although intervention provided superficial relief, it came too late to have a significant impact on the patients' mental health. The data "suggests the difficulty of establishing a mental health regimen for such disasters,"[22] especially if months or years have passed since the exposure to the trauma.

Third, with the exception of the study mentioned above, most treatment was provided at the initiation of patients, with very limited proactive psychological treatment offered to victims. Outside of the major medical centers, such as St. Luke's International Hospital, most facilities treated the physical needs of the victims and did not address their psychological needs. Group debriefings or counseling sessions were rare, and patients typically had to seek psychiatric care themselves.

Fourth, there is a stigma attached to victims of violence in Japan that is distinct from the perception of victims in the United States. Socially, victims are often considered troublemakers and are isolated from their families and coworkers. Institutionally, "Japan is often described as lagging 20 years behind Western countries in terms of the support provided for violence victims."[23] Victims of the sarin attack received neither social nor monetary support. When it comes to psychological damage experienced by victims of the subway attack, they "have received neither compensation nor any kind of recovery assistance from either the guilty party [as they would in a case resulting in physical injury], the government, or society."[24]

---

20. This assertion is supported by the general consensus expressed by participants at a conference sponsored by the Japan Society in Tokyo in 2000.

21. Asukai, "Health Effects Following the Sarin Attack," p. 4.

22. Ibid.

23. Takako Konishi, "Cultural Aspects Of Violence Against Women In Japan," *Lancet*, Vol. 355, No. 9217 (May 20, 2000), p. 1810. Konishi notes that since the events of 1995, there has been an increased impact of violence on victims, especially women. He also notes, however, that "this increased awareness has yet to be incorporated into Japan's health-care system."

24. Futaba Igarashi, "Victim's Rights in Japan," *Japan Echo*, December 2000.

Implications for the United States

Is the United States any more prepared in 2003 to handle the psychiatric consequences of a terrorist attack with weapons of mass destruction than Japan was in 1995? The short answer is "somewhat." The federal government has focused a good deal of attention and resources, particularly since 9/11, on mitigating the physical effects of an attack. However, fear management is relatively new for most academics, emergency response practitioners, and policymakers and has received inadequate attention.

A mass-casualty or mass-fatality terrorist attack will overwhelm local and state resources. There is no comprehensive response plan for fear management; this translates to a lack of preparedness on the part of federal, state, and local governments. The following section outlines the resources in place to address the psychological needs of victims.

FEDERAL RESOURCES

Agencies' responsibilities for terrorism are detailed in the Federal Response Plan. Under the plan, the Federal Emergency Management Agency (FEMA) is designated as the lead federal agency for consequence management. However, FEMA focuses on physical rescue and recovery operations and provides relatively little by way of mental health counseling in times of disaster. The mental health services that FEMA coordinates are provided by the Center for Mental Health Services (CMHS), which can offer basic resources to communities. After a presidentially declared disaster, for example, states can apply for Crisis Counseling Program grants to provide mental health services that help disaster survivors recognize common psychiatric responses and deal with them in the short term.[25]

In addition, FEMA grants funds to local agencies that provide mental health services in emergencies. One such program provides services to states for approximately one year following a presidentially declared disaster. The program's efforts to respond to psychological needs following major disasters have grown dramatically over the 22 years since it was established. Funds, which of course are allocated according to the needs of response operations in any particular year, reached $60 million in 1994 and $30 million in 1995.[26] The National Disaster Medical System provides

---

25. For more information, see <http://www.samhsa.gov/centers/cmhs/cmhs. html>.

26. Flynn, "Disaster Mental Health," p. 122.

additional resources through the Disaster Medical Assistance Teams that focus on mental health.

The Federal Response Plan divides up response activities into 12 Emergency Support Functions. The plan calls for the Department of Health and Human Service (HHS) to act as the lead federal agency for Emergency Support Function Number 8 Health and Medical Services. The primary agency for mental health care within HHS is the Substance Abuse and Mental Health Services Administration (SAMHSA). The mission of this subgroup is to "assist in assessing mental health needs; provide mental health training materials for disaster workers; and provide liaison with assessment, training, and program development activities undertaken by federal, state, and local mental health officials."[27]

There is a Crisis Counseling and Assistance Program under the Center for Mental Health Services that is "designed to provide supplemental funding to the states for short-term crisis counseling services to people affected by a presidentially declared disaster."[28] Two programs may be funded at the state's request: immediate services to help the state or local agencies "respond to disaster victims with screening, diagnostic, and counseling techniques, [and] outreach services such as public information and community networking." A program for longer-term needs can provide up to nine months of crisis counseling, community outreach, and education services. Both programs are designed for residents of the affected area or those who were in the area at the time of the disaster.

NONGOVERNMENTAL ORGANIZATIONS

Several nongovernmental organizations play a role in the current mélange of disaster mental health care efforts, including the American Red Cross, the American Psychiatric Association, the American Psychological Association, and the American Counseling Association. In fact, FEMA's web site refers individuals suffering from disaster-related stress to the American Red Cross or the Salvation Army.

During disasters, several organizations work with the Red Cross to provide mental health services to disaster victims. The American Counseling Association, the American Psychological Association (APA), and the National Association of Social Workers have all signed separate memoranda of understanding with the Red Cross that set out agreements for dealing with the mental health aspects of disaster relief operations. These

---

27. Federal Response Plan, ESF #8–10, "Health and Medical Services Annex," April 1999, p. 124.

28. For more information, see <http://www.fema.gov/r-n-r/dec_guid.htm>.

organizations can mobilize massive human resources to a disaster scene. For example, the American Psychological Association's Disaster Response Network consists of 1,500 volunteer psychologists integrated into Red Cross services.[29]

Public and private medical facilities are also integral to the provision of mental health care after traumatic events. "In theory, accredited hospitals are to have plans for dealing with disaster; in fact, few hospitals and fewer communities have disaster plans to minimize post-traumatic psychological sequelae," the after-effects of a disease or injury.[30] In an era of downsizing and cost containment, private medical facilities may be unprepared to "flex" to meet the urgent care needs of high numbers of psychological patients.

What Remains to Be Done?

It is too early to analyze either the long-term psychological needs of the victims or the effectiveness of the existing mental health programs after the attacks on the World Trade Center or the anthrax attacks. But, as with many aspects of consequence management, the current system can certainly be improved to meet the needs of individuals and communities after a terrorist attack. At present, few first responders have received training specific to psychological traumas involving weapons of mass destruction. Second, the mental health needs of victims are underestimated. Third, the structure overemphasizes the federal role in disaster management and ignores the immediate mental health care role of first responders, particularly emergency medical workers. Fourth, there is a tendency among mental health organizations in the United States, unlike in Japan, to focus on the needs of emergency workers instead of victims, whereas both populations will require assistance. Fifth, even when victims are given due consideration, the net is cast narrowly and does not always include family, friends, witnesses, and others who are emotionally affected by the disaster. Finally, intervention tends to be tailored to the short-term needs of victims rather than to long-term recovery.

Current plans rely too heavily on federal resources at the expense of

---

29. Institute of Medicine National Research Council, "Prevention, Assessment, and Treatments of Psychological Effects," in *Chemical and Biological Terrorism: Research and Development to Improve Civilian Medical Response* (Washington, D.C.: National Academy Press, 1999), p. 171.

30. A. David Mangelsdorff, "Lessons Learned And Forgotten: The Need For Prevention And Mental Health Interventions In Disaster Preparedness," *Journal of Community Psychology*, Vol. 13 (July 1985), pp. 239–257 at p. 250.

local assets. Mental health needs cannot be addressed by the federal government alone. Nor does federal law provide sufficient resources to meet the need. Executive orders such as Presidential Decision Directive 39 may relegate domestic terrorism response to the federal arena, but responsibility for stress and other effects on rescuers is not part of federal policy, justified on the basis that, "the federal government does not have primary responsibility for consequence management, but supports state and local governments in domestic incidents.'"[31] The federal government has the responsibility for, but neither the institutional investment in nor the capability to pursue, a comprehensive disaster mental health response plan.

Much of the mental health planning in the United States deals not with the large numbers of victims who will require care but focuses on the mental health needs of rescue workers. In some nongovernmental organizations such as the Red Cross, for example, "top priority for mental health services is to Red Cross volunteers as well as other disaster responders. . . . The second priority is providing services to victims and their families."[32] However, governmental and nongovernmental programs aimed at rescue workers' mental health are insufficient. The APA and the U.S. Public Health Service have both observed that services under existing federal programs are inadequate to meet these needs. In its final report on the mental health response to the 1995 Oklahoma City bombing, the APA judged mental health and stress management services to responders as "quite extensive and impressive" but cited the need for "well-planned and adequately funded long-term disaster mental health services."[33]

Moreover, there are victims far beyond the immediate perimeter of the attack scene. Friends, family, the worried well, colleagues, and concerned citizens may all suffer from emotional distress after an attack. In "A National Survey of Stress Reactions after the September 11, 2001, Terrorist Attacks," a telephone study done to assess the immediate mental health effects of September 11, 44 percent of the adults surveyed reported

---

31. Carol W. Lewis and Morton Tenzer, "The Heroic Response to Terror: The Case of Oklahoma City," *Public Personnel Management*,Winter 2000, pp. 617–635.

32. H.E. Marcus, "Disaster Mental Health Services," *The Internet Journal of Rescue and Disaster Medicine*, Vol. 1, No. 2 (2000) <http://www.icaap.org/iuicode?86.1.2.2>.

33. The Oklahoma City operation was the first time that the FEMA funded critical incident stress management services for rescue workers; federal funding through FEMA is for short-term crisis intervention only. Funding for critical incident workshops through the 1996 Anti-Terrorism and Effective Death Penalty Act addressed longer lasting effects. Lewis and Tenzer, "The Heroic Response to Terror," p. 6.

one or more substantial symptoms of stress, and 90 percent had one or more symptoms at least to some degree. The survey concluded that in general, after the September 11 attacks, adults and children across the country displayed substantial symptoms of stress. Another post–September 11 analysis suggests that "there is no systematic way to treat all of those who might need help" after an attack, because affected individuals are not confined to the area of the attack but are spread throughout the country.[34]

RECOMMENDATIONS

Filling the gaps in the U.S. mental health response plans and capabilities is vital to the overall domestic preparedness effort. One of the purposes of terrorism is to inflict terror. More than natural disasters—or even other intentional, man-made disasters—terrorist attacks can inspire panic, fear, and long-term psychological distress in the victims and the community as a whole. Preparing an appropriate response can reduce the incidence of psychological problems among at-risk individuals and communities.

Further establishing the need for a fear management initiative is evidence that "disasters have been found to produce two kinds of effects, ones caused by the event itself and others brought about by society's response to the disaster."[35] In other words, an individual may be able to handle the psychological trauma of the actual disaster but can be adversely affected by the federal government's uncoordinated or unsympathetic response to the disaster. In addition to mitigating effects caused by the disaster itself, government and non-government response personnel must avoid inflicting an additional psychological burden on victims through insufficient planning or inept implementation.

The recommendations presented here for establishing a mental health plan for mass-casualty terrorism are broken down by phase of disaster.[36] For example, while communication with the public is vital

34. Maggie Farley and Charles Ornstein, "US Mental Health Suffers a Major Blow," *New York Times*, September 22, 2001.

35. Don Hartsough, "Legal Issues and Public Policy in the Psychology of Disasters," in Richard Gist and Bernard Lubin, eds., *Psychosocial Aspects of Disaster* (New York: John Wiley and Sons, 1989), pp. 283–308 at p. 289. Individuals may experience "feelings of hopelessness brought about by the way in which victims are managed following the disaster." Ibid., p. 290.

36. The structure of these recommendations is borrowed from Morgan and Camper, who advocate that: "a strong fear management program should focus on a longitudinal approach to fear management, i.e., supporting a multi-stage intervention program that uses all major management modalities to emphasize preparatory and response ac-

through all phases of a disaster, it may take different forms before, during, and after an attack. Similarly, while improved security is best undertaken before a disaster—at best, deterring an attack—visible improvements *after* a disaster can help reassure citizens, thus lessening the psychological tension associated with the attack.

COMMUNICATION

BEFORE: PUBLIC EDUCATION WITH REALISTIC THREAT ASSESSMENT.   In Japan, there was no notable education about or warnings of terrorism with weapons of mass destruction prior to the subway attack. Nor was there any open discussion about Aum Shinrikyo as a potential threat to the population. This made the attack even more shocking to the Japanese people. In the United States, government officials have been increasingly vocal regarding the WMD terrorist threat since 1995, stimulated by Tokyo's experience, and particularly since the anthrax attacks in 2001. However, the government and the media are emphasizing not the low probability of attack but the potential for catastrophic consequences and lack of U.S. preparedness. This type of communication between policymakers and the public is not productive: it fails to explain how the threat assessment is reached and what is being done to improve the country's preparedness.

The federal government has issued numerous alerts to the nation since 9/11, calling for a heightened state of vigilance in preparation for potential terrorist attacks. The alerts do not mention a specific threat but often convey unsubstantiated or overly broad intelligence. Many in Congress and the public, as well as some counterterrorism experts, argue that vague alerts alarm people without telling them how to respond. Others are concerned by the "crying wolf" phenomenon—an imprecise alert system that keeps people constantly on edge will contribute to complacency as the public views the threats as not credible and commonplace. Finally, many state and local officials are worried that maintaining a high level of security commensurate with the alerts is stretching their already strained budgets.

Efforts to remedy these concerns are currently being made by the Office of Homeland Security as well as police and security officials, who have implemented a five-step alert system in which colors indicate the level of the threat. Government officials must take this one step further by communicating both what the threat is, and how the assessment has

---

tions taken pre- and trans-event, not just those taken post-event." Morgan and Camper, "Fear Management," p. 1.

been made. An educational campaign to inform citizens of the nature of potential weapons and appropriate responses is a necessary complement.

DURING: WORKING WITH AND THROUGH THE MEDIA.   A good way to communicate with the public, of course, is through the media, but it is not simple. The media has the potential to be a hindrance. For instance, irresponsible media coverage can cause problems by "increas[ing] convergence to the scene both by the curious and by those with genuine concerns. By their own convergence, both in person and by telephone [members of the media] can create pressures on managers for information to the point where media demands interfere with effective response. They can spread rumors and so alter the reality of disaster, at least to those well away from it, that they can bias the nature of the response."[37]

However, the media can also be helpful—and making sure that it is helpful is the job of a well-prepared, rehearsed, and implemented response plan.[38] A potential plan for local and state agencies that will need to deal with media includes eight components:

*   establish what media outlets exist and what they can do;
*   establish the media's potential in disaster;
*   develop a plan for dealing with the media and do that planning in cooperation with them;
*   identify those persons capable of putting the plan into effect;
*   test the plan with the media playing an active role in the test;
*   evaluate and revise the plan in light of the test, ensuring that the media's criticisms are taken into account;
*   make sure the plan becomes known to all those involved in the disaster response, including the public;
*   make sure the plan is constantly revised in light of changing conditions, regular tests, and actual experience.[39]

---

37.   "They can and do create myths about disasters, myths which will persist even among those with contrary disaster experience." Joseph Scanlon, Suzane Allred, Al Farrell, and Angela Prawzick, "Coping with the Media in Disasters: Some Predictable Problems," *Public Administration Review,* special issue (1985), pp. 123–133 at p. 124.

38.   "All of these problems, however, can be managed and controlled because of two key facts: One is the media behave much the same way in disasters as at other times. The other is that media behavior at all times is highly predictable. This means it may be demanding, but planning for media in one disaster can be relatively efficient because it is possible to predict from long experience precisely what the media will do." Ibid., p. 124.

39.   Ibid, pp. 124–125.

Moreover, full disclosure to the media (within reasonable bounds) is critical and withholding information is often detrimental. The media have alternative sources of information, including the public itself. Word of mouth works very quickly so that information gets around even in a media blackout. Officials should be concerned with getting out accurate information, especially after misleading rumors begin to circulate: "Rumors can be stopped very quickly if they are identified and corrected over the air. They should not be ignored", or they will proliferate.[40]

AFTER: SHARING INFORMATION WITH THE PUBLIC. In the days and weeks following the sarin attack:

Tokyo's millions moved under a cloud of fear. Taxi drivers reported a surge in business as people avoided the subways. Commuters who had no alternative were seen sniffing subway cars before boarding. Fewer people dozed in their seats. The most common of sounds—a person coughing, a child's scream, a can rattling down the aisle—was enough to send ripples of alarm through the car. One day after the attack, one subway line was stopped while a foul-smelling package was investigated. It contained fish.[41]

Could government action have alleviated the feelings of fear described above? Despite the fact that the police raided Aum Shinrikyo's compounds wearing full personal protective equipment and carrying canaries as sentinels, they refused to publicly link the cult to the attack. Aum experts David Kaplan and Andrew Marshall observed that, "to the public, the intense speculation on whether a religious group had gassed Tokyo's subways was almost as unbelievable as the attack itself. . . . For the next week, as a mesmerized nation watched live on television, police began unearthing a mammoth stockpile of chemicals at Mount Fuji . . . police estimated that Aum's stockpile held more than 200 kinds of chemicals, including all the key elements for producing sarin."[42] Yet, these raids were not reassuring to the public. A statement of innocence recorded by cult leader Shoko Asahara was played across the national media. No arrests had been made. "In contrast to the cult's loud declarations of inno-

---

40. Ibid, p. 129. "The media should also be told that they should report all the facts possible. The evidence suggests that the public can deal with the facts. There is no need to hold back disturbing information because it is feared it might cause panic. The real danger lies in not informing people of dangers and what they should do about them."

41. David E. Kaplan and Andrew Marshall, *The Cult at the End of the World: The Incredible Story of Aum* (London: Hutchison Press, 1996) p. 255.

42. Ibid., p. 257.

cence, Japanese authorities seemed intent on keeping the public in the dark."[43]

Open investigation of Aum Shinrikyo by police and information-sharing with the Japanese public about the sarin attack by the government would have given the public a way to think about the potential destructiveness of that cult and chemical weapons. Instead of pursuing this course, "during these anxious days, Tokyo learned a painful lesson in the tactics of modern terrorism. Once the terrorist has displayed the dreadful destruction he is capable of, there is no need to launch another attack to disrupt a city and hold its population ransom. As one journalist noted, the mere threat of another attack 'paralyzed Tokyo almost as effectively as nerve gas itself.'"[44] Concerns that the public cannot handle information about the situation and appropriate response are misconceived. Public health and disaster response experts believe that full disclosure is usually preferable to withholding information, and it helps curb the public's tendency to speculate and to act based on that speculation.[45]

INFRASTRUCTURE PROTECTION

BEFORE: TRAINING AND EXERCISES.   Large- and small-scale exercises are an integral part of an emergency response service's training regime. Exercises that are designed to simulate an actual mass-casualty attack allow responders to practice activities that can be used in more routine operations as well as skills that are specific to such an attack. The skills and protocols practiced in training can be more readily applied during the disaster, which leads to a successful performance and the feeling of being more in control during the operation.

Over the past several years, new players—including public health departments—have been incorporated into the design and play of emergency response training and exercises. However, some key players are still overlooked, including private medical practitioners and the media. Both are critical to fear management. In "TOPOFF," a large-scale simula-

---

43. Ibid., p. 259.

44. Ibid., p. 271.

45. "Public reactions to an outbreak of meningitis suggest that infectious disease and infection control specialists who routinely deal with contagion can help prevent panic by using the mass media and personal outreach in neighborhoods and at people's workplaces to provide credible, accurate information." Thomas A. Glass and Monica Shoch-Spana, "Bioterrorism and the People: How to Vaccinate a City Against Panic," *Clinical Infectious Diseases*, January 15, 2002, p. 218.

tion first conducted in May 2000 (involving a simultaneous, hypothetical release of chemical, biological, and radiological agents in three large U.S. cities), there were physicians standing by to help victims, but no psychiatrists or mental health professionals.[46] To create and, if necessary, implement appropriate disaster mental health plans for responding to an attack the medical community must be consulted and included in exercises.[47]

The media also need to become fully active participants in these exercises. At present, they may be invited to observe or to act in a contrived manner that does not accurately reflect modern media outlets. It has been posited that it would "make more sense to convince some local media to act in a simulation the way they would in a real event. They should be asked to cover not the exercise but the simulated event: to try to press for information from already harassed officials; to try to crash official lines."[48] This will help emergency responders and public officials to understand how to best work with the media to calm the public and to convey important information to the citizenry.[49]

DURING: MANAGING CONVERGENCE.   There is a popular conception that civilians and rescue workers will flee a site that has been attacked. This is not supported by the literature on other disasters. "Although erroneous popular images focus on the flight of people *out of* the stricken area, a major problem communities actually face is convergence, or the movement of people and resources *into* the stricken area."[50] The press,

---

46.   Eve Kupersanin, "FBI Psychiatrist Urges Colleagues to Prepare to Aid Terrorism Victims," *Psychiatric News,* July 20, 2000, reprinted in *The Beacon,* Vol. 3, No. 7 (April 2001), p. 3.

47.   See also Scott Sleek, "Learning How To Calm Public Panic In The Event Of A Chemical Attack," *American Psychological Association Monitor,* Vol. 29, No. 6 (June 1998) at <http://www.apa.org/monitor/jun98/panic.html>.

48.   Scanlon et al., "Coping with the Media," p. 130.

49.   Media has the potential to be a help or a hindrance. For instance, they can cause problems by "increas[ing] convergence to the scene both by the curious and by those with genuine concerns. By their own convergence, both in person and by telephone, they can create pressures on managers for information to the point where media demands interfere with effective response. They can spread rumors and so alter the reality of disaster, at least to those well away from it, that they can bias the nature of the response. They can and do create myths about disasters, myths which will persist even among those with contrary disaster experience." Ibid., p. 124.

50.   Kathleen J. Tierney, "The Social and Community Contexts of Disaster," in Richard Gist and Bernard Lubin, eds., *Psychosocial Aspects of Disaster* (New York: John Wiley and Sons, 1989), p. 24. Beyond the immediate convergence of first responders, concerned individuals, and worried well, "in federally declared disasters, shortly after the immediate emergency period concludes (usually within 3 or 4 days after impact), an-

friends and families of the victims, volunteers, curious onlookers, and response personnel who have not been assigned to the response may all converge at or near the scene. In many disasters, managing convergence diverts resources that might otherwise be applied to disaster rescue and recovery operations. Despite this evidence that convergence, not flight, is the common human response to disaster, many experts have speculated that in a terrorist attack, as opposed to a natural disaster or conventional terrorist attack, the reaction will be the opposite. It is difficult to refute this hypothesis because most studies of human behavior have focused on natural disasters. However, one analyst argues that:

"Technological disasters tend to elicit a different pattern of public response than do natural disasters. Whereas publics tend to be reluctant to evacuate in natural disasters, evacuation from technological disasters tends to exceed official expectations. Factors contributing to this difference are the lack of familiarity and greater perception of threat associated with the latter. Technological disasters, unlike natural disasters, result in a greater reliance upon governmental authorities and a reduced use of community and family social networks."[51]

However, the experience in Tokyo suggests that convergence will occur after a terrorist attack as well. In fact, "convergence did happen in the sarin incident even though the event was so spread out."[52] During the attack, bystanders entered the subways to assist emergency workers; after the attack, concerned citizens, friends and family of the victims, and media from around the world converged on the attack area seeking information.

One of the best ways to reduce convergence is by sharing information with the public. A good public information campaign that regularly updates the public on the situation removes the need for concerned family, worried well, and curious outsiders to enter the stricken area to get the information first hand. Experts agree, for example, that "the communication of the risk to individuals following a bacteriologic attack will be critical to how communities and individuals respond."[53]

---

other more formalized type of convergence begins as representatives of federal agencies and other relief organizations come to the community to offer various kinds of disaster assistance." Ibid., p. 27.

51. Roger Kasperson and David Pijawka, "Societal Response to Hazards and Major Hazard Events: Comparing Natural and Technological Hazards," *Public Administration Review,* Vol. 45, special issue (January 1985), p. 17.

52. Interview with Nozomu Asukai, November 1, 2000.

53. Holloway et al., "The Threat of Biological Weapons," p. 259.

Full disclosure can also alleviate telecommunications convergence, which can overwhelm the communication infrastructure. Spokespersons can ask people to stay away from the scene and refrain from calling emergency phone numbers unless they are facing a genuine emergency. They can also reduce the number of nonemergency calls by shifting to a "comprehensive news policy"—by giving out information that answers questions before people call to ask them, reporting on areas not hit by disaster so people do not wonder if friends in those areas are affected, and so forth.[54]

AFTER: IMPROVED SECURITY MEASURES AND LAW ENFORCEMENT. Improved security measures and timely law enforcement safeguard the public from future attacks and offer visual reassurance of individual safety. The official reaction to the sarin attack was to heighten security: "cars were searched, cyclists stopped, litter bins and coin lockers sealed. In department stores and stadiums, security guards [asked owners to identify their bags]."[55]

Achieving a sense that a positive change has resulted from an otherwise terrible incident is critical to the psychological recovery of individuals and the rebuilding of the community. For many victims, prosecuting the perpetrators provides a sense of closure and justice that facilitates recovery. Furthermore, involving victims in the law enforcement phase of disaster recovery, such as the litigation phase of the process, is as important as providing proactive response roles for victims during the later stages of disaster recovery. In Tokyo, the legal process has not served to assuage the psychological impact suffered by survivors. On the contrary, "survivors and victims' families say they feel their rights have been overlooked, while the rights of the defendants, the members of Aum on trial for the gas attack and a raft of other heinous crimes, have been closely guarded."[56] For example, cult leader Asahara was placed under medical supervision free of charge, whereas victims are paying for medical care and litigation. In Tokyo, a National Police Administration survey found that "additional fear and frustration were expressed regarding the prolonged trial of [Asahara], as well as recent reports confirming that current Aum members are involved in a major effort to rebuild and recover their organization."[57]

---

54. Scanlon et al., "Coping with the Media," p. 129.

55. Peter Haworth, "The Treatment Of Shell Shock: Cognitive Therapy Before Its Time," *Psychiatric Bulletin,* No. 24 (2000), pp. 225–227.

56. Tetsushi Kajimoto, "Aum Three Years Later: Victims Struggle for Redress," *Japan Times,* March 18, 1998.

57. "Victims of Subway Attack Still Suffer," February 2, 1999.

Rapid law enforcement is also key to recovery. In Tokyo, resentment over the drawn out legal process lingers. In fact, "71 percent of the respondents expressed hope for an early conclusion of [Asahara's] trial."[58] The general public expressed a desire to put the episode behind them, as represented by the litigation process. At the same time, many victims feel that they are being forgotten. A neurologist treating PTSD patients notes that "with the memory of the incident fading in most people's minds, survivors still suffering post-traumatic stress disorder are receiving less public sympathy."[59]

PSYCHOLOGICAL ASSISTANCE

BEFORE: PREPARING RESPONSE PERSONNEL.   Response agencies prepare rescue workers for the physical demands of their work. They should also emphasize three aspects of mental health training: preparing response personnel for their own psychological trauma; training response personnel to help manage the trauma experienced by victims; and training psychiatric workers to respond to disasters caused by weapons of mass destruction.

In standard training, little attention is given to the mental health needs of first responders until after an attack.[60] Failure to consider the mental health needs of responders during the planning and training phases can have adverse results. Studies indicate that response personnel play conflicting roles in an emergency: they may be torn between family and professional responsibilities; they must decide between moving to safety or converging on the scene; and they are likely to suffer psychological effects from extended exposure to the trauma.

Additionally, traditional first responders—fire, police, and emergency medical technicians—need to be sensitized to the psychological needs of victims. Mental health staff should have the opportunity to educate emergency planners and public officials about how laypeople and response personnel each respond to emergency situations. "A tremendous mythology exists regarding human behavior in disaster. For example, a common misperception is that panic and looting are common occurrences following a disaster. *Accurate* information, in this case, that panic and looting are extremely rare in natural disasters, can help planners and

---

58. Ibid.

59. Kajimoto, "Aum Three Years Later."

60. Institute of Medicine National Research Council, "Prevention, Assessment, and Treatments," p. 168.

responders to base their action plans for deployment of staff and materials on a more realistic prediction of what may be needed."[61]

Concurrently, psychiatrists need to be trained in the specifics of responding to a terrorist attack, such as "the effects of, and treatment for, the chemical and biological agents that my be used in a terrorist incident."[62] Mental health professionals also need training in how to work in a contaminated environment, where protective gear or at least a gas mask may be needed.

DURING: RAPID RESPONSE WITH ROLES FOR VICTIMS AS WELL AS PROFESSIONALS. The popular image of a first responder is a trained municipal employee such as a firefighter, police officer, or emergency medical technician. In a terrorist attack, the first responders may be untrained bystanders, such as the transit workers in the subway attack. Additionally, in a mass-casualty attack, there may not be enough trained professionals to aid the victims. Hence, it may be necessary to craft roles for victims in the response effort. Experience has shown that "nonprofessional citizens are capable of full and useful participation in times of crisis."[63] This may hold true for victims at the scene as well as for civic groups that are already organized and have some infrastructure in place that may aid response workers.

Providing roles for victims has a secondary benefit. A terrorist attack is by its nature particularly stressful.[64] However, "it is not the stress that is dangerous to individuals but rather their inability to cope with it that is significant."[65] Experts believe that an individual's ability to change their situation has a great impact on the onset and severity of psychological distress.[66] "The assignment of simple work tasks that facilitate the care of other patients can help restore function to the psychological casualties. The recovery environment should be constructed to create a sense of

---

61. Garaventa Myers, "Mental Health and Disaster: Preventive Approaches to Intervention," in Richard Gist and Bernard Lubin, eds., *Psychosocial Aspects of Disaster* (New York: John Wiley and Sons, 1989), p. 201.

62. Cleto DiGiovanni, Jr., "Domestic Terrorism With Chemical Or Biological Agents: Psychiatric Aspects," *American Journal of Psychiatry*, Vol. 156, No. 10 (October 1999), pp. 1500–1505.

63. Glass and Shoch-Spana, 'Bioterrorism and the People," p. 219.

64. Stress, according to Hans Selye, is the "non-specific response of the body to any demand made upon it." E.E. Flynn "Victims of Terrorism" in Paul Wilkenson and Alasdair Stewart, eds., *Contemporary Research on Terrorism* (Aberdeen, Scotland: Aberdeen University Press, 1987), pp. 337–356, p. 348.

65. Ibid., p. 349.

66. Ibid.

safety and to counteract the helplessness induced by the terrorist act."[67] Hence, establishing proactive roles for victims may be the first and most important step toward their psychological recovery.

AFTER: EARLY PROACTIVE PSYCHOLOGICAL INTERVENTION FOR VICTIMS AND RESPONDERS. Experts agree that early intervention is one key to preventing ASD and PTSD or mitigating the severity of these conditions.[68] "Intervention during a crisis and prior to the development of psychological symptoms has been found effective in reducing subsequent emotional problems."[69] *Immediate* intervention may not always be the best option; each person must be allowed to grieve at his or her own pace and be counseled when it is appropriate to their needs. In fact, even when the first opportunities for intervention are missed, it is still possible to mitigate long-term effects within the first month after exposure.[70] The importance of *early* intervention, however, was starkly revealed in Tokyo. Although treatment provided months or even years after the attack relieved some symptoms, test results indicate that the underlying psychological disorders were not adequately resolved with delayed treatment.

The method of early intervention and treatment must, of course, be determined by professionals on an individual basis. In general, however, group debriefings have been used to mitigate effects and can help identify those who need further assistance.[71] This is an easy method of early intervention that allows victims to share their stories and identify points of concern. Critical incident stress debriefing has been popularly adopted by rescue organizations. These group meetings are for all personnel in the group, regardless of whether or not symptoms are present, and are led by a combination of unit leaders and mental health professionals.[72]

---

67. Holloway et al., "The Threat of Biological Weapons," p. 255.

68. The "underlying theme of all the interventions is an *educative one,* with the main intervention objective being the provision of *accurate information* to residents concerning a near-by disaster. Theoretically, such information would prevent the formation of stress-arousing rumors and would allay the unrealistic fears of residents." Glenn E. Shippee, Richard Bradford, and W. Larry Gregory, "Community Perceptions of Natural Disasters and Post-Disaster Mental Health Services," *Journal of Community Psychology,* Vol. 10, No. 1, pp. 23–28 at p. 27.

69. Mangelsdorff, "Lessons Learned and Forgotten," at p. 250.

70. "The capacity to identify in the acute trauma phase those individuals who are at risk of developing chronic PTSD provides an opportunity to prevent the development of chronic PTSD through early intervention." Bryant et al., p. 1780.

71. Holloway et al., "The Threat of Biological Weapons," p. 259.

72. There is little evidence to indicate whether or not debriefings are effective. Insti-

Intervention by trained professionals is only one aspect of a fear management program. "Disasters generate highly novel circumstances that require disaster mental health workers to adopt creative and flexible approaches to interventions that deviate from the usual ways of providing mental health services in the familiar treatment settings left at home."[73] There is also a significant role for community groups, trained laypeople, and victims. "Experience in the U.S. crisis counseling program, at the federal level, has consistently shown that a blend of professionals and trained nonprofessionals is the most effective provider mix."[74] Community groups can augment the cast of mental health professionals, bringing a greater sense of community support to the victims and providing useful roles for individuals who might otherwise join the ranks of the worried well or emotionally distressed.[75] Moreover, "even in the most severe disasters, nonvictims typically outnumber victims, so the community retains the ability to provide for itself."[76] Whereas the number of mental health professionals available on scene in the immediate aftermath of a disaster is small, the number of noncritically wounded civilians should be large enough to allow them to craft an effective support network. This is often more in tune with victims' needs than an influx of outside professionals.[77]

---

tute of Medicine National Research Council, "Prevention, Assessment, and Treatment," p. 168.

73.   John Weaver, Robert Dingman, Jane Morgan, Barry Hong, and Carol North, "The American Red Cross disaster mental health services: Development of a cooperative, single function, multidisciplinary service model," *Journal of Behavioral Health Services and Research,* Vol. 27, No. 3 (August 2000), pp. 314–320 at p. 318.

74.   Flynn, "Victims of Terrorism," p. 112.

75.   "There are several important policy implications of this investigation for the design of post-disaster mental health services for communities that are afflicted by a natural or man-made disaster. The results suggest that post-disaster mental health services should be extended to include those residential areas not directly affected by the disaster. That is, current disaster planning for mental health and crisis intervention services usually includes only those areas that are directly affected . . . yet, present research indicates that mental health facilities in communities adjacent to areas in which a disaster occurs should have a contingency plan ready for implementation." Shippee et al., "Community Perceptions," p. 27.

76.   Tierney, "The Social and Community Contexts of Disaster," p. 23.

77.   For example, "when the Mississippi River and its tributaries flooded St. Louis, Missouri in the spring and summer of 1993, 250 mental health professionals stood ready to help the thousands whose lives the floods would affect. It turned out, however, that most of the flood victims sought instead the support of community leaders they knew and trusted." See Carol S. North and Barry A. Hong, "Project CREST: A

Working within the community might also remove the stigma that can still surround psychiatric care. Reluctance to seek help due to stigmatization, although perhaps less extreme in the United States than in Japan, is also a major barrier to psychological recovery particularly for rescue workers.[78] Thus, requiring all police officers in a community to attend sessions run by community members removes the barrier an individual officer might feel about reaching out for help on his own, exposing a larger population to beneficial treatment. A trusted leader, such as a member of the clergy or of the community, can also help ease this transition from the role of helper to that of one receiving help that any first responder must make if he or she is to benefit from psychological intervention.

Conclusions: Taking Some of the Terror out of Terrorism

Mark J. Morgan and Paul M. Camper, authors of "Fear Management" note that, "History teaches us that the greatest numbers of victims or casualties arise from the indirect psychological consequence—FEAR."[79] Several contemporary academics have issued reminders that terrorism is the use of violence designed to inspire fear and terror. Since Aum Shinrikyo's 1995 subway attack, several countries have undertaken plans to deter terrorist attacks with weapons of mass destruction and to mitigate its consequences should it occur. However, few officials have developed or practiced plans that mitigate the fear and anxiety that result from terrorism. "[P]lanning and preparation for biological attacks and their attendant psychological consequences can diminish the terrorists' ability to

New Model for Mental Health Intervention After Community Disaster," *American Journal of Public Health,* Vol. 90, No. 7 (July 2000), pp. 1057–1058 at p. 1057.

78. Following the September 11, 2001, attacks, the New York City Police Department ordered that all 55,000 employees attend mental health counseling, "to relieve the stress and strain imposed by the attack on the World Trade Center and its aftermath." The program was paid for by a private nonprofit foundation (The Police Foundation, which has raised $10 million for the project) and carried out at Columbia University. The program was mandated in part because police officers were not seeking voluntary treatment, which was also available. According to a spokesperson, "We wanted to destigmatize it so that no one thinks that they are being singled out because they are having a problem, but rather to universalize it so that it is clear that it's a problem affecting everyone." The New York City Fire Department has not instituted mandatory counseling but has added $3 million to its counseling unit and counselors have been visiting fire houses. Richard Lezin Jones, "New York Police Officers Face Counseling on Sept. 11 Events," *The New York Times,* November 30, 2001 at A1.

79. Morgan and Camper, "Fear Management," p. 1.

achieve their overall goal—the induction of terror," therefore they are essential for the United States as it faces a newly heightened state of affairs where mass destruction terrorism is a very real threat.[80]

The U.S. experience with terrorism has been a chilling one, claiming several thousand lives and impacting millions more. The entire country has witnessed the psychological damage that such attacks can inflict. The greatest concern for first responders engaged in domestic preparedness is saving lives. This mission, of course, is paramount and should not be seen as trivialized in the call for prioritization of mental health response. As their name implies, weapons of mass destruction have the potential to create thousands of fatalities and scores of casualties. Mitigating their physical effects is, rightly, the first priority. History has shown, however, that not all terrorist attacks with weapons of mass destruction create mass fatalities. Indeed, the sarin attack and the recent anthrax attacks in the United States resulted in fewer than 20 fatalities total. The psychological casualties, on the other hand, numbered in the thousands in each scenario. Hence, plans must account for what, until now at least, has been the predominant result of WMD terrorism: psychological damage.

The psychological impact of a terrorist event need not cripple the community. The deleterious psychological effects of terrorism can be ameliorated if a well-defined mental health plan and adequate training are incorporated into emergency response plans. Such a plan should include all the tools of fear management.

---

80. Holloway et al. "The Threat of Biological Weapons," p. 261.

Chapter 10

Supporting the National Strategy for Homeland Security: The Role of the National Guard

Phillip Oates

The terrorist attacks against the nation on September 11, 2001, have brought about a resurgence of patriotism, a major military campaign, and a significant increase in federal budgets and programs for homeland security. Our international coalition and the military campaign in Afghanistan have been successful because of effective diplomacy and appropriate use of information, politics, economics, and military power. Equally important efforts are occurring at home. Increases in federal spending are adding billions of dollars to the tasks of improving interagency coordination, intelligence collection, security planning, emergency management, and military programs. The president's supplemental Fiscal Year 2002 Budget request and his Fiscal Year 2003 Budget for homeland security will constitute one of the largest increases in history to improve domestic preparedness and emergency response programs.

Even with this increase in spending, the nation will still be unable to afford the cost of establishing and funding new agencies and programs that exist solely for the prevention or response to major domestic terrorist attacks. It will also be politically difficult to take funding from other important national priorities to establish these new capabilities. The difficulties of are of funding new programs are began to surface within a year of the September 11 attacks. Politicians and legislators at city and state levels of government—and to a lesser degree at the federal level—persist in concentrating emergency response funding on the kinds of events, such as natural disasters, that are most likely to occur. There is less willingness to appropriate dollars for the capabilities that are necessary to fully respond to major emergencies such as a terrorist attack using weapons of mass destruction with a low probability of occurrence. This trend exists in spite of the fact that such a contingency would result in catastrophic damages and enormous long-term negative consequences to the nation. Fortunately, the nation does not have to start completely anew to build new response capabilities. Existing agencies, programs, and procedures at federal and state levels do provide a good foundation for the improvement of capabilities to protect against major acts of terrorism.

A similar situation exists in the Department of Defense (DoD), where current structures and resources must be leveraged to establish new domestic military capabilities. As decision makers in DoD begin to take these steps, it will become increasingly important to protect the basic framework of budgets, resources, and programs that exist to accomplish the department's core military requirement to deploy forces and win the wars that protect our critical national interests overseas. The guidance that flowed from the Office of the Secretary of Defense to establish a new domestic military capability without increasing the overall number of military personnel in joint billets was probably a reflection of these concerns. Additional emphasis was also made on the needs to control spending and preserve war-fighting capabilities. The next phase of this effort should be the identification of the primary military forces for homeland security. These forces will likely and mainly come from the National Guard.[1]

Predominant use of the National Guard for homeland security against major acts of terrorism is appropriate for three key reasons. First, the National Guard already has a significant emergency response capability that would provide a firm foundation for a larger role in homeland security. Second, the Constitution of the United States establishes the authority to employ the National Guard in significant and leading domestic roles against terrorism. Third, because active duty forces provide our nation's leading military resources for rapid deployment and expeditionary warfare, these forces are less available as a contingency force for domestic missions and might be completely unavailable in the event of a major overseas deployment. Existing laws also restrict the use of federal military forces in domestic law enforcement roles but afford the National Guard much greater latitude in domestic operations.

The enormous consequences of the terrorist attacks on September 11, 2001, have forced our nation to focus its efforts and resources on developing new capabilities, structures, and procedures for homeland security. The purpose of this chapter is to develop and recommend the terms of reference and appropriate roles for the Combatant Command for Home-

---

1. Point Paper on Homeland Security, Adjutants General Association of the United States (February 25, 2002).

land Security by using the National Guard as the "base piece" for this effort.[2] The paper begins with a brief discussion of the different categories of military service in our nation. Next is a consideration of the missions, structures, and procedures of the National Guard that should be relied upon in this era of greater emphasis on homeland security. That consideration leads to a discussion of the state and national roles for the National Guard in homeland security. Finally, the paper discusses operational focus of the Combatant Command for Homeland Security. The paper concludes with other changes to consider as homeland security becomes a defining mission for the DoD.

Categories of Individual Military Service

It is important to establish a common understanding of the different categories of individual service in the military as the military role for homeland security is being constructed. There are two titles and a state status that define these categories of service: Title 10, Title 32, and State Active Duty.

Title 10 defines the parameters for all federal military forces—Active Duty and Reserve—and the National Guard when federalized. The Posse Comitatus Act of 1878 prevents these military forces from performing domestic law enforcement roles unless specifically authorized by presidential order. These forces are established, funded, and controlled at the federal level. Their liability also lies at the federal level.

Title 32 defines the National Guard forces belonging to the states and following jurisdictions: Guam, Puerto Rico, the Virgin Islands, and the District of Columbia. The Posse Comitatus Act does not apply, so these military forces may be used in a domestic law enforcement role. They are federally funded, but the forces remain under the local control. The state governor retains full authority as the commander-in-chief. Because these National Guard forces are federally funded, they must be federally established at the level of Service Secretary or higher. Liability exists at both the federal and state or territorial levels. Federal liability exists for torts (civil wrongs), but there is no indemnification for the state or territory.

State Active Duty defines the National Guard forces of the individual states and territories when they are performing state or territory func-

---

2. "Base piece" is a U.S. Army Field Artillery term that establishes the point of beginning for accurate adjustment of cannon firing. The "base piece" is the howitzer that fires the first shot in an engagement and serves as the point of adjustment for the firing of all other guns in the battalion. In this paper the "base piece" serves as the point of beginning and subsequent adjustment of capabilities for homeland security.

tions (normally in response to an emergency or disaster). Again, the Posse Comitatus Act does not apply, so these military forces may be used in a domestic law enforcement role. Funding is normally the responsibility of the state or territory that has called up these forces. As in Title 32, these forces are under the command and control of the governor. Any liability for the use of these forces remains at the state or territorial level.

In summary, the governor remains the commander-in-chief of the National Guard in a state or territory under the two categories of military service where law enforcement roles are always possible (Title 32 and State Active Duty). Title 32 forces, however, are established and funded at the federal level and State Active Duty forces are established and funded by the state or territory. Title 10 forces are federally established, federally controlled, and federally funded, and they are not permitted to play a law enforcement role unless directed to do so by the President of the United States.

Activation of National Guard members in Title 32 or State Active Duty status reinforces the emergency powers of the governor that are established in the U.S. Constitution and encourages a strong state or territorial role in an emergency or disaster. Title 32 and State Active Duty categories of service also enhance the state or territory's ability to provide resources and support to first responders—a major tenet of the Federal Response Plan.[3] Title 10 forces tend to be less supportive to first responders because of the greater centralization of command, control, and planning that is commonly a characteristic of Active Duty forces.

There are a number of other advantages that Title 32 and State Active Duty National Guard forces bring to a state or territory during an emergency or disaster. First, when National Guard members are kept in "state" roles, they are seen as the military members of the community and often have a greater stake in the success of the effort. Second, National Guard leaders are often more willing than Active Duty leaders to allow members to work individually or in small units on a decentralized basis with other agencies. Third, many activated National Guard members come from the agencies being supported. These individuals add significant value to the National Guard because they bring together the knowledge, experience, and understanding of their agency and the mili-

---

3. First published in 1992, the Federal Response Plan is an agreement among 27 Federal departments and agencies and the American Red Cross. This agreement provides a mechanism to provide federal assistance and resources to state and local governments during a major emergency or disaster. It implements the Robert T. Stafford Disaster Relief and Emergency Assistance Act and is a supplement to other federal emergency operations plans.

tary. This dual expertise is in itself synergistic and thus is valuable to the interagency process. Fourth, these categories of military members are authorized to perform law enforcement functions in accordance with the rules of engagement and the laws of the states or territories.[4]

National Guard Missions and Resources

The 2001 Quadrennial Defense Review (QDR) provides a blueprint that is guiding the transformation of the military from the threat-based force structure of the Cold War to a capabilities-based strategy for the future. It provides a DoD assessment of current and projected military capabilities and requirements to Congress. A significant conclusion of the 2001 review is the need for greater military capabilities to defend the nation against major acts of terrorism. The following excerpt reflects the new emphasis.

- The protection of the nation's homeland is a primary mission for DoD.
- Homeland security is not the only mission for Reserve Component forces.
- The National Guard and the Reserves both provide capabilities for power projection and homeland security.
- Right-sizing the force is necessary to achieve new transformation goals.
- Experimentation is a key tenet of transformation.
- Interagency communication and cooperation could be improved by leveraging the capabilities of the National Guard and the Reserves.
- The worldwide proliferation of ballistic missiles and other weapons of mass destruction significantly increase the threat of massive terrorism against the homeland of the United States.[5]

With this summary of the 2001 defense review in mind, each state and territory should have a National Guard that is organized, trained,

---

4. It should also be noted during this discussion of categories of service and command relationships that the National Guard in the District of Columbia has a unique command structure that differs from that of the states and territories. That difference is not germane to the ideas and concepts in this paper and is therefore not discussed.

5. Summary of pertinent points in the September 30, 2001, Quadrennial Defense Review Report is provided by Lieutenant General (ret) Jay M. Garner, President, SY Technology. The full report may be accessed at <www.defenselink.mil/pubs/qdr2001.pdf>.

and equipped for missions in three major areas: mobilization missions for wartime contingencies; homeland security missions; and force provider missions. These three major mission areas, explained in more detail in the following paragraphs, might be conceptualized as three legs of a stool—in this case the "mission" stool for the National Guard of a state or territory. Mobilization missions are performed under the stipulations of Title 10. Homeland security missions are normally performed under Title 32 or State Active Duty status but could be carried out with a Title 10 status if the National Guard were federalized. Force provider missions are performed under the stipulations of Title 32, with procedures in place to immediately transition individuals to a Title 10 status.

The specific National Guard force structure that exists today in states or territories was established to focus primarily on combat and mobilization for wartime contingencies. That paradigm is changing. Now that the National Guard is assuming major responsibilities for homeland security, there will be a greater interest in establishing combat support and combat service support organizations. There will also be a redefinition of "mobilization." Because of the cost of maintaining single purpose forces, the National Guard will evolve into a primary force structure of different military organizations that are fully capable of performing tasks across the spectrum of mission requirements—from military support of civil authorities to homeland security to mobilization for wars fought overseas. Although a multi-purpose force is more cost-effective, the approach brings some risk, as National Guard deployments overseas would leave the homeland less protected. Some portion of the National Guard, therefore, should be dedicated solely to the homeland security mission.

The provisioning of National Guard operational forces to the active duty military within the homeland is another mission concept that already exists and is one that will become increasingly important in the future. In this concept, the state or territory's National Guard functions as a daily and operational "force provider" to active duty commands, performs missions such as air defense, space surveillance, missile defense, and manning operations centers. This force provisioning by the National Guard frees active duty forces for expeditionary roles. It also often gives the National Guard missions that are important for homeland security, such as missile defense.

The organizational structures of the National Guard elements that perform "force provider" roles are normally unique to specific missions or functional requirements. The personnel filling these roles are usually full-time Guardsmen and -women who have been recruited, trained, equipped, and professionally developed by the National Guard, but who are operationally and tactically controlled by the active duty commander.

On a day-to-day basis, during routine operations and training, the military members of these units work under Title 32 status (and are still somewhat available for state roles) but hostile or specified operational events immediately transfer them to a Title 10 status.

The event driving this change in military status might be an unknown aircraft's incursion into the Air Defense Identification Zone of North American Aerospace Defense Command or an enemy ballistic missile launch. In other words, these types of hostile or operational events will immediately transfer military units from state to federal control. A memorandum of agreement between the governor, the National Guard, the appropriate federal authority, and each military individual establishes the procedures that permit military units or members to serve in state roles and outlines the conditions that change the military status.

National Guard organizations that are required to mobilize and deploy rapidly in wartime contingencies normally have equipment and structures that are virtually identical to those of active duty organizations. These rapid deployment National Guard organizations are given a high priority in the allotment of resources for training, equipment, personnel, and repair parts. On the other hand, National Guard organizations whose equipment or structure is dissimilar to that of active Army or Air Force organizations are ones that do not play key roles in major contingencies. These organizations receive less support from the active Army or Air Force for the acquisition of resources and funding necessary to maintain a high level of readiness. Many in the National Guard would, therefore, caution against a National Guard structure tailored uniquely for the homeland security missions. A dissimilar military organizational structure performing a dissimilar mission such as homeland security would certainly find difficulty in competing for resources within the DoD.

The same "contingency plan" linkage that drives the prioritization of resources for budgets, manning, equipping, training, and spare parts could also serve as an appropriate model for the allocation of resources for national contingencies in homeland security. Just as the early deployment units in major wartime contingencies receive the highest priority for resources, the homeland security units responsible for the missions of greatest importance to the nation could similarly be given the highest priorities for resources.

Another, more aggressive approach to ensure that adequate resources are available to the National Guard for homeland security would be to give budget authority for major homeland security programs to the combatant commander of the new command in charge of homeland security. The armed services and the DoD, however, would probably resist this suggestion, because it is an approach that reduces their overarching control of budgets, priorities, and programs. There is a successful precedent for this type of approach. Congress gave the Commander of United States Special Operations Command (USSOCOM) similar budget authority through Major Force Program 11 at a time when the leadership of the Army, Navy, and Air Force repeatedly failed to meet congressional expectations for the funding of special operations programs. That budget authority for USSOCOM had a significant positive impact on improving the readiness and capabilities of special operations forces—improvement that was readily apparent during the recent war in Afghanistan.

Heretofore, the National Guard has traditionally looked to the armed services (the Army and the Air Force) and to Congress for resources to fund programs, requirements, operations, maintenance, and construction. The Guard, however, has not been able to significantly leverage the support from combatant commanders to increase resources and establish new programs.[6] Although combatant command priorities may ultimately cascade to the National Guard, these resources do not improve capabilities quickly or accomplish near-term transformation. With the advent of a new Combatant Command for Homeland Security, the National Guard will finally have a champion to influence priorities and programs that accomplish rapid transformation of capabilities for these new roles and missions.

A Concept for the National Guard Role in Homeland Security

The majority of military organizations assigned to each state or territory's National Guard should, with a single organizational structure, be able to accomplish two different missions—mobilization for major war and homeland security. This dual capability force structure in the Army National Guard should consist primarily of light infantry, military police, air defense, engineers, medical, communications, aviation, and civil support organizations. Similarly, the dual capability force structure in the Air National Guard should consist primarily of security police, combat communications, medical, tactical airlift, combat search and rescue, air defense, and aerial refueling organizations. Both Army and Air Guard forces should have robust intelligence capabilities and the ability to operate in contaminated and hazardous environments. Some National Guard forces, however, should be dedicated solely to homeland security requirements, especially in areas where the nation cannot afford risk. This is

---

6. One result of the Goldwater-Nichols legislation of 1986 was greater authority for combatant commanders to influence the resources and priorities of the armed services.

especially important because major mobilization or deployment of the National Guard overseas could render many organizations unavailable to defend our nation's most critical sites at home—possibly when they are needed most.

As suggested earlier, the National Guard organizations with the responsibilities to provide the quickest support to civil authorities would be granted a higher priority in the allocation of resources for homeland security missions (i.e., the resources for training, manning, equipping, and replacing). Organizations with missions to protect sites deemed most critical to the nation would likewise be given a higher priority in resource allocation.

For the most part, the personnel structure of the National Guard organizations devoted to mobilization and homeland security missions would continue to consist of traditional (part-time) National Guard members. Activation for full-time duty could be determined by contingency plan requirements for specific warning categories being established by the Office of Homeland Security.[7] Homeland security tasks, missions, and contingency plans could be developed according to two geographical categories: national sites of importance and sites that are important to the states and territories. Contingency plans would identify the military force packages and tasks appropriate to each level of threat warning, as well as the other private and public responsibilities for protection. In the lower categories of threat warning for the military, this might involve the integration of information activities with other agencies. At a higher level, security forces might be involved. At an even higher level, a plan might call for fully armed defense of a critical site. At a recovery level, recovery assistance across the spectrum of consequence management might be enlisted.

After authorization by the governor, the protection of critical sites of specific interest to the individual states or territories would come from National Guard forces that have been elevated to State Active Duty status. Payment for these state military forces would normally be the responsibility of the respective states or territories. After authorization by

---

7. DoD's war plans identify missions, tasks, forces, and the deployment sequence for each military organization and establish the training and readiness requirements for contingency operations. That same approach, expanded to include private and non-DoD agency participation, should be a part of contingency planning for the "terrorism" threat and warning system developed by the Office of Homeland Security. Additional requirements for funding, training, and exercise responsibilities must also be established for each different category of warning. Force packages and responsibilities of all tasked agencies would be identified for each critical site or contingency mission.

federal authority, the protection of sites critical to the national interest would come from National Guard forces with a Title 32 status. Payment for the use of Title 32 forces would be the responsibility of the federal government.

An Organizational Nucleus for Homeland Security in the National Guard

The National Guard Counter-Drug Support Program (CDSP) provides an apt model for a small full-time organization of approximately 30 personnel that could significantly improve interagency capabilities for homeland security. As seen in the CDSP, such organizations should provide National Guard resources and manpower to other "homeland security" agencies on a continuous basis.

The CDSP, established by Congress in 1989, has had continuous funding since its inception through annual appropriations to the National Guard Bureau. This budget provides pay and allowances for full-time (Title 32) personnel and for the operations and maintenance costs of the military equipment and other resources used to support drug law enforcement agencies in drug demand reduction and counterdrug support operations. A federally approved governor's plan makes National Guard resources available (within the constraints of the annual budget) to agencies at all levels of government to achieve the drug missions.

The CDSP demonstrates a model that provides an exponential improvement in the capabilities of every participating agency. It enhances the operations and interoperability of agencies by providing a mechanism to improve coordination, communications, training, and planning. How is this done? The CDSP can be thought of as the hub of a bicycle tire. The multiple agencies with a drug-related focus can be thought of as the tread of the tire. Spokes, obviously, connect the hub to the tire. In this analogy, the spokes represent the conduits of information, coordination, and assistance that run between the CDSP hub and the individual agencies. Although the hub does not roll on the ground, it holds the wheel of agencies together and ultimately helps all agencies to roll more smoothly and effectively together. By functioning as a supporting agency, not as a supported or primary agency, the CDSP produces a synergistic effect that improves all agencies.

A similar approach might produce equally important improvements to agency cooperation, interoperability, and communications in the areas of preventing and responding to major acts of terrorism in our nation. This proposed National Guard Homeland Security Support Program could provide daily coordination, integration, and assistance between agencies such as the Federal Bureau of Investigation (FBI) and the Federal Emergency Management Agency (FEMA). The full resources of the National Guard would be made available (within the limitations of budgets and pre-established agreements) to manage flows of information and intelligence, while improving all players' abilities to plan, train, exercise, and operate together. Law enforcement roles would be possible for these Title 32 forces within the constraints of the federally approved governor's plan.

The Operational Context and the Role of a Combatant Command for Homeland Security

Establishing a Combatant Command for Homeland Security—United States Northern Command (USNORTHCOM)—on October 1, 2002, was a clear indication that DoD will implement major changes to meet the requirements of the national strategy for homeland security. The military roles in meeting these new requirements could be leading efforts or supporting efforts. When the military has superior capabilities and full legal authority to deter, preempt, prevent, or defeat terrorism, it could perform a leading role and receive support from other federal agencies.[8] A lead military effort might occur during the execution of missions such as air defense or missile defense against major acts of terrorism. When other agencies possess better capabilities and authority to deal with a situation, the military would likely be in support of those federal agencies. Domestic law enforcement is a good example of a situation where the military might play a supporting role. In most consequence management scenarios, the active duty military role is normally one of providing support to civil authorities and lead federal agencies.

Since the Combatant Command for Homeland Security is obviously a military organization, it is helpful to use doctrinal military terms to define the roles and operational context for the command. Terms such as "area of responsibility" describe the parameters of a particular mission. Other doctrinal terms such as "tactical," "operational," and "strategic" define operational contexts for military organizations. These same terms will help define the operational context and the roles of the Combatant Command for Homeland Security.[9]

---

8. This language is from the draft mission statement for USNORTHCOM, as briefed at the Adjuncts General Association of the United States (AGAUS) Conference on June 16, 2002, to deter, preempt, prevent, or defeat threats and aggression aimed at U.S. territories, its population, and its possessions.

9. Major Adrian Bogart of the Maryland Army National Guard provided suggestions

A state or territorial border might be used to establish the area of operational responsibility for a National Guard organization performing a homeland security mission. This type of approach would help the state and federal levels of government maintain the balance of power established in the Constitution while providing a· military context for homeland security operations. From a doctrinal perspective, these state or territorial National Guard operational areas would be considered the tactical levels of homeland security. This is the level where all forces—Title 10, Title 32, federal DoD, federal non-DoD, and state and local agencies—converge to support the emergency response efforts of the governors and first responders across the nation. Defining the tactical military area of operation by state or territorial borders is an approach that is also consistent with the guidance of the Federal Response Plan. This approach to establishing National Guard forces parallels a similar approach used by FEMA. As an ancillary benefit, this military model would also enhance the command and coordination lines between National Guard forces and Active Duty forces of a standing joint task force and U.S. Northern Command.[10]

The collective and adjacent state areas of operation could be organized around the 10 FEMA regions, and these areas could then become the operational levels of homeland security for the nation.[11] The operational level of homeland security refers to the area where an organization such as Joint Force Headquarters–Civil Support would be able to enlist the full complement of regional resources. Strategic levels of homeland security could be organized around the 1st and 5th Army areas of responsibility which divide the continental United States into two major regional areas (an eastern area and a western/central area that includes Alaska but not Hawaii).

Significant terrorist attacks might require an even larger strategic area. If terrorist attacks were to occur in rapid succession in multiple locations across the nation, the strategic area for operations might stretch to the full area of responsibility for the entire Combatant Command for

---

to the author for this operational context of the Combatant Command for Homeland Security.

10. This observation was from Lieutenant General (ret) Jay M. Garner.

11. 10 FEMA regions exist to facilitate the coordination and provision of federal assistance for emergency response and recovery operations. A multitude of different boundaries and regions exist across the spectrum of federal agencies (both military and nonmilitary). It is therefore much simpler for all of these agencies that have a role in homeland security to plan their support around the existing FEMA regions that currently define emergency operations planning.

Homeland Security. The strategic level of homeland security becomes the level where all strategic resources, both national and international, are brought together to win a major military campaign.

The U.S. Northern Command would be designated as the supported combatant command responsible for national military participation in the incident command system, the unified command system, or the command post system of lead federal agencies. It is also likely that USNORTHCOM and North American Aerospace Defense Command will be designated as separate commands under a single combatant commander. Interagency coordination of this supported combatant command would take place in a Joint Interagency Coordination Group. Supporting combatant and unified commands would normally include those of Joint Forces Command, Space Command, Special Operations Command, and Transportation Command. The Commander of U.S. Northern Command will be given coordination authority over the Coast Guard in scenarios that require maritime and coastal protection and response. Component service commands and functional service capabilities for USNORTHCOM would normally be provided by Joint Forces Command. The Combatant Command for Homeland Security will, therefore, have a comprehensive array of supporting forces to help " . . . deter, preempt, prevent, or defeat threats or aggression aimed at U.S. territories, its population and possessions."[12] The commander of U.S. Northern Command should also take the following actions, to enhance overall capabilities to accomplish and provide for the homeland security of the United States of America:

- Make use of the Defense Planning Guidance (DPG) and the Joint Strategic Capabilities Plan (JSCP) processes to ensure the military has robust capabilities that address and fully support the crisis response and consequence management pillars of homeland security.
- Assume responsibility for the disparate civil support agencies, functions, and activities that exist across the DoD, to include Military Support to Civil Authorities (MSCA) and the Director of Military Support (DOMS) from the Secretary of the Army.
- Use the significant tools available to a combatant commander— Integrated Priority List (IPL) and Joint Requirements Oversight Council (JROC)—to influence the rapid transformation of the National Guard to perform a lead military role in homeland security.
- Assist in developing the Joint War-Fighting Capability Assessment

---

12. This quote was taken from the draft mission statement for USNORTHCOM.

(JWCA) to validate the joint military and interagency approach to homeland security.

- Coordinate and establish joint requirements, tactics, techniques, and procedures for homeland security with federal departments and agencies.
- Develop missions and critical tasks for the national strategy for homeland security.
- Facilitate interagency coordination, training, and exercises for homeland security.
- Allocate assigned forces (active, reserve, and National Guard) for homeland security missions and training.
- Validate training and readiness through a Deployable Joint Task Force Augmentation Cell (DJTFAC) and through training and assistance teams from the 1st and 5th Army.
- Provide a DJTFAC to the states or territories that are performing a significant homeland security mission (to augment the limited capabilities of the National Guard Headquarters to coordinate, command, and control forces).
- Coordinate, analyze, and help disseminate national intelligence.
- Assume responsibility for Joint Task Force–Six (Counter-Drug) from Joint Forces Command.[13]
- Serve as the supported combatant command commander with primary responsibility to coordinate overall military support to the lead federal agencies and governors for homeland security operations.

Other Changes to Consider

As homeland security requirements become more vital in defining the organization, structure, and procedures in the National Guard, it is important to consider other changes that might enhance our nation's capabilities to protect the homeland against attacks or incidents involving weapons of mass destruction. The following proposals offer various ideas and topics for consideration as we continue this effort.

First, governors could be given coordination authority over all active duty and reserve forces (Army and Air Force) performing military support to civil authorities in their state or territory. This would give the governor full oversight of the active duty military in support of civilian authorities and a better chance to influence the direction of that support. This would further reinforce the leadership role of states and territories.

---

13. This suggestion was from Lieutenant General (ret.) Jay M. Garner.

Second, in some circumstances, it might be desirable to have the option to change reserve forces to a Title 32 status and assign them to a governor. This would admittedly require a significant change of current statutes. It would, however, allow the governor of a state or territory to have operational control of additional combat support and combat service support forces which may be extremely important for consequence management purposes.

Third, the DoD could develop a program that would establish exchange assignments for military personnel in "homeland security" agencies such as the Department of Homeland Security, Department of Health and Social Services, FBI, and FEMA. More senior leaders in the National Guard of the future will obviously need greater expertise and understanding of the procedures and operations of the major agencies that perform significant homeland security roles.

Fourth, more combat support and combat service support capability could be placed in the National Guard of the future. Tomorrow's National Guard forces must be equally capable of performing overseas mobilization roles and domestic security roles—out of a single organizational structure. The large and heavy division formations that were built for the Cold War are less advantageous for these dual requirements which need smaller and lighter formations. Future Army National Guard combat forces should probably be no larger than brigade size. Army Aviation units should consist primarily of cargo and utility aircraft.

Fifth, the Federal Response Plan could be expanded to provide a formal mechanism to funnel all federal assistance and resources to state and local governments to accomplish the national strategy for homeland security. The expansion of this important plan should build on the current provisions and procedures for providing federal assistance and resources for natural disasters and other emergencies. State and regional response plans and assistance compacts should be a mandatory part of the overall planning process. These plans and compacts could provide a soft match to the federal appropriations for specific homeland security programs.[14]

Sixth, budget authority for major homeland security programs could be given to the Combatant Command for Homeland Security. The precedent for this approach was described earlier in this paper—Congress gave budget authority to the commander of USSOCOM for special operations programs. This unique approach to budgeting is normally resisted

---

14. A soft match at the state level is a match that substitutes actions such as the adoption of specific laws or procedures for the hard match in state dollars that is normally required for federally funded programs.

by the DoD and its services, but it could serve to ensure that the department devotes sufficient resources to the military capabilities for homeland security.

Summary

Just as fighting and winning wars overseas is a vital and defining mission for our country's military forces, a second major mission area is becoming equally important to the National Guard and to other components of the Department of Defense. That mission is protecting our homeland and way of life against any attack or threat of attack by terrorists with weapons of mass destruction. The military, however, is only one part of the solution. Comprehensive homeland security capabilities to adequately prevent and protect against terrorist attacks and the capabilities to adequately manage the consequences of any attacks that occur will require the full and appropriate use of resources at all levels of government and the private sector.

Chapter 11

Homeland Security and War-Fighting: Two Pillars of National Guard Responsibility

Paul D. Monroe, Jr.

Prior to September 2001, the United States felt confidently prepared to fight major regional conflicts virtually anywhere in the world in much the same manner that it did during World War II. After all, Operation Desert Storm had ended quickly, U.S. interventions in Grenada, Panama, and Bosnia were successful, enforcement of the no-fly zone in Iraq was going well, and, except for a few "warm spots," the world was at relative peace. But it is not difficult to walk on water when the pond is frozen; the true test comes with the spring thaw. That "thaw" exploded with devastating fury on September 11, 2001, and dramatically changed the U.S. view of warfare, especially when considering the theater of operations in which future wars will be fought. The United States immediately realized a previously inconceivable fact: it must forever place a laser-like focus on the homeland as a potential theater of operations.

Despite impressive technological advancements, this nation's basic plans for warfare have changed at a relatively slow pace since World War II and even more slowly since the end of the Cold War. U.S. armed forces have only recently begun planning the transformation necessary to meet new challenges. The new federal organization for homeland security, together with the requisite military transformation, must effectively prepare the nation to meet new challenges to its security. More importantly, this transformation must provide a lasting federal institutional solution for the security of the American people and their way of life.

Whatever the organizational result, the United States must be prepared to develop "its many national capabilities to mitigate, prepare for, respond to, recover from, and learn from threats known and unknown."[1] The General Accounting Office's *June 2002 Report to Congress on Combating Terrorism* stated that, " without central leadership and an overarching strategy that identifies goals and objectives, priorities, measurable outcomes, and state and local government roles, the efforts of more than 40 federal entities and numerous state and local governments were fragmented."[2]

Among these national capabilities is the military response to acts of terrorism. However, discussions within the Department of Defense (DoD) and the homeland security community often center on the National Guard's federal wartime *versus* its state homeland defense missions as if these two pillars of the Guard's responsibility were mutually exclusive. Colonel Michael Fleming of the Florida National Guard states in his article for the August 2001 issue of the *ANSER Homeland Security Journal:* "The debate over future roles of the National Guard is often conducted through examination of either the federal or state mission while excluding the one over the other." Colonel Fleming also emphasizes that, "This approach does not acknowledge the synergy and dynamics of these two simultaneous National Guard missions."[3]

The two missions are complementary. The required skills and deployment procedures for wartime missions are also applicable to homeland security requirements. The National Guard has historically performed these two missions concurrently. Homeland security has been the responsibility of the National Guard since the beginning of the republic. As the United States became involved in overseas wars, so did the National Guard as the primary reserve force of the Army and Air Force.

However, since 9/11 and the new focus given to homeland security, it has been incorrectly assumed that the National Guard can perform its state homeland security function only if it significantly reduces its federal wartime focus. DoD has defined its responsibility for homeland security and has moved quickly to provide an immediate response to any future terrorist attacks against the United States, in the near term, by creating regional rapid reaction forces. The Department of Defense has also established the United States Northern Command, or USNORTHCOM, a joint command that will provide the national military strategy for homeland security, in support of the Federal Response Plan. This plan de-

---

1. Michael J. Hillyard, *Organizing for Homeland Security* (Carlisle, Pa.: U.S. Army War College, Spring 2002), p. 76.

2. General Accounting Office, *Report on Homeland Security* (Washington, D.C.: June 2002), p. 4.

3. Colonel Michael P. Fleming, *National Security Roles for the National Guard* (Arlington, Va., August 2001), p. 1.

scribes federal responsibilities and how states receive support from the federal government during disasters, acts of terrorism, and other catastrophes.

In developing these initial rapid reaction forces, DoD considered only active duty forces. The National Guard has not been included in the discussions, in any major way, regarding its future role in homeland security. Yet, the National Guard has been the traditional military first responder in domestic emergencies and disasters. It has the experience, training, and long-time relationships with state and local first responders. Homeland security has been the mission of the National Guard since 1636. There has been no military entity with more experience at performing homeland security duties. The National Guard is, therefore, best positioned to assume the lead military role in homeland security.

As the primary reserve force for the active army, the National Guard has participated in every war and national emergency in which the United States was involved since the nation was founded. Any effort to remove one of the main National Guard missions in an attempt to emphasize the other is shortsighted. The Army National Guard constitutes 54 percent of the Army's combat power, and the Air National Guard is fully integrated into the Expeditionary Aerospace Force. Both the Army and Air National Guard are an indispensable part of the National Military Strategy. The National Guard is fully engaged in joint, operational, and contingency operations.[4] The discussion on roles and missions for the National Guard must include procedures for enhancing its dual core competencies.

Although homeland security is a federal responsibility, the first response to a terrorist attack is executed by the state affected. DoD must allow the National Guard to focus its training on homeland security in addition to its role as part of the active forces. Although the National Guard is deployed most often as military first responder to state emergencies, 90 percent of its training is devoted to its wartime mission. The National Guard must be organized, funded, and equipped to provide this lead role in homeland security effectively.

Federal Organizations and Homeland Security

Until recently, the Office of Homeland Security attempted to coordinate the homeland security activities of all federal organizations holding specified responsibilities in planning and response to acts of terrorism

---

4. Ibid, p. 4.

and other threats to the homeland. It is anticipated that the Department of Homeland Security (DHS) and USNORTHCOM will assume most of these functions. While the federal government is not solely responsible for planning and implementing the homeland security effort, the answer devised must be a national response. The existing Federal Response Plan and the U.S. Government Interagency Domestic Terrorism Concept of Operations Plan (CONPLAN) acknowledge that the laws of the United States assign primary authority to state and local governments to respond to terrorist acts. Additionally, the federal CONPLAN "serves as the foundation for further development of detailed national, regional, state, and local operations, plans, and procedures."[5]

However, there is often a lack of awareness in state and local responders of current federal programs. A national survey commissioned by the congressionally-established Gilmore Commission revealed that at least 43 percent of those responsible for the initial response to acts of terrorism were unaware of the related federal assistance programs.[6] The existing organization for homeland security fails to provide the necessary coordination and sharing of information needed to prevent acts of terrorism. In addition, there is also no existing system that may adequately produce and distribute thoroughly analyzed and timely intelligence to agencies that require such information. Although OHS has recommended improvements in operational efficiencies within federal agencies, major deficiencies remain.

It is therefore evident that any federal plan designed to protect against future terrorist actions or to react to the effects of an actual attack must be synchronized with the security and response plans developed by each state. To qualify for federal resources, each state has been asked to create a state plan for responses to terrorism and other state emergencies. Such plans address the threats to the state, identify potential targets, allocate available resources, and delineate the responsibilities of the various state agencies as well as lines of authority and coordination between federal, state, and local entities in the event of state emergencies or disasters. The federal government would remain responsible for developing guidelines, providing oversight, maintaining a coordinating role, and, ulti-

5. Federal Emergency Management Agency, U.S. *Government Interagency Domestic Terrorism Concept of Operations Plan.* (Washington, D.C.: Federal Emergency Management Agency, January 2001), p. 2.

6. Advisory Panel to Assess Domestic Response Capabilities for Terrorism Involving Weapons of Mass Destruction, *The Third Annual Report to Congress,* RAND, Arlington, Va., December 15, 2001.

mately, providing necessary funding, equipment, and personnel authorizations for the homeland security plan.

Since the National Guard falls under the command and control of the state's governor (unless federalized) state security and response plans will include the National Guard as the first military responder in support of state or local civil authorities. The planning for military response, like law enforcement and fire response, begins at the state level and is consolidated at the regional and national levels. Only by consolidating the state plans into a federal response plan that includes the Department of Defense's military response plan, which will be formulated by USNORTHCOM, can the nation adequately prepare for and respond to future threats to homeland security.

The federal responsibility must include the planning and coordination of all federal resources to best support the requirements of state and local governments to prevent an attack or to respond quickly, should an attack occur. The developing DHS will likely be the lead federal agency in regard to preparation for and response to threats to homeland security and must consider the capabilities of all of the participating agencies when formulating policy concerning homeland security.

An excellent model for homeland security is the present National CounterDrug Program. This program is administered by the Office of National Drug Control Policy (ONDCP), which provides controlling policy to several federal agencies that are responsible for counterdrug activities. The office writes the national drug control policy for the president based on his guidance. Federal and state agencies and local governments that have counterdrug responsibility develop plans based on this federal policy. The adjutant general develops the state plan for the governor. The governor, the state attorney general, and the adjutant general review and sign the plan prior to forwarding it to ONDCP. Once plans are submitted, the office reviews them for compliance with its policy and provides federal funding in accordance with approved plans.

A reorganization of any federal or state agency is not required to implement ONDCP policies. The agency or state plan for drug control is sufficient to obtain federal resources and develop the necessary coordination between agencies and different levels of government. This same practice can be applied to homeland security and emergency operations. Once DHS becomes operational, it would create the national homeland security policy for the president. All other governmental agencies, at all levels, would produce directives implementing the policy published by the Department of Homeland Security. The approved plans would ensure distribution of appropriated funds, equipment, and methods of coordination and mutual support. State plans would be developed by each state's adjutant general or emergency manager and would include the plans for local first responders.

State Organizations and Homeland Security

The state security and response plans are the first step in developing a successful homeland security plan. These state plans are usually based on the state and local guidelines published by the Federal Emergency Management Agency (FEMA).[7] Each state plan includes the governor's vision for the security of the public and his or her support to local first responders. The public and the media expect civil authorities and the state to be responsible for disaster planning and response at the local level. Recent examples, in addition to the events of 9/11, include the 1995 Oklahoma City bombing, seasonal hurricanes in Florida, tornados and floods in the Midwest, and earthquakes in California. The federal government has always supported state and local governments with resources and assistance in such instances. This process must be expanded to address new homeland security missions, such as acts of terrorism.

Some states, depending on their size and the development of their urban areas, will require designated rapid reaction forces as part of their National Guard structure, similar to the Army National Guard Air Defense units of the 1960s and 1970s. Portions of these units were staffed with full-time National Guard soldiers. Large states with dense or widely dispersed population areas and a large National Guard force would be organized to respond to emergency situations anywhere in the state. These forces would also have a secondary responsibility to respond to regional threats. Smaller states, with a smaller guard force and less geographical area to cover, would contribute to a regional force.

To organize all the National Guard regionally, which was the concept for the Civil Support Teams initially organized by FEMA, would cause unnecessary delays in responding to an incident—increasing the possibility of loss of life, damage to infrastructure, and regional stability. Experience has shown that communications and transportation flows are quickly disrupted following a terrorist event. The delay caused by having to deploy a response capability geographically separated from the location of the attack only compounds the incident.

The World Trade Organization demonstrations in Seattle and the Los

---

7. Federal Emergency Management Agency, *SLG 101: Guide for All Hazard Emergency Operations Planning* (Washington, D.C.: Federal Emergency Management Agency, April 2001), at 6.

Angeles riots exemplify how quickly first responders can be overwhelmed. In the latter, first responders from both the city and county of Los Angeles had been preparing for civil unrest for weeks before the actual riot. The terrorist attacks on New York City and Washington, D.C., illustrate that not even the preparation time that existed for the Los Angeles planners will be available. Past emergency deployments have demonstrated that no matter how ready the force, responding from a "standing start" significantly impacts the recovery process. Without a rapid reaction force, a standby force would need to be alerted, assembled, and deployed, delaying support to first responders, impeding recovery, and placing public safety at greater risk.

In addition to population distribution and geographic considerations, the lead federal agency must also analyze potential threats and targets that states possess before determining how to allocate federal resources and assistance. States also vary in the organization of their emergency response systems. Within each of the states and territories, control and employment of emergency management, the National Guard, fire response, and law enforcement also differ. In 26 states, for example, the Adjutant General is also the emergency manager. In some states, the Adjutant General is the homeland security advisor, while others have established a separate homeland security office. A carefully coordinated federal plan is the obvious solution when there are significant differences in the responsibilities of the emergency managers, adjutants general, law enforcement officials, fire supervisors, health service managers, and those responsible for the maintenance and security of the infrastructure system.

The Los Angeles riots also demonstrated that there is a sharp learning curve for active duty military forces responding to domestic emergencies. Once the National Guard was federalized, they were required to respond to the active duty Task Force Commander. A lack of understanding of the federal role and a misapplication of *posse comitatus*, which limits the use of federal active duty forces in the enforcement of civil laws, made the federalized forces less effective than the National Guard had been in its state status.[8] For example, the Task Force Commander prevented any unit in a federal status from providing direct assistance to local authorities. He erroneously thought this to be a violation of *posse comitatus*. However, since the president had declared a state of emergency, those duties similar to those previously being carried out by the California National Guard in a state status could also have been per-

---

8. Susan Rosegrant, *The Flawed Emergency Response to the 1992 Los Angeles Riots (Part C)*, Kennedy School of Government Case Study Program, Cambridge, Mass.: September 1, 2000, p. 17.

formed by federal forces. Rapid reaction forces, composed of well-trained, well-equipped military personnel located in several states, must be a critical element of any homeland security plan. They can quickly form a regional force to reinforce the effort of any state within the region should the need arise. Requirements beyond the capability of the regional rapid reaction force would dictate the support of federal forces. However, the National Guard possesses the organization, experience, and the critical relationship with local first responders needed for successful execution of homeland security missions and is, therefore, the logical choice for performing the rapid response mission and for assuming the lead military role in homeland security.

The National Guard and Homeland Security

The National Guard is the ideal choice for primary military responder to threats to homeland security because of both its experience with this responsibility and the manner in which it is organized. The force structure in the Army and Air National Guard consists of combat, combat support, and combat service support. Combat support units, which are essential to homeland security missions, are military police, engineer, reconnaissance, communications, and intelligence forces. Equally important are the combat service support units, such as medical, aviation, transportation, and quartermaster organizations.

Organizations currently exist in the Army and Air National Guard that permit the Guard to satisfy both its wartime and homeland security missions. The National Military Strategy and the specific requirements of the Army and Air Force determine the manner in which the National Guard is organized. The National Military Strategy must include the security of the homeland as a primary mission for the DoD. The National Guard is the logical military component for that mission. DoD should organize and equip the National Guard to execute both its wartime and homeland security missions.

The Air National Guard, in particular, possesses combat, combat support, and combat service support capable of performing both wartime and homeland security missions. The Air Guard is an active partner with the Air Force in satisfying the requirements of the Aerospace Expeditionary Force and defending the homeland. Fighter, airlift, air refueling, and air rescue organizations support both missions. Inherent in these units are the security police, engineers, medical, and communications units needed to help fulfill these commitments.

This seamless system was in force at the time of the September 11, 2001, attacks. At that time, Air Guard units were already deployed in support operations in the Middle East and were also conducting missions in Bosnia and Kosovo. Other Air Guard units were providing all air defense for the entire United States. The response of these air defense units to the attacks in New York City and Washington, D.C., was immediate.

A similar system can be developed for the Army National Guard, without an increase in its overall strength authorization. Although there are currently not enough military police, light infantry, engineers, medical, aviation, or communications units to satisfy federal and state requirements for the Army National Guard, combat, combat support, and combat service support units can be shifted between components to develop the force structure required for homeland security. This force structure would still designate most National Guard units to support active duty forces, and National Guard heavy combat forces would remain oriented toward providing immediate response to the Army's overseas commitments. The light combat support units, however, would be focused on homeland security, with a secondary role for overseas warfare and peacekeeping and nation-building missions. These forces need to be identified in the state plan, based on an analysis of identified threats.

Making It Happen: Recommendations

The National Guard has the unique advantage of having more than 450,000 soldiers and airmen strategically located in more than 2,900 communities and 33,200 National Guard facilities throughout the United States.[9] Each National Guard force can be tailored to meet the needs of its state. Cities require well-equipped firefighters, medical response personnel, and law enforcement officers to respond to emergencies. The military homeland security force is similar in that it requires well-equipped, ready National Guard response forces. In each instance, the size of the force must be tailored to satisfy the perceived threat, to reduce response time, and to limit damage to people and property. The allocation of the National Guard responders must be based on this same need and the acceptable response time.

Equipping the National Guard's homeland security force, however, presents a significant challenge for three reasons. First, the armed forces are in the process of transformation and have the problem of maintaining what is essentially a legacy force (the Cold War structure) while evolving at the research and development phase to develop an objective force—one that will exist to combat future threats. Second, there is a shortage of

---

9. Reserve Forces Policy Board, *Reserve Component Programs* (Washington, D.C.: Reserve Forces Policy Board, March 2000), at p. 53.

equipment for homeland defense. Third, the equipment that is available to the National Guard is not always compatible with the modern equipment of the Army or with that of the first responders. There are two solutions to the equipment problem; both involve additional funding. The first solution is for Congress to authorize the purchase of additional military equipment to make the National Guard compatible with the Army. The second solution is to gain congressional authorization for purchasing commercial off-the-shelf equipment that would make the National Guard more compatible with local first responders.

The best solution would combine these ideas. Equipment required for peacekeeping and nation-building should be provided by DoD as part of the military service procurement process. This, in turn, would ensure that all components for the total weapons or equipment system are provided along with the new equipment training required for soldiers. Also, as in past occasions, commercial off-the-shelf equipment could be used as a substitute for unavailable military equipment. Because commercial equipment is readily accessed, without the associated cost of research and development, it is usually less expensive than the military equipment (as temporary replacements). For the most part, the homeland security force could deploy for peacekeeping missions, if not the war-fighting missions, with commercial off-the-shelf equipment.

As suggested earlier, the National Guard homeland security forces would comprise combat and support units that best meet the needs of each state's homeland security plan. These requirements must be recognized in a national military strategy that also considers homeland security as a primary mission for DoD. The same forces required for a major theater war could be used for homeland security, nation-building, and peacekeeping missions. The National Guard homeland security forces would be deployed within the state in a Title 32 state status with all the benefits and services accorded active duty personnel. Title 32 of the U.S. Code places state military forces in a federal status but leaves them under the command and control of the governor. Soldiers and airmen that performed security duty at airports around the nation were in a Title 32 status. When employed regionally or as a peacekeeping or nation-building force outside the state, National Guard units would be deployed in a Title 10 federal status. Title 10 of the U.S. Code places state military forces in a federal status under the command and control of the active Army or Air Force. Soldiers and airmen mobilized and sent overseas or in support of federal installations were in a Title 10 status.

National Guard homeland security units would train concurrently for their homeland security and war-fighting missions. Consideration should be given to establishing homeland security regions, similar to how the Nunn-Lugar-Domenici Act provided one Weapons of Mass Destruction (WMD) Civil Support Team for each FEMA Region in 1996. (Subsequent legislation has expanded the number of teams to 18 and then to 32. Federal legislation is now being considered to expand these teams to at least one in each state). The most densely populated state in each homeland security region would be designated the regional command and control headquarters.

Combat Support Military Police Brigades are best organized to provide this function. These brigades are light, highly mobile forces that possess the necessary command, operational, administrative, and logistical capabilities to effectively execute homeland security missions. They also provide the support activities required of a multifunctional, higher headquarters for all other types of forces that would make up the National Guard homeland security force. Other states within the region would have homeland security forces of battalion or company size, depending on the size and population of the state. Battalions should be military police, light infantry, or reconnaissance forces of 500 to 700 personnel each. Separate homeland security companies would have similar force structure of 150 to 200 personnel each.

The National Military Strategy would govern the number of military police, light infantry, reconnaissance, and other forces that comprise homeland security and the war-fighting forces. Homeland security forces would also train with local first responders, much like the WMD Civil Support Teams train. They would also train periodically with the regional force. Training centers within each established region would also be used to serve as a location where the National Guard homeland security force and other first responders could build relationships necessary to work together in a crisis. These centers may also serve as mobilization bases for the war-fighting force.

The homeland security mission, however, must also extend beyond response to a WMD attack. Natural disasters and other civil emergencies that threaten the security of the people must be included in homeland security plans, limiting the tendency to develop additional vertical organizations in response to the most recent event. An analysis of the homeland security tasks will identify the response required for the security and safeguarding of persons and property; evacuation of populations; support to law enforcement; transportation services; communications support; command, control, and coordination; search and rescue; and other similar activities. These tasks mirror the missions essential to both terrorist acts and natural and civil disasters. No distinction should be made between the missions designed to safeguard the citizenry during terrorist attacks and other events requiring the same support. The training and organization that the National Guard maintains for homeland security is also directly applicable to Military Support to Civil Authority requirements.

The deployment of the National Guard in Title 32 state status under the command and control of the governor ensures continuity of operations and gives the Governor and Adjutant General the flexibility necessary to anticipate future needs and to adjust the force accordingly. Title 32 status, under state control, also ensures that the military will avoid the potential legal problems of *posse comitatus.* As previously stated, the National Guard should be placed in a Title 10 federal status only when deployed outside the borders of its state—and only when the unit gaining command is an active duty Army or Air Force unit.

Conclusions

Jack Spencer and Larry Wortzel suggest in their essay, "The Role of the National Guard in Homeland Security" for *The Heritage Foundation Backgrounder,* that the asymmetric threats that characterize current security challenges require the United States to revise its Total Force Concept.[10] According to this school of thought, the National Guard should continue to support the National Security Strategy of the active duty forces. The National Guard homeland security forces identified in each state's plan must be federally funded to train and equip themselves and, as Spencer and Wortzel claim, "to help train state and local officials to respond to a weapon of mass destruction event, while continuing to prepare to support the active forces in a general war."[11] The National Guard should maintain working relationships with state and local authorities, particularly with medical and hazardous materials responders and county and city emergency managers. Since the National Guard is the military force with the strongest and longest relationship with local first responders, logic dictates that the National Guard continues to be the first military responder.

Designating a homeland security force, including identifying a standing element, is essential for ensuring immediate response to any attack or civil disaster. Clearly, the U.S. homeland is no longer impervious to terrorist attacks, and homeland security must be the primary mission of DoD. To best support national security and local public safety, the Na-

---

10. Jack Spencer and Larry Wortzel, "The Role of the National Guard in Homeland Security," *Heritage Foundation Backgrounder,* Number 1532 (April 8, 2002), pp. 2–3.

11. Ibid.

tional Guard of each state must possess the capability to provide the primary military response to the Army and Air Force, be able to execute homeland security missions, and provide support to civil authority when required. Properly supported, the National Guard can provide protection without restricting the individual freedoms to which Americans are accustomed. Correctly structured, the National Guard is the logical and ideal military component to perform the homeland security mission as the primary military responder.

Chapter 12

The Two-Hat Syndrome: Determining Response Capabilities and Mutual Aid Limitations

Rebecca F. Denlinger
with Kristin Gonzenbach

Imagine that the National Weather Service has reported a severe thunderstorm advisory with tornado watches covering the entire metropolitan area. As the torrential rains begin in county after county, reports of downed trees and power lines, trapped people, and damage to buildings start to pour into 911 emergency centers. A tornado the size of a city block has touched down in four metro counties and is still moving. Emergency managers are sending fire apparatus, ambulances, and police in every direction to assist trapped and injured people, but many responders cannot reach incident scenes because trees and debris have blocked roads. Counties invoke mutual aid from neighboring municipalities and open emergency operation centers. The state activates its own center and begins to receive calls for assistance.

The storm passes. Citizens continue to call for help. Responders are still having trouble traversing blocked roadways, and off-duty personnel cannot reach staging areas. By the time the storm ends, devastation extends across 12 counties. All these counties call up off-duty personnel for emergency shifts and cancel all scheduled days off.

However, an unanticipated problem surfaces. Many emergency workers, particularly fire and rescue employees, work at more than one public safety agency. When contacted, many of the off-duty employees are at work on their second jobs at these other agencies. Calling them in means they will have to abandon assigned duties at private ambulance services, local hospitals, and neighboring fire departments. Calling in these employees narrows the pool of personnel for nearby volunteer fire departments.

"Public safety agency" is an umbrella phrase for a vast group that includes police, fire, emergency medical services (EMS), 911 communications, public health, emergency management, and sheriff's agencies. Public safety employers are likely to have developed call-up plans designed to increase the number of personnel available to perform the agency's mission in time of disaster. Call-up plans assume that off-duty personnel will report to work when contacted to expand the agency's capability.

An informal survey of public safety workers found that many have some type of secondary employment, often at another public safety agency. This dependence on one another may critically affect public safety agencies in time of disaster. Of particular concern is that extended breaks between long shifts allow firefighters and EMS personnel to make commitments to more than one agency. The "secondary" employer is likely to depend upon the employee as much as the "primary" employer. The survey, conducted in the Atlanta metropolitan area, found that among 16 fire departments, an average of 22.2 percent of employees hold two or more public safety positions. Moreover, a significant percentage of the public safety workforce has commitments to the military reserve or National Guard. If those agencies activate these employees, other agencies could lose up to 13 percent of their workforce.[1]

Many firefighters have either emergency medical technician (EMT) or paramedic certification and often use those certifications to work for other public safety agencies, hospitals, or private ambulance companies. This raises questions about how many EMS workers are actually available in a given area should these employers need to expand service. Are two agencies counting on the same person to be available when planning for a disaster? Does a geographic area actually have the number of emergency medical responders necessary to handle a crisis? Every jurisdiction must develop a strategic disaster plan that includes the spectrum of service providers, or it may be left underserved in a disaster.

The Two-Hat Syndrome

The *two-hat syndrome* is the dynamic in which public safety workers hold at least two public safety positions. In an emergency, these workers might be called upon to perform both jobs, to wear both hats. Because each employee would be able to fill only one position, public safety agencies should identify which employees wear more than one hat and discuss how critical each of those hats is to each employer.

The *two-hat syndrome* prompts a series of initial questions: where does

---

1. Excerpt of Two Hat Project Survey, Cobb County Fire and Emergency Services, June 2002.

an individual's primary duty lie when personnel call-ups occur? What planning do agencies need to do to overcome their reliance on the same individuals? How does the *two-hat syndrome* affect a community's actual response capability?

These questions lead to others, equally compelling and problematic:

- How many of an agency's employees are military reservists and how would their activation affect staffing?
- Can communities rely on public safety agencies to increase their capability enough to remain effective in a disaster?
- If an employee works for two agencies, who decides where the employee will report if called up by both agencies?

All these questions must be asked and answered to formulate a successful personnel call-up strategy. Furthermore, until public safety officials share the information that they learn when asking these questions, no agency can be certain it has a reliable call-up plan in place.

The Two-Hat Project Survey

The Two-Hat Project survey, conducted in 23 counties and involving 48 local government and private agencies and two state agencies, showed that communities might not have a firm grasp of what personnel will be available in a disaster. Many agencies operating within the 14-county metropolitan area participated in the survey. None of the agencies was able to readily identify the number of employees who wear two or more hats, where these people worked, or how this might affect disaster response plans. When asked about the likelihood that this syndrome would have an impact on his agency, one respondent stated, "It is not an issue for us, because our agency is their primary employment."[2]

Other conflicts often arise when career fire and rescue personnel compose a considerable portion of volunteer agencies in other jurisdictions. If these personnel respond to their primary employers, fewer will be available to serve volunteer fire departments. Counties and municipalities also often hire private ambulance contractors to transport patients in their communities. The Two-Hat Project survey found that many of these private ambulance companies employ significant numbers of off-duty firefighters and EMS workers. In one case in Cobb County, Georgia, 33 percent of an ambulance company's workforce was off-duty firefighters.

---

2. Louis Graham, chief deputy sheriff, DeKalb County, Georgia, interview, May 9, 2002.

Owing to a nationwide shortage of health care workers, a growing number of EMTs and paramedics are also being recruited for part- and full-time employment in local hospitals. This adds to the quandary of whether enough EMTs and paramedics are available to respond in a major crisis.

The two-hat survey also found that some smaller police agencies in the Atlanta, Georgia, metropolitan area are having a difficult time attracting qualified personnel because the salaries that they offer are typically lower than those in larger, neighboring jurisdictions. Some of these smaller agencies are therefore hiring off-duty personnel from larger public safety departments to work on a part-time basis. For example, the Police Chief of Powder Springs, a small suburb within Cobb County, reported that 32 percent of his sworn personnel work part-time and that more than one-half of those are firefighters and paramedics from other public safety departments. Firefighters from other departments also constitute one-third of his Special Weapons And Tactics (SWAT) team. A countywide disaster may thus have a serious impact on Powder Springs' ability to field enough personnel. Despite its excellent mutual aid relationships with the Cobb County police and sheriff's departments, Powder Springs should explore how it will address its needs in the event of a wider disaster.[3]

Another major consideration, particularly in more rural regions, is to plan who will wear which hat in a disaster. For example, in many rural areas the local sheriff may also be the director of the emergency management agency (EMA), police chief of a small city within the county, and head of security for the local hospital. Plans must be in place to determine who will fill these roles should it be necessary to staff more than one during a crisis. Interviews with chief officials of public safety agencies revealed that these officials often fit the two-hat profile, and they had not considered the problem or their own limitations when planning for disaster. Top public safety managers who are also assigned critical roles in their community EMAs often seemed to fit this description.

Events such as the 9/11 terrorist attacks at the World Trade Center and the Pentagon, Hurricane Andrew's landfall near Miami in 1992, and the floodwaters of 1994 in southwestern Georgia required lengthy emergency and cleanup operations and unusually high availability of essential personnel. Any call-up plan must provide higher-than-normal levels of service over extended periods of time.

---

3. L. Rick Richardson, Police chief, Powder Springs, Georgia, telephone interview, May 15, 2002.

FURTHER SURVEY RESULTS

Overall, 47 law enforcement, fire, rescue, 911 emergency centers, emergency management agencies, and private ambulance companies responded to our request to survey their employees. The survey indicated that the *two-hat syndrome* affects most dramatically fire and rescue, private ambulance, and emergency management agencies, as a significantly higher percentage of their personnel work in other public safety agencies than do employees of law enforcement agencies and 911 emergency centers.

According to the survey results, police and sheriff's department personnel were the least affected by the *two-hat syndrome*. Of the 20 law enforcement agencies responding, 15 reported that less than one percent of their employees had made commitments to another public safety agency. A small city in the Atlanta suburbs reported the highest percentage, 11.1 percent.[4] However, police agencies would suffer if the number of fire and rescue responders is inadequate to cover call volume during and after a disaster. Simply stated, the less effective any part of the workforce required to manage a disaster, the longer it will take to complete a phase of disaster response.

The survey also indicated that a military call-up would affect police and sheriff agencies more than fire and rescue agencies. One law enforcement agency reported that 13 percent of its personnel have military obligations.[5]

On average, fire and rescue departments indicated that 22.2 percent of their fire and rescue personnel work for at least one other public safety agency. A fire department where 56.2 percent of its personnel work at another public safety agency was the most dramatic example. In another agency, 38 percent fit the *two-hat syndrome* description, and, of those individuals, 25 percent work full-time at another agency.[6] This particular city is not surrounded by well-staffed fire departments from which it can immediately draw significant mutual aid. It is critical that this city's disaster plan includes provisions to address this problem. The city must plan realistic call-up procedures, determine how long personnel may take before returning to its resource pool, and consider what effect a call-up might have on other local public safety agencies.

As in many jurisdictions, one of the largest counties in the Atlanta

---

4. Excerpt of Two-Hat Project Survey, Cobb County Fire and Emergency Services, June 2002.

5. Ibid.

6. Ibid.

area maintains several private ambulance contracts. As a result of the study, the county discovered that 33 percent of one ambulance firm's 42 employees also work full-time as firefighters in the same county.[7] When the county fire department became aware of this conflict, it reexamined its strategic disaster response plan and began reworking it to address the potential shortage of firefighters and ambulance personnel. In a disaster, ambulance company managers will work with officials in the county emergency operations center to staff and dispatch ambulances from fire stations until personnel issues stabilize.

A major finding from the survey is the high percentage of employees of emergency management agencies who fit the *two-hat syndrome* description. Few agencies have the financial resources to fund a fully staffed and separate EMA, and this is not unique to smaller agencies. Even in large municipalities, personnel find themselves wearing two hats in a disaster and even during routine operations. For example, Atlanta's Fulton County found that 25 percent of critical county emergency management agency personnel are also key officials in their fire or other public safety departments, while adjacent Cobb County found that 50 percent of such personnel wear two hats.[8] The smaller the agency, the greater the impact will be if those wearing two hats do not report for duty during a disaster. And in the case of large jurisdictions, a disastrous incident is likely to magnify the impact of absent or overworked personnel.

Few agencies indicated what would occur if the county's emergency operations center were activated and the EMA director is also the fire chief, for instance. Have provisions been made to fill the chief's role if he or she is lost to the emergency operations center? As a result of shift work, public safety organizations have built in redundancy at many levels and positions, but, in top command ranks, this is almost never the case. No second or third shift of chiefs and deputy chiefs remains at home, while another is at work. When disaster strikes, chief officers must be prepared to immediately break into shifts in order to maintain command capability.

For this reason, Miami/Dade County Fire and Rescue found it necessary to change its disaster plan after Hurricane Andrew struck. U. S. Fire Administrator Dave Paulison, Miami/Dade fire and rescue chief at the time, reported that after the first week of disaster operations following Andrew's landfall, his staff had burned out from managing a spike in

---

7. Ibid.

8. Ibid.

emergency calls from the typical 400–500 to more than 3,000 per day. Following this experience, Miami/Dade changed its hurricane plan to an all-hazards disaster plan. Among other adjustments, the plan now calls for command staff to immediately form two platoons that work in 12-hour shifts. Interestingly, Miami/Dade Fire and Rescue's line personnel remain in standard three-platoon format even during disaster operations, working 24-hour shifts—an aspect of the plan that the chief and his staff did not find necessary to change after Hurricane Andrew.[9]

Agencies such as 911 emergency centers and state public safety agencies are not immune from the *two-hat syndrome*, although this survey did not include adequate responses from these types of agencies to draw firm conclusions.

Overall, the survey reveals that the *two-hat syndrome* is a concern for most public safety agencies, directly or indirectly. Awareness of the problem is the first step in identifying and addressing any significant impact it may have.

THE PLANNING AND PREPARATION PROCESS

As jurisdictions develop their strategic plans for responding to disasters, they should practice their departments' call-up plans and reassess them based on the outcomes. Should agencies lose employees to military commitments, plans should address who will back up any critical positions left vacant. Local governments must also coordinate disaster plans with private ambulance companies, public health officials, and local hospitals. If a hospital's employees work for other public safety agencies, it should compare call-up plans with those agencies.

Jurisdictions must also determine whether each plan is practical. On 9/11, New York City firefighters and police faced multiple high-rise building fires, two plane crashes, structural collapses on a scale never before experienced, a monumental rescue problem, and major uncertainty about what was going to happen next. Emergency managers decided to call up *all* off-duty fire and rescue personnel in the first recall of the entire fire department in more than 50 years.[10] This created a tremendous management problem concerning how to deploy and feed all of the personnel who reported and how to ensure that they remained rested. A transition plan to move to a split work force had to be executed as the fire depart-

---

9. David Paulison, U.S. fire administrator, telephone interview, May 10, 2002.

10. Harvey Eisner, "Terrorist Attack at New York World Trade Center" *Firehouse*, April 2002, pp. 61–62.

ment changed its shifts to 24 hours on and 24 hours off to sustain operations over the ensuing days and weeks.[11] Because of the number of firefighters missing in the destruction, many surviving firefighters refused to go home for days at a time, further challenging the department to ensure that these members could perform their duties safely.

Disasters With and Without Notice

Interviews with chief administrators from several public safety agencies who have been involved in major incidents explored how disaster plans worked during a crisis, and how the administrators changed their plans in light of these experiences. These administrators emphasized the need to prepare before an incident and review and revise plans after every major incident. Following are two accounts of disaster responses that highlight how managers have changed their disaster preparedness plans since the events had transpired.

DISASTER WITH NOTICE

In 1994, Crisp County was one of several counties in southwest Georgia devastated by massive flooding of the Flint River. Community leaders had as many as three days to prepare for this disaster. Crisp County, one of nine counties hit hardest by the flooding, was able to evacuate thousands of people from their homes in advance, request that state agencies prepare to implement disaster plans, and organize emergency command centers. Authorities also inventoried their resources, located and reinforced weaknesses in their response plans, and activated evacuation plans for hospitals, jails, schools, and other facilities.[12]

When the flooding occurred, authorities in various counties implemented their disaster plans. Crisp County authorities had already asked the National Guard to supplement the county's police presence. After the floodwaters receded about 10 days later, the county requested additional support from the Georgia Emergency Management Agency and the Georgia Department of Corrections for cleanup operations. In a major cooperative effort, agencies from as far as 200 miles away made mutual aid to flood-damaged areas available for weeks after the flood.[13]

Crisp County Sheriff Donnie Haralson reported that by identifying

---

11. Ibid.

12. Donnie Haralson, Sheriff, Crisp County, Georgia, telephone interviews, May 9, 2002 and May 15, 2002.

13. Ibid.

available personnel resources and calling for mutual aid and state assistance, the county maximized its ability to mitigate the flood's dangers and its aftereffects. The county has further developed its policies and procedures for managing a disaster. For example, the county's disaster plan now details the locations of emergency operations centers, alternate locations for those centers, the number, type, and sources of vehicles needed, and what resources other communities may make available. Crisp County has also identified its personnel resources and knows how long it will take to activate them as well as how long it can provide in-house personnel before requesting mutual aid. Sheriff Haralson further noted that a thorough plan should include the ability to change gears, if necessary, during a crisis. The 1994 flooding has helped the county develop procedures and chronologies for various scenarios. Sheriff Haralson reports that today the community is comfortable with its disaster plan and confident in its personnel call-up strategy.[14]

DISASTER WITHOUT NOTICE

By 9 A.M. eastern standard time (EST) on September 11, 2001, much of the world was watching a series of horrifying events unfold in New York City. Then, at 9:43 A.M. a jetliner hit the Pentagon. Arlington County, Virginia, which provides fire protection for the Pentagon, promptly dispatched its fire department. Although the county typically responds to at least one call for service at the Pentagon daily, the department's familiarity with the complex did not prepare responders for the scene that they encountered that morning.[15] The scale of devastation and injuries exceeded the capacity of the department's resources.

The Washington-area news media were already poised to cover the disaster. Within minutes, every television network nationwide was reporting the Pentagon crash. As in New York, Arlington administrators made the decision to call up all of their personnel. Because the county's dispatch center was inundated with calls and unable to take the time to notify fire personnel, administrators enlisted the media's help. Within one half-hour, television and radio stations across metropolitan Washington had broadcast the call-up to viewers and listeners. More than 95 percent of the county's public sector personnel received these messages and reported to stations and staging areas within two hours. The Arlington Fire Department realized almost immediately that it would have to tran-

---

14.   Ibid.

15.   Ed Plaugher, Fire Chief, Arlington County, Virginia, telephone interview, May 13, 2002.

sition to a platoon schedule to sustain lengthy round-the-clock operations. The department assigned personnel to three platoons, working 12-hour shifts with 24 hours rest between shifts.[16]

In this case, Fire Chief Ed Plaugher was also the county disaster coordinator for the Arlington emergency management agency. He stated that in many situations, one person simultaneously filling the roles of fire chief and county disaster coordinator can work well. In the attack on the Pentagon, however, each role became a full-time job. Because staffing strategic centers with officials from assisting agencies took nearly 21 hours, Chief Plaugher admitted that after 10 or 12 hours it was difficult to manage both roles well. In a true disaster, additional trained personnel should be available to take over key roles assigned to individuals wearing more than one critical hat, and planning should account for this type of long-term incident management.[17]

Arlington County is unusual in that it maintains a full-time emergency management agency (EMA) staff which reduced some of the demands on Chief Plaugher. However, most agencies cannot afford to fund a dedicated EMA staff. This is one reason why so many key officials take on multiple disaster roles and, then, must deal with all of the associated responsibilities during a major incident.

Chief Plaugher believes that secondary employment commitments were not an issue for Arlington County during this crisis and was unaware if Arlington County Fire's total personnel call-up had a negative impact on any other agency. He says that Arlington County Fire employees must consider the agency their primary employer. He added that this incident was the call of a career for most firefighters and that "they weren't going to miss it for anything."[18] This insight reinforces the concern that firefighters on duty at one employer may be likely to leave those assignments to report to a second employer during a major incident. While the jurisdiction suffering the disaster would enjoy its full complement of employees, the other employer may no longer be prepared to respond to a secondary strike, to maintain normal service levels, or to provide mutual aid to a stricken jurisdiction. Identifying the number of employees holding more than one public safety position and exploring how that situation may affect both agencies is critical.

Plaugher advised that most fire and rescue agencies surrounding Arlington County are career departments, which may minimize the like-

---

16. Ibid.

17. Ibid.

18. Ibid.

lihood that many of his employees hold another position of firefighter in a nearby department. He did indicate, however, that volunteer agencies are prevalent across the state.[19] Also, in the past year, the International Association of Fire Fighters passed a rule prohibiting its members from serving as volunteer firefighters. In a region with a unionized workforce, this rule might reduce the likelihood that firefighters would hold more than one firefighting position. However, the rule will not limit, and may indeed increase, the possibility that firefighters will hold other types of secondary employment.

The Arlington County Fire Department has also made a number of policy and procedural changes in its disaster plan since the Pentagon incident. It has changed its call-up strategy to add the ability to build up its force gradually rather than calling in all off-duty personnel at once. The department has also begun utilizing an automated telephone system for notifying personnel, thereby removing this critical and staff-intensive assignment from its dispatch center—a sort of second hat. Chief Plaugher and his staff do not want to rely again on the media to notify personnel, as they did in the Pentagon incident. The department is also developing a different approach for deploying technical teams for lengthy operations, as the numbers of these trained personnel are limited and they must be fed and sheltered on-site or nearby. The department is amending its plan to address those needs.[20]

When asked about the impact of the Pentagon incident on the Arlington County budget, Chief Plaugher pointed out that county administrators knew about the call-up plan, and that they viewed the extra cost as a necessary expense. Plaugher said that he had exercised authorized discretion, and he is confident of the parameters set for department managers in his jurisdiction. Clearly, developing and discussing disaster plans are keys to successfully managing such a major incident.[21]

What Other Disasters Can Teach Us

Agencies can learn about the *two-hat syndrome* from the problems encountered in managing these recent disasters. First, agencies must plan to rotate personnel on and off shift to maintain a strong and alert work force and take into account employees who have off-duty obligations of any type. Second, a thorough and well-communicated personnel call-up plan

19. Ibid.
20. Ibid.
21. Ibid.

will manage employee expectations and preparation before a disaster occurs. Third, practicing these call-up plans will help reveal any problems, including those that result from the *two-hat syndrome* and will allow agencies to develop solutions for those problems.

Cobb County Fire and Emergency Services is developing a call-up plan capable of providing half of its total staff for immediate duty while making the other half of the work force available in 12 to 24 hours. All personnel will then work either 12 hours on and 12 hours off or 24 hours on and 24 hours off, with leave canceled until normal operations resume.

Although a major emergency might tempt the Cobb County Fire Department's administration to execute a total personnel call-up, the department has opted to develop the ability to hold half its force in reserve to provide a sustained response. Supporting elements include mutual aid from Cobb County's immediate neighbors and the Georgia Mutual Aid Group, a seasoned organization that can draw on the resources of more than 50 fire and EMS departments from around the state. A region-wide survey is being conducted to identify and address problems that the *two-hat syndrome* may cause in Cobb County's or others' call-up plans.

Part of Cobb County's call-up plan takes into account reasonable travel time. If off duty, many of the county's firefighting personnel must travel an extended distance to reach their Cobb assignments. The plan also recognizes that a number of the department's employees may be called up for military service. A practice run-through of this call-up plan will reveal how quickly half the total staff actually become available, and administrators can modify the plan accordingly. Activation plans should be practiced to determine their true feasibility and allow for necessary adjustments.

Planning Is Key

Communities depend on public safety agencies to respond effectively to any disaster, and most have developed some type of strategic disaster response plan. The Federal Emergency Management Agency has recently tied federal disaster funding to the development of a detailed strategic plan that identifies risks in a community, details how to protect important assets, and develops plans for handling an emergency response. Public safety officials should look within their organizations to determine whether the *two-hat syndrome* is a problem. Officials must also share this information with agencies that provide mutual aid.

Agencies must practice any activation plan to test its effectiveness. Every official contacted during the research stated that she or he had made changes to call-up plans after using them in a disaster. As a result of the policy and procedural changes Miami/Dade County fire officials made after Hurricane Andrew, emergency personnel managed a much more effective response when a ValuJet airliner crashed nearby four years later.[22]

If a community discovers that the *two-hat syndrome* would significantly affect disaster mitigation, informed planning and preparation are the keys to overcoming its effects. The biggest obstacle for any agency is the unverified belief that it operates in isolation. Because virtually every public safety agency depends on other agencies for support during a crisis, the chance that the *two-hat syndrome* will directly affect every agency increases significantly. Agencies should be aware of their mutual aid capabilities and limitations and prepare for how those may dictate changes in their strategy. Public safety administrators who fail to gain insight into the *two-hat syndrome* and to consider, consult, and cooperate accordingly, may fail their communities in the face of disaster.

---

22. David Paulison, U.S. Fire Administrator, Former Fire Chief, Miami/Dade County, Florida, telephone interview, May 10, 2002.

Chapter 13

Sustaining Domestic Preparedness: Challenges in a Post-9/11 World

David Grannis

Until September 11, 2001, U.S. domestic preparedness was a subject of interest to relatively few people beyond the professional communities involved. Few government officials, academics, or think-tank experts with an interest in homeland defense were concerned with the overall sustainability of domestic preparedness programs.

The terrorist attacks on the World Trade Center and the Pentagon, shortly followed by the mailing of envelopes containing anthrax spores, directed massive attention to all aspects of homeland security. Prior to 9/11, the threat of terrorism was perceived to be too low to invest deeply in and to think long-term about domestic preparedness. The sustainability of domestic preparedness programs, therefore, was not a particularly high concern for the U.S. government. The current environment—in which additional terrorist attacks are considered inevitable—poses two major challenges.

First, the current political, social, and security climate in the United States has provided the impetus for significantly larger domestic preparedness budgets at the federal, state, and local levels. If no further terrorist attacks occur, this elevated level of spending will be difficult to maintain, especially if federal, state, and local budget difficulties continue.

Second, with so much focus on domestic preparedness (and terrorism prevention), there is a push to devote monetary and nonmonetary resources exclusively to enhance security. Doing so would diverge from a more appropriate focus on all-hazards and dual-use based approaches to domestic preparedness. Keeping the right focus while under pressure to make gains in national security presents a challenge that affects the sustainability of all domestic preparedness programs.

Domestic Preparedness and the Pre-9/11 Sustainability Challenge

Domestic preparedness comprises federal, state, and local programs that plan for and build capabilities to respond to terrorist attacks on the U.S. homeland, especially attacks with weapons of mass destruction and disruption.[1] The programs began in earnest in 1996 with the Defense against Weapons of Mass Destruction Act of 1996, which was passed in reaction to the terrorist attacks against the World Trade Center in New York City in 1993 and the Alfred P. Murrah Federal Building in Oklahoma City in 1995.[2]

Domestic preparedness now encompasses the development and maintenance of federal response capabilities as well as the training and equipping of first responders—those police officers, firefighters, emergency operations workers, environmental and hazardous materials personnel, nurses and doctors, emergency medical personnel, and public health employees who would be the first to come into contact with, for example, a chemical or biological weapon in the aftermath of an attack with such a weapon. Limited progress was made between 1996 and 2001 in coordinating the response efforts of the first responders and governmental stakeholders. Mutual aid plans at the local level and intergovernmental coordination between federal, state, and local response entities are examples of these efforts.

Before the 9/11 terrorist attacks and subsequent anthrax mailings, it seemed possible that the developing domestic preparedness programs would not be sustained.[3] The absence of a large-scale terrorist attack or any incident involving a weapon of mass destruction (WMD) against the

---

1. Weapons of mass destruction include chemical, biological, nuclear, and radiological weapons. The characteristics of biological and chemical weapons, including principally the possibility to significantly mitigate consequences with prompt action after an attack, make these two classes the most relevant for domestic preparedness.

2. The Defense Against Weapons of Mass Destruction Act was part of the Fiscal Year 1997 Defense Authorization Act signed on September 23, 1996 (Public Law 104–201). It is more commonly referred to as the Nunn-Lugar-Domenici amendment.

3. See, for example, Richard A. Falkenrath, "The Problems of Preparedness: Challenges Facing the U.S. Domestic Preparedness Program," Belfer Center for Science and International Affairs Discussion Paper 2000–28 (John F. Kennedy School of Government, Harvard University, December 2000); and Amy E. Smithson and Leslie-Anne Levy, *Ataxia: The Chemical and Biological Terrorism Threat and the U.S. Response* (Washington, D.C.: Henry L. Stimson Center, October 2000).

United States suggested that government attention and resources could be shifted from domestic preparedness to more immediate needs.[4] The resulting concern was that either or both of two key components—operational readiness and program sustainability—could be degraded.

OPERATIONAL READINESS

Operational readiness refers to the ability of the first responders to react quickly and efficiently in a both previously planned and rehearsed manner to an event—whether a terrorist attack, natural disaster, or otherwise. Operational readiness requires that new personnel be trained and that all personnel keep up with best practices and changes in policy. It also means conducting exercises to test and practice domestic preparedness skills and procuring, maintaining, and distributing equipment in working order. Because federal assets to support local WMD response are scattered throughout different departments, sustaining operational readiness is necessary at the federal and local levels and must be maintained in the coordination between the two. The sustainability challenge is particularly acute when practitioners are not devoted solely to terrorism response, as more common tasks will naturally divert attention, training time, and use of equipment.

Operational readiness depends on the amount of training, equipping, and integration of first responders at the local and regional levels; federal stocks of expertise, equipment, vaccines, and other medical treatments; legal authorization to act in maximally efficient ways; education of public officials and media outlets; "surge capacity" to adapt hospitals and other facilities to WMD response; and a workable and tested plan for possible scenarios of attack. WMD response readiness will tend to decline over time because individual pieces of equipment and training will deteriorate unless carefully monitored and maintained. Stockpiles of medications, vaccines, and antidotes can either lose their efficacy or degrade into toxic compounds over time, and equipment such as chemical and biological detectors, decontaminating materials, and protective suits eventually become obsolete. Skills learned by first responders, if not practiced and enhanced, will fade to the point that practitioners are unable to follow established response protocols.

---

4. The use of anthrax (unsuccessfully) and sarin (with moderate success) by Aum Shinrikyo created some concern among U.S. policymakers and provided a climate for the passage of the Nunn-Lugar-Domenici amendment. The Rajneeshee cult used salmonella to influence local voting in Wasco County, Oregon, but with little national attention or repercussions. See, for example, Jonathan B. Tucker, ed., *Toxic Terror: Assessing Terrorist Use of Chemical and Biological Weapons* (Cambridge, Mass.: MIT Press, 2000).

PROGRAM SUSTAINABILITY

Program sustainability refers to the maintenance of adequate funding and effective management of preparedness programs and efforts to keep domestic preparedness as a policy priority. While local-level funding for domestic preparedness is crucial and local communities provide the response capabilities, program sustainability is even more important at the federal level. State and local governments and agencies look to the federal government for financial support and the provision of specialized equipment. Poor federal program support is likely to lead to poor local program sustainability. Like operational readiness, program sustainability is subject to changing forces such as the availability and willingness to spend government funds and other issues that occupy the time of policymakers.

A further challenge to program sustainability is the tension between federal and local responsibilities. The federal government has the greatest risk of facing a terrorist attack (as it faces risks across the entire country). Yet while the federal government plays a role in the management of the response, the initial handling of an event falls by necessity to local responders. The personnel who respond daily to injury, illness, and everyday hazards—who are not devoted exclusively to domestic preparedness—are the first responders in a terrorist event. Moreover, benefits associated with domestic preparedness efforts beyond WMD preparedness and response—such as improved public health monitoring and joint training of law enforcement and emergency response personnel—accrue at the local level. Thus, both the federal and local governments must sustain a high level of domestic preparedness, despite each seeing the other as bearing more significant responsibility.

Domestic preparedness is unique among government programs because of the complexity of actors involved and skills and resources needed. Preparedness requires the integrated efforts of more than 40 federal departments and agencies, all U.S. states and territories, the private sector, and a large, diverse group of potential first responders. This complexity implies the need for oversight and coordination from the top, as well as bottom-up support from the responder groups and their local funders.

To accomplish the task of coordination, President George W. Bush appointed Governor Tom Ridge to direct the Office of Homeland Security (OHS). The executive order creating the office, signed on October 8, 2001, has put forth mission to "develop and coordinate the implementation of a comprehensive national strategy to secure the United States from terrorist threats or attacks." The Office of Homeland Security, however, was perceived to be an insufficient response to fighting a "war on terrorism."

Thus, in early June 2002, President George W. Bush proposed the creation of a new Department of Homeland Security, which was passed in late November 2002. The Department of Homeland Security, headed by former OHS Director Ridge, is responsible for coordinating efforts within its jurisdiction at the federal level and with state and local stakeholders.

The creation of the Office and Department of Homeland Security bodes well for sustaining domestic preparedness. The existence of dedicated government bodies ensures that domestic preparedness will continue to have institutional advocates, complete with budgetary authority and their own personnel to maintain.

Post-9/11 Sustainability Challenges

As a result of terrorist activity on and after 9/11 and the enormous response across the United States, the previous sustainability concerns—underinvestment and low priority for responders with more pressing daily tasks—have become outdated. Other developments, however, have created new challenges.

"BOOM OR BUST" PRIORITIZATION

The first sustainability challenge is the possible reemergence of an earlier concern: in the absence of new terrorist attacks or any significant homeland security threats in the next couple of years, lawmakers and first responders may turn away from domestic preparedness and focus on other needs. This is especially likely if the United States and its allies prove successful in dismantling al Qaeda and other known terrorist groups. Current critics of past domestic preparedness efforts have pointed to the unwillingness of the government and the populace to sustain attention to terrorism, even after the 1993 World Trade Center bombing, the 1995 Oklahoma City attack, the 1998 U.S. embassy bombings in Africa, and the 2000 attack on the USS Cole.

The huge increase that is expected in domestic preparedness funding at the federal, state, and local levels makes future preparedness budgets a likely target for cuts. Funding for homeland security increased to approximately $38 billion in President Bush's 2003 budget from $19.5 billion in 2002, with an additional $5.1 billion in a summer 2002 supplemental appropriation.[5] These increases are matched by expanded budgets at state,

---

5. The $5.1 billion appropriation, which was part of a supplemental spending package for homeland security and defense, was rejected by President George W. Bush on August 13, 2002. "Bush Rejects $5.1 billion in Spending," CNN (August 13, 2002) at <www.cnn.com/2002/ALLPOLITICS/08/13/bush.spending/index.html>.

county, and city levels across the country. Funding at the state level is especially precarious, as many states are experiencing budget shortfalls and are prevented by law from running operating deficits.

The likelihood of a boom-to-bust problem is, however, relatively low: because further terrorist attacks against the United States are likely, the possibility of a drop in attention to domestic preparedness is less probable. And if not in the United States, attacks elsewhere in the world will keep attention on the specter of terrorism.

Second, organizational changes made since 9/11 greatly decrease the chance of lapses in program sustainability. As noted above, the creation of the Office and Department of Homeland Security, new homeland security positions in all U.S. states and many cities, and an increase in the number of security advisors in most federal departments have institutionalized the government's commitment to homeland security.

Third, the changes requested in the president's budget are mostly increases to agencies' base budgets rather than onetime purchases. This includes the $3.5 billion requested for first responder support, meaning that the funds will spread beyond the Washington, D.C., beltway. While the increase in domestic preparedness funding at all levels makes these accounts more attractive for politicians or responder group personnel to use in other ways, budgetary inertia will favor sustainability. The current military debate over eliminating "nontransformational" programs demonstrates the political difficulty in cutting any funding stream, regardless of its worth. The massive increases in funding support for domestic preparedness may be changed at the margins, but it is highly unlikely it will be seriously reduced.

SETTING THE RIGHT PRIORITIES

The sudden attention to homeland security has created a need to take steps to reduce the vulnerability of the United States to terrorist attacks and to improve response capabilities. This is true for elected officials wishing to appear strong on security, for businesses seeking to minimize losses from a threatened consumer base, and for those who provide security—first responders and others—to demonstrate that they are able to both defeat terrorist plots and respond to attacks when they occur. With so much focus on domestic preparedness (and terrorism prevention), there is a push to devote resources exclusively to security. This is largely based not on expertise (as the experience with domestic preparedness before 9/11 is insufficient to guide policymakers and security providers), but on perceived need.

The result of this new attention and need to react is a sustainability challenge to domestic preparedness. The concern is that preparedness will shift from its current focus on an all-hazards approach, which emphasizes functions that apply to terrorist and nonterrorist situations alike, to terrorism-specific initiatives. In addition, domestic preparedness may begin to move in the wrong direction. One possible pitfall is that the government will spend its energy preparing to counter the last attack rather than uncovering future threats. Another problem related to programmatic direction is the lack of prioritization. While airport security and anthrax response need to be improved, for example, they exist within a larger portfolio of security shortcomings. A knee-jerk reaction to bolster airport security, as embodied in the newly created Transportation Security Administration, will divert attention and resources from more general needs, such as improved intelligence and broad-based response capabilities. As media reports of threats and vulnerabilities emerge, domestic preparedness will veer from one need to another in an *ad hoc* manner, unless a strategy and prioritization of needs governs the system.

The following trends threaten to change the homeland security mission, resulting in less appropriate alternatives:

1. *All Homeland Security, All the Time.* Merging 22 agencies into a Department of Homeland Security will bring focus to federal homeland security and domestic preparedness and should improve the coordination of federal, state, and local efforts. All of the agencies involved in the consolidation, however, have nonsecurity functions that must be preserved in the new department. The same dilemma plays out on the local scene: first responders have to be prepared to prevent and respond to terrorist activity, but they spend most of their time on other missions such as criminal investigation, fire fighting, and nonterrorist-related search and rescue operations.

The pre-9/11 strategy was to have domestic preparedness mesh, to the greatest extent possible, with other first responder goals. The incident command system for structuring a response was needed as much for terrorism as it was for natural disasters and major fires. Interoperable radio communications assist any response effort involving multiple groups, regardless of the event. To some extent, single-use assets are required. Some post-9/11 efforts have provided assets used only for specific terrorism events, such as stockpiles of vaccine and increased use of WMD civil support teams. Policymakers, however, should rely to the greatest extent possible on dual-use preparations.

The focus on homeland security should not unduly divert funds or attention from other, more traditional functions. To the extent possible, equipment and procedures for domestic preparedness should also apply to other roles. Not only will this maximize efficiency of procurement and training, but also skills and equipment needed for domestic preparedness will be kept in good working order.

2. *Fighting the Last War.* Just as with the Department of Defense, the homeland security effort has placed inordinate focus on past attacks as compared with previously untargeted sites or methods. For example, the Transportation Security Administration, established by Congress in the immediate aftermath of 9/11, has hired tens of thousands of airport screeners and deployed a fleet of explosive detection systems. At the same time, spending on port, rail, highway, and other transportation security has received little attention.

It is always easier to focus on security systems that have already failed, and the public has a right to expect improvements in systems that terrorists have exploited. Past attacks may not foreshadow future ones, however, and history is only one criterion of priorities for spending and action.

3. *Doing Too Much.* The steps taken to prevent and prepare for further terrorist attacks have been far reaching, *ad hoc,* and conducted in the absence of a good sense of threats, vulnerabilities, or priority needs. Without risk assessment and national domestic preparedness strategies in place, money and attention are likely to be lavished on targets or other needs that are extremely unlikely to come under attack.

Domestic preparedness has always faced the prospect of a low-probability, high-consequence attack—such as the attacks of 9/11. Previously domestic preparedness levels were an insurance policy in case response assets were needed; subsequently, domestic preparedness is seen as response assets needed for future attacks. This view can be extended to preparing for an attack against every possible target, regardless of the likelihood that such an attack may occur. The total allocation of domestic preparedness funding, as well as prioritization among competing preparedness needs, should be subject to cost-benefit analyses and trade-offs with other government and first responder missions.[6]

Recommendations

The following recommendations provide guidance on improving the sustainability of domestic preparedness programs and operations. Some

---

6. For a treatment of risk analysis in determining domestic preparedness spending, see Richard A. Falkenrath, "Analytic Models and Policy Prescription: Understanding Recent Innovation in U.S. Counterterrorism," *Studies in Conflict and Terrorism,* Vol. 24, No. 3 (2001), pp. 159–181.

recommendations will increase sustainability to the detriment of other objectives; others have relatively small costs.

RECOMMENDATION 1: RESPONSIBLE GOVERNMENT ENTITY

Sustaining domestic preparedness will be easier if there is a clear organizational home for domestic preparedness issues and an entrenched organizational bureaucracy to fight for those interests. Disaggregated responsibility, as existed between 1996 and 2001, requires domestic preparedness supporters to fight among other agency responsibilities for attention and funding.

The establishment of a Department of Homeland Security has been a positive step toward the creation of a federal nexus for domestic preparedness. Congress granted significant powers to the secretary, and Secretary Ridge will have a staff larger than all cabinet departments except the Defense Department and the Department of Veterans Affairs and an initial budget of roughly $37.5 billion. The Department of Homeland Security is an institutional force for the continued funding and priority of domestic preparedness, overcoming sustainability problems inherent in keeping domestic preparedness control in other departments with conflicting funding needs.

The Department of Homeland Security will also have its own dedicated (see recommendation 3) section in the president's budget request to Congress for annual spending, which will facilitate domestic preparedness sustainability. This will include its own research and development capabilities and funds to allocate grant programs to state and city governments and responder groups. The department will assist in oversight of exercises at the local and regional levels and conduct national exercises and simulations.[7]

Congressional reorganization is also necessary to oversee and fund an effective and efficient homeland security effort. As virtually every congressional committee in both the Senate and House can claim some jurisdiction over homeland security, consolidating or better defining responsibility will require dedication from congressional leadership. The House Select Committee on Homeland Security is a promising start but an insufficient reorganization, by itself, for efficient Congressional oversight

---

7. The Office of Homeland Security, Homeland Security Council, and any other future White House groups charged with overseeing and coordinating homeland security efforts across the federal bureaucracy will still be a necessary component, in addition to the creation of a department. The Department of Homeland Security does not include all federal homeland security functions, and the secretary cannot direct or coordinate programs in other departments.

and action. Especially important for the sustainability of funding is the creation of an appropriations subcommittee for homeland security with jurisdiction over Department of Homeland Security spending and related programs across the federal government.

It is difficult to monitor and measure operational readiness to respond to emergencies. The Department of Homeland Security should work with states, cities, and first responder groups to develop metrics for measuring operational readiness. This will require identifying desired response capabilities and a judgment of who should be capable of performing which tasks.

Federal, state, and local response units should be judged against the developed metrics, as should federal offices providing training or equipment.[8] Once objective measurements are done, more attention can be given to maintaining equipment and changing current procedures to sustain the desired level of preparedness.

Simulation exercises are critical for training and for measuring readiness. Large-scale exercises involving agencies at all levels of government (like TOPOFF and Dark Winter) should occur annually. Smaller exercises at the state, county, or city level should be carried out periodically to test readiness and identify shortcomings. Provisions should be made to disseminate lessons learned from all exercises to responders and planners in other geographic areas. Exercises should be made as realistic as possible, but they should stop short of significantly interrupting the cities or towns where they are staged, as disruptions to everyday life will decrease local politicians' willingness to allow exercises to continue.[9] Responders must

---

8. Measuring requires that some entity be available to assess the results. Possible groups to conduct judgments are private or nonprofit institutions, state governors' offices, and federal organizations such as the Government Accounting Office and the Office of Management and Budget.

9. Where technically and legally feasible, the Department of Homeland Security and Environmental Protection Agency should identify harmless chemicals and bacteria that can be used in simulations and exercises to replicate the experience of an attack. This will not only provide better experience in measuring and educating first responders about contamination and detection but will also provide a danger-free way of making the responders more comfortable with WMD response. Exercises with real but harmless agents has an unfortunate precedent in tests done in California to test bacterial dissemination, which was problematic more for its exposure of the unwitting public to bacterial agents. Domestic preparedness exercises should minimize actual agent

be prevented from receiving information on exercises in advance, as prenotification undermines the ability to determine readiness.

Finally, money should be set aside to compensate federal, state, and local responder groups to replace equipment and supplies as needed. Waiting for the beginning of new accounting periods to replace used material will decrease readiness if stocks are depleted and inflexible funding cannot replace materials until the next period.

RECOMMENDATION 3: BUDGET PREPARATION AND APPORTIONING RESPONSIBILITY

As part of the federal coordination process, the Homeland Security Council or the Office of Management and Budget should prepare for Congress a description of all federal spending on domestic preparedness as part of a homeland security budget. A unified figure for the federal government's spending would provide Congress with a better picture of federal domestic preparedness efforts and would help pass parts of the total domestic preparedness budget through the congressional budget and appropriations processes.

Currently, the Office of Management and Budget collects general budget data on the government's preparedness efforts against terrorism and weapons of mass destruction from relevant agencies. WMD preparedness figures are divided into training and equipment for first responders, special response teams, federal planning and exercises, public health surveillance, and other relevant capabilities. This effort should be formalized and submitted to the relevant congressional subcommittees when the annual budget is formulated.

Second, the Homeland Security Council, in conjunction with the Office of Management and Budget, the Department of Homeland Security, the National Governors Association, city and county organizations, and first responder associations, must delineate federal responsibilities for domestic preparedness and state and local responsibilities. One sensible suggestion is to place the spending onus on the entity that derives the greatest everyday benefit from the product or service purchased.[10]

---

contact with the general public to minimize public hysteria and civil liberties infringements. Involvement in WMD exercises should never be allowed to interfere with the primary jobs of first responders, and contingency plans should be made for adjusting exercises if a real emergency occurs. Similarly, exercises should not be designed to unduly hamper normal traffic or other everyday activities.

10. Ivo H. Daalder, I.M. Destler, David L. Gunter, Paul C. Light, Robert E. Litan, Michael E. O'Hanlon, Peter R. Orszag, James B. Steinberg, *Protecting the American Homeland: A Preliminary Analysis* (Washington, D.C.: Brookings Institution, 2002).

RECOMMENDATION 4: DUAL USE AND LEVERAGING

The structure and goals of domestic preparedness programs have great importance for the effort's sustainability. The goal of the programs should be to maximize the ability to prepare for and respond to a range of terrorist attacks or emergencies on U.S. territory.

For this goal to be realized in a sustained manner, local responders must be prepared to follow exacting procedures for extremely unlikely eventualities without degrading their daily operations. This implies a trade-off between specialization and maximum readiness with attention to more commonplace needs. Domestic preparedness should thus be thought of as part of the existing all-hazards approach to disaster management rather than as a separate entity, and to the maximum extent possible, domestic preparedness capabilities should be developed in ways that benefit other responsibilities. For example, improving domestic preparedness is nearly certain to improve public health, disaster response, law enforcement operations, military capabilities in contaminated environments, and international assistance capabilities.

As noted earlier, WMD response should be made the responsibility of those with related missions who are sure to be present when an attack occurs. Stockpiles of equipment maintained at the local level should be made available for purposes other than domestic preparedness causes, provided there is a mandatory procedure for replacing them in a suitable time period. When equipment needed for domestic preparedness is not dual-use, such as anthrax vaccines or sarin detectors, it should reside with specialists in emergency management (often at the county or state level) rather than with the usual first responders.

WMD response should also be included in instruction programs for the response communities: the fire and police academies, medical school for doctors and nurses, and similar educational activities.[11] Having all first responders pass examinations or take courses to develop their preparedness skills, and then requiring that all responders be certified in order to receive federal money, creates a baseline readiness standard and incentives for attaining it. Requiring recertification at intervals of two or three years will also help to sustain readiness.

Personnel in state emergency preparedness offices and at the county level should be made responsible for monitoring and coordinating the domestic preparedness efforts among the traditional responder community (firefighters, police, hazardous materials workers), the public health and medical communities, and the media.

---

11. See also Amy E. Smithson and Leslie-Anne Levy, *Ataxia*, chap. 7.

RECOMMENDATION 5: INSTITUTIONALIZATION

To the extent possible, domestic preparedness needs to become institutionalized and automated within the participating communities. Creating protocols or automated tasks that increase response effectiveness will decrease the chance that sustainability will fail. Some of these protocols will require the responder community to change standard procedures, such as requiring personnel to wear extra protective clothing and requiring departments to bring weapon detectors to deployment sites. Other protocols, such as notifying specific people upon a high level of hospital admittance or unusual veterinary activity, may be automated through computer protocols triggered by data entry. To the extent that technologies can be used independent of human activity (e.g., detectors placed in strategic sites to monitor for WMD and relay results to a central facility), automation can replace training or attention without risking sustainability.

Because not all responders can be sufficiently trained in the use of domestic preparedness equipment or procedures, one or more federal agencies, as coordinated by the offices identified in recommendations 1 and 2, should publish "procedure sheets" for various circumstances. A sole agency, preferably the Federal Emergency Management Agency due to its lead responsibility in federal-state-local coordination could, for example, mimic the military's practice of codifying maintenance standards for equipment to instruct the personnel charged with maintaining equipment caches. The Centers for Disease Control and Prevention have begun, and should continue, to take responsibility for publishing guidelines to be distributed to every hospital in the country for identifying and treating suspected diseases or chemical reactions.[12]

Finally, response to weapons of mass destruction should be made part of the training that firefighters, police, hazardous materials workers, public health personnel, doctors, and nurses are required to complete before employment. While this instruction is conducted locally and is sometimes private, federal legislation should mandate that standards for training be set by the relevant federal agencies and that training academies be trained directly by the federal experts.[13]

Conclusion

The post-9/11 environment drives policymakers and first responders to emphasize domestic preparedness programs and priority. This focus on

---

12. Ibid. chap. 6.

13. Ibid. pp. 298–303.

preventing and preparing for future terrorist attacks—without regard to long-term sustainability or efficiency of the system—raises the real possibility that efforts undertaken now either will not survive or will be inefficient or counterproductive later.

To create and shape a system in which domestic preparedness continues to work and leverage everyday needs, sustainability must be included as an integral part of the effort. The major needs for sustainability are: an institutional advocate for domestic preparedness; an emphasis on an all-hazards approach; and a way to keep training and equipping for WMD response as a regular part of first responder functions.

The creation of a Department of Homeland Security was a critical step in ensuring sustainability, especially in the fight for federal funding for domestic preparedness programs. A strengthened White House coordination role through the Homeland Security Council is also necessary to ensure the proper integration of domestic preparedness efforts across the federal government.

Finally, the nature of domestic preparedness as an all-hazards program must be preserved. Rather than WMD response being added to a long list of training and equipment needs for police, fire, medical, and other emergency workers, the tools and procedures for domestic preparedness should be grafted onto everyday needs. Only by using dual-use equipment and overlaying WMD response actions can responders and their equipment remain ready for an emergency on a sustained basis.

About the Authors

Graham Allison. *Douglas Dillon Professor of Government and Director, Belfer Center for Science and International Affairs, John F. Kennedy School of Government, Harvard University.* From 1977–89, Allison served as Dean of the Kennedy School. Under his leadership, a small, undefined program grew twenty-fold to become a major professional school of public policy and government. In the first term of the Clinton administration, he served as Assistant Secretary of Defense for Policy and Plans where he coordinated Department of Defense (DOD) strategy and policy toward Russia, Ukraine, and the other states of the former Soviet Union. He has authored or co-authored more than a dozen books and 100 articles, including, most recently, *Realizing Human Rights: From Inspiration to Impact* (2000) and *Avoiding Nuclear Anarchy: Containing the Threat of Loose Russian Nuclear Weapons and Fissile Material* (1996). As Executive Director of the Commission on America's National Interests, he served as principal author of its report, *America's National Interests* (2000). His first book, *Essence of Decision: Explaining the Cuban Missile Crisis* (1971) was recently released in an updated and revised second edition (1999) and ranks among the best-sellers in political science with more than 300,000 copies in print. He has been a member of the Secretary of Defense's Defense Policy Board for Secretaries Weinberger, Carlucci, Cheney, Aspin, Perry, and Cohen. He was a founding member of the Trilateral Commission, a Director of the Council on Foreign Relations, and a member of many public committees and commissions.

Andrei Kokoshin. *Director of the Institute for International Security Studies of the Russian Academy of Sciences.* Kokoshin is a scientist, scholar and author, and is a Deputy of the Russian Duma. He is a former First Deputy Minister of Defense in Russia as well as a former member of Russia's Security Council. From 1994 to 1997, Dr. Kokoshin served with former U.S. Defense Secretary Bill Perry as Co-Chairman of the Russian-American Committee on Defense Industry Conversion. He is world-renowned as an expert in Russian high-tech industries and often speaks for the technologically advanced sectors of the economy. Since 2000, he has served as vice chairman of the Committee on Industry, Construction and High Technologies of the Duma and is also the Chairman of Expert Councils for biotechnologies and information technologies. Kokoshin is a member of the Russian Academy of Natural Sciences and served as the acting vice president of that body from 1998–1999. In 2000, he was appointed chairman of the Russian National Council for the Development of Education. He has an engineering degree in radioelectronics and a doctorate in political science. Kokoshin is the author of 12 books on international security, political and military affairs, and defense industry policy.

Peter S. Beering. *Indianapolis Terrorism Preparedness Coordinator.* Peter Beering is the Indianapolis Terrorism Preparedness Coordinator. Mr. Beering has overseen the training of more than 6,000 public safety, EMS, haz-mat, and medical personnel under the Nunn-Lugar-Domenici program and is one of ten experts who trained mayors and senior city officials in terrorism preparation and response for the Department of Defense. He is a member of the State and Local Advisory Board of the National Domestic Preparedness Office. The architect of the Indiana Omnibus Anti-Terrorism Act of 2001 (enacted before the September 11 attacks), Beering has testified before the Indiana General Assembly and before the U.S. Congress. Beering is the lead author of "Winning Plays: Essential Guidance From the Terrorism Line of Scrimmage" which has been entered into the Congressional Record three times since its release. He is the National Director of Security Initiatives for USFilter, one of the nation's largest water and wastewater management companies; he is the former Deputy General Counsel for Indianapolis Water Company. He has published several articles on infrastructure security and threat assessment and a series of articles on terrorism preparedness and response for various industries and professions. He continues his sixteen-year relationship with the Indianapolis/Marion County Prosecutor's Office where he is Special Prosecuting Attorney for Arson and Bombings. He is a Master Fire fighter, a Certified Fire Investigator, a faculty member for the Bureau of Alcohol, Tobacco and Firearms National Academy, and a teacher of Criminal Law, Evidence Law, and Terrorism Policy and Response at Indiana University.

Juliette N. Kayyem. *Executive Director of Executive Session on Domestic Preparedness, John F. Kennedy School of Government, Harvard University.* Kayyem is Executive Director of the Executive Session on Domestic Preparedness at the John F. Kennedy School of Government, a terrorism and homeland security research project at Harvard University. From 1999–2001, she served as former House Minority Leader Richard Gephardt's appointment to the National Commission on Terrorism. Before that, she was a legal advisor to the Attorney General and Counsel to the Assistant Attorney General for Civil Rights at the U.S. Department of Justice. In related areas, she serves as a member of the bipartisan Constitution Project's program on Liberty and Security, the Council on Foreign Relations, the American Bar Association's committee on National Security Law, and the Advisory Committee of the Migration Policy Institute. She has also served as adjunct faculty at Boston University School of Law and has taught at the Institute of Politics at the Kennedy School of Government. She has testified before Congress and serves as an advisor to a number of governmental and private institutions. She writes frequently in the field of counterterrorism law, domestic preparedness, and the legal implications of U.S. national security strategy. Her work has appeared in the *New York Times*, the *L.A. Times*, the *Christian Science Monitor*, and the *Washington Post* as well as academic journals such as the *Boston Review, National Defense*, and *Studies in Conflict and Terrorism*. Ms. Kayyem also serves as an analyst for NBC News and National Public Radio WBUR's On Point. She is a 1991 graduate of Harvard College and a 1995 graduate of Harvard Law School.

Clarence Harmon. *Former Mayor, City of St. Louis, Missouri.* Harmon served as the Mayor of the City of St. Louis from April 1997 through April 2001. Harmon was St. Louis' 48th mayor. As mayor, he established a public-private partnership that created St. Louis' first downtown development action plan and created a health care system to serve the indigent. He also made great strides to restore faith in government by making city government more responsive, more efficient, and more user-friendly through initiatives such as the reorganization of the city's development agencies. Prior to being elected mayor, he was Director of Business Development for United Van Lines, the nation's leading household goods moving company. He joined United Van Lines, Inc., in December 1995, following a twenty-six year career with the St. Louis Metropolitan Police Department, including four years as Chief of Police. He holds an M.A. in Criminal Justice Administration and Public Administration from Webster University and a B.S. from Northeast Missouri State University.

Frances Edwards-Winslow. *Director, Office of Emergency Services for the City of San Jose and Director, San Jose Metropolitan Medical Task Force.* Dr. Edwards-Winslow's career has included 11 years as San Jose's Director of Emergency Preparedness, university teaching, criminal justice research and planning, and one year as acting assistant fire chief in San Jose. In addition to being a member of the Harvard Executive Session on Domestic Preparedness, she is a member of the Stanford University Bioterrorism Working Group, the U.S.-Germany Project, and recently completed work on the Committee on Evaluation of the Metropolitan Medical Response Team Program of the National Academy of Sciences, Institute of Medicine. The report has been published by the National Academy Press as *Preparing for Terrorism: Tools for Evaluating the Metropolitan Medical Response System Program.* She has published articles and book chapters on emergency management topics, including three chapters in the *Handbook of Crisis and Emergency Management,* "The First-Responder's Perspective," a chapter in *The New Terror: Facing the Threat of Biological and Chemical Weapons,* from the Hoover Institution at Stanford University, and an article on collaborative leadership in the Drucker Foundation's *Leader to Leader Magazine.* She received the Public Official of the Year 2002 award from *Governing Magazine.* She is a frequent speaker at professional conferences and represented emergency management on the five night "Bio War" series on *Nightline with Ted Koppel.* She is an adjunct teacher for three California universities and is an emergency management consultant to Federal Emergency Management Agency (FEMA), The Association of Bay Area Governments, the Jason Project, cities in Japan, and Santa Clara University.

David Dixon. *FAIA. Principal, Goody, Clancy & Associates, Boston.* Mr. Dixon directs planning and urban design for GC&A, a Boston-based firm with a national practice in planning, urban design, and architecture. He has led significant revitalization initiatives in recent years in Boston, Cleveland, Chicago, Providence, and a variety of other cities. The *Wall Street Journal* described his vision for redevelopment around Chicago's Cabrini Green public housing as a model for "rebuilding mixed-income neighborhoods." Mr. Dixon has been invited to talk about urban issues at national conferences sponsored by the American Institute of Architects (AIA), the Congress for the New Urbanism, the MacArthur Foundation, the Urban Land Institute, and other national organizations. He was asked by the AIA to participate in the society's first national conference on terrorism following September 11, 2001. Mr. Dixon is a Fellow of the AIA and has received national honor awards from the AIA, the Congress for the New Urbanism, the Society of College and University Planners, the

American Society of Landscape Architects, and other professional organizations. He is the 2003 president of the Boston Society of Architects, an advisor to the AIA's national Regional and Urban Design Committee, and co-director of the Civic Initiative for Livable New England.

Patricia E. Chang. *Research Assistant, Executive Session on Domestic Preparedness, John F. Kennedy School of Government, Harvard University.* Patricia is a recent graduate of Amherst College where she graduated *magna cum laude* in Political Science and Women and Gender Studies. Her senior year thesis was entitled, "Our Sweat, Our Daily Bread: Women Garment Workers in New York's Chinatown" and was focused broadly on women's role in the global garment industry. Her past working experiences have included interning for a national magazine, for an electronic publisher of books on line, and researching social exclusion and poverty issues at the Bunting Institute at Radcliffe University. In the fall of 2003, Chang will attend the Kennedy School of Government as a master's candidate, focusing on Peace and International Security Studies.

Robert F. Knouss. *Chief Medical Advisor to the Assistant Secretary for Public Health Emergency Preparedness, U.S. Department of Health and Human Services.* Knouss is the Chief Medical Advisor to the Assistant Secretary for Public Health Emergency Preparedness at the Department of Health and Human Services. Previously, Knouss served as the Director of the Office of Emergency Preparedness for over six years, where he directed the federal health response to the September 11, 2001 attacks as well as many other public health emergencies. He was also the Director of the National Disaster Medical System (NDMS) in the U.S. Department of Health and Human Services. Knouss was trained at the University of Pennsylvania and, prior to that, at the University of Wisconsin. He entered the Public Health Service and was first Chief of the Physician Education Branch in National Institute of Health (NIH) and Director of the Division of Medicine in the Health Resources Administration. Among his numerous assignments, Knouss has directed the Public Health Service's refugee health activities in the Cuban-Haitian and Southeast Asian refugee crises. Knouss was for ten years deputy director of the Pan America Health Organization and, in his more distant past, was a staff member for the Senate Committee on Labor and Human Resources.

Robyn Pangi. *Former Research Associate, Executive Session on Domestic Preparedness, John F. Kennedy School of Government, Harvard University.* Ms. Pangi is a 2000 graduate of the Master in Public Policy Program at the John F. Kennedy School of Government. In addition to this volume, she is coeditor of the forthcoming *Countering Terrorism: Dimensions of Prepared-ness* (MIT Press, 2003). She is author of "Preparing for Terrorism: What Governors and Mayors Can Do," "Consequence Management Following the Sarin Attack in the Tokyo Subway System," and co-author of "Inter-governmental Challenges of Combating Terrorism," and "Preparing for the Worst: Mitigating the Consequences of Chemical and Biological Ter-rorism." She received her bachelor's degree from Columbia University.

Phillip Oates. *Former Commissioner of the Department of Military and Vet-erans Affairs and Emergency Services and Adjutant General, State of Alaska.* As an Army infantry officer, Oates culminated a thirty-year active duty ca-reer as Chief of Staff of the 6th Infantry Division, Commander of the Dragon Brigade for XVIII Airborne Corps, and Chief of Staff of Alaskan Command, a subordinate unified command of United States Pacific Com-mand. As a Commissioner, he is currently responsible for emergency ser-vices and homeland security as well as veterans affairs, a military youth academy, counterdrug support, and civil military support for the State of Alaska. As Adjutant General, he commands Alaska's Army and Air Na-tional Guard that include an Army Brigade level task force and two Air Force wings. Oates holds a B.S. in Psychology from Louisiana College and an M.A. in Public Administration from the University of Missouri at Kansas City. He also was a U.S. Army Fellow at the John F. Kennedy School of Government, Harvard University.

Paul D. Monroe, Jr. *Adjutant General, California National Guard.* Monroe was appointed as Adjutant General on April 28, 1999. As Adjutant Gen-eral, he leads the largest National Guard force in the United States and authorizes more than 18,000 Army and 4,900 Air National Guard mem-bers. He has held several staff assignments with the Office of the Adju-tant General and was appointed as the Assistant Adjutant General for Plans and Mobilization in April 1994 and was promoted to the rank of Brigadier General in July 1995. He received his B.S. in Public Administra-tion from the University of San Francisco and completed programs at the Army Officer Candidate School, Signal Officer Basic Course, Infantry Officer Advanced Course, Military Police Officer Career Course, Com-mand and General Staff College, and the U.S. Army War College.

Rebecca F. Denlinger, *Chief, Cobb County Fire & Emergency Services, Marietta, Georgia.* Denlinger began her career with Cobb County Fire & Emergency Services in November 1977 as a firefighter and has advanced through the ranks to the position of Fire Chief. Appointed Fire Chief in

April 1997, she manages a department of 606 employees with a $49 million annual budget. She is the fire service representative on the Georgia Board of Public Safety, the Georgia Homeland Security Task Force, and the Georgia Emergency Management Agency Area 7 All Hazards Council. Denlinger is a Board member of the Metropolitan Chiefs Section of the International Association of Fire Chiefs. She is a member of the National Homeland Security Advisory Group for Georgia's 8th Congressional District Representative Saxby Chambliss, the Women Chiefs Fire Officers Association, and the Southeastern Association of Fire Chiefs as well as many others. Denlinger holds certification in the State of Georgia as a Firefighter, Emergency Medical Technician, and Smoke Diver, and is a PADI certified Open Water Diver. Denlinger was the recipient of 2002 Georgia Fire Official of the Year award, received Cobb County's "Golden Goose" Award in February 2002, an award of excellence to a person who exemplifies teamwork and leadership as a public servant, and was recognized by Georgia Commission on Women as an honoree at Georgia Women in Public Safety in March 2001. Denlinger has studied in Germany, at Manchester College in Indiana, and is currently enrolled at Thomas Edison State College.

Kristin H. Gonzenbach. *Managing Partner, Callahan Management Strategies, LLC.* Callahan Management Strategies, LLC, is a consulting firm assisting local and state governments to operate at optimum efficiency and effectiveness. Kristin began her career as a Police Officer and then Security Inspector for two Department of Energy nuclear facilities focusing on counterterrorism preparedness. She worked as a Management Assistant to a County Manager and eventually began consulting to local governments regarding spending, cost savings and improvements, capital expenditures, personnel issues, and conducting research projects. Most recently, she has been working with DeKalb County, Georgia (pop. 700,000), analyzing their fire and EMS service delivery. Her study led to the integration of those departments, where she is currently a member of the integration team. Kristin received her undergraduate degree in Administration of Justice from Wichita State University in Wichita, Kansas and her graduate degree in Public Finance from Rockefeller College, the Public Affairs and Policy School of the State University of New York in Albany, New York.

David Grannis. *Senior Policy Advisor to Congresswoman Jane Harman.* Grannis is Senior Advisor to Congresswoman Harman on terrorism, intelligence, and defense issues. He worked as a Research Assistant for the

Executive Session on Domestic Preparedness in 1999 while a student at the John F. Kennedy School of Government. He wrote a master's thesis on sustaining domestic preparedness. David formerly worked at the National Research Council's Board on Chemical Sciences and Technology and holds a Master of Public Policy degree from the John F. Kennedy School of Government and a B.A. in chemistry from Cornell University.

Index

BCSIA Studies in International Security

Published by The MIT Press

Sean M. Lynn-Jones and Steven E. Miller, series editors
Karen Motley, executive editor
Belfer Center for Science and International Affairs (BCSIA)
John F. Kennedy School of Government, Harvard University

Allison, Graham T., Owen R. Coté, Jr., Richard A. Falkenrath, and Steven E. Miller, *Avoiding Nuclear Anarchy: Containing the Threat of Loose Russian Nuclear Weapons and Fissile Material* (1996)

Allison, Graham T., and Kalypso Nicolaïdis, eds., *The Greek Paradox: Promise vs. Performance* (1996)

Arbatov, Alexei, Abram Chayes, Antonia Handler Chayes, and Lara Olson, eds., *Managing Conflict in the Former Soviet Union: Russian and American Perspectives* (1997)

Bennett, Andrew, *Condemned to Repetition? The Rise, Fall, and Reprise of Soviet-Russian Military Interventionism, 1973–1996* (1999)

Blackwill, Robert D., and Michael Stürmer, eds., *Allies Divided: Transatlantic Policies for the Greater Middle East* (1997)

Blackwill, Robert D., and Paul Dibb, eds., *America's Asian Alliances* (2000)

Brom, Shlomo, and Yiftah Shapir, eds., *The Middle East Military Balance 1999–2000* (1999)

Brom, Shlomo, and Yiftah Shapir, eds., *The Middle East Military Balance 2001–2002* (2002)

Brown, Michael E., ed., *The International Dimensions of Internal Conflict* (1996)

Brown, Michael E., and Šumit Ganguly, eds., *Fighting Words: Language Policy and Ethnic Relations in Asia* (2003)

Brown, Michael E., and Šumit Ganguly, eds., *Government Policies and Ethnic Relations in Asia and the Pacific* (1997)

Carter, Ashton B., and John P. White, eds., *Keeping the Edge: Managing Defense for the Future* (2001)

de Nevers, Renée, *Comrades No More: The Seeds of Political Change in Eastern Europe* (2003)

Elman, Colin, and Miriam Fendius Elman, eds., *Progress in International Relations Theory: Appraising the Field* (2003)

Elman, Colin, and Miriam Fendius Elman, eds., *Bridges and Boundaries: Historians, Political Scientists, and the Study of International Relations* (2001)

Elman, Miriam Fendius, ed., *Paths to Peace: Is Democracy the Answer?* (1997)

Falkenrath, Richard A., *Shaping Europe's Military Order: The Origins and Consequences of the CFE Treaty* (1994)

Falkenrath, Richard A., Robert D. Newman, and Bradley A. Thayer, *America's Achilles' Heel: Nuclear, Biological, and Chemical Terrorism and Covert Attack* (1998)

Feaver, Peter D., and Richard H. Kohn, eds., *Soldiers and Civilians: The Civil-Military Gap and American National Security* (2001)

Feldman, Shai, *Nuclear Weapons and Arms Control in the Middle East* (1996)

Feldman, Shai, and Yiftah Shapir, eds., *The Middle East Military Balance 2000–2001* (2001)

Forsberg, Randall, ed., *The Arms Production Dilemma: Contraction and Restraint in the World Combat Aircraft Industry* (1994)

Hagerty, Devin T., *The Consequences of Nuclear Proliferation: Lessons from South Asia* (1998)

Heymann, Philip B., *Terrorism and America: A Commonsense Strategy for a Democratic Society* (1998)

Heymann, Philip B., *Terrorism, Freedom, and Security Winning without War* (2003)

Howitt, Arnold M., and Robyn L. Pangi, eds., *Countering Terrorism: Dimensions of Preparedness* (2003)

Kayyem, Juliette N., and Robyn L. Pangi, eds., *First to Arrive: State and Local Responses to Terrorism* (2003)

Kokoshin, Andrei A., *Soviet Strategic Thought, 1917–91* (1998)

Lederberg, Joshua, ed., *Biological Weapons: Limiting the Threat* (1999)

Shaffer, Brenda, *Borders and Brethren: Iran and the Challenge of Azerbaijani Identity* (2002)

Shields, John M., and William C. Potter, eds., *Dismantling the Cold War: U.S. and NIS Perspectives on the Nunn-Lugar Cooperative Threat Reduction Program* (1997)

Tucker, Jonathan B., ed., *Toxic Terror: Assessing Terrorist Use of Chemical and Biological Weapons* (2000)

Utgoff, Victor A., ed., *The Coming Crisis: Nuclear Proliferation, U.S. Interests, and World Order* (2000)

Williams, Cindy, ed., *Holding the Line: U.S. Defense Alternatives for the Early 21st Century* (2001)

The Robert and Renée Belfer Center for Science and International Affairs

Graham T. Allison, Director
John F. Kennedy School of Government
Harvard University
79 JFK Street, Cambridge, MA 02138
(617) 495-1400
http://www.ksg.harvard.edu/bcsia   bcsia_ksg@harvard.edu

The Belfer Center for Science and International Affairs (BCSIA) is the hub of research, teaching and training in international security affairs, environmental and resource issues, science and technology policy, human rights and conflict studies at Harvard's John F. Kennedy School of Government. The Center's mission is to provide leadership in advancing policy-relevant knowledge about the most important challenges of international security and other critical issues where science, technology, and international affairs intersect.

BCSIA's leadership begins with the recognition of science and technology as driving forces transforming international affairs. The Center integrates insights of social scientists, natural scientists, technologists, and practitioners with experience in government, diplomacy, the military, and business to address these challenges. The Center pursues its mission in four complementary research programs:

- The **International Security Program** (ISP) addresses the most pressing threats to U.S. national interests and international security.

- The **Environment and Natural Resources Program** (ENRP) is the locus of Harvard's interdisciplinary research on resource and environmental problems and policy responses.

- The **Science, Technology and Public Policy** (STPP) program analyzes ways in which science and technology policy influence international security, resources, environment, and development, and such cross-cutting issues as technological innovation and information infrastructure.

- The **WPF Program on Intrastate Conflict, Conflict Prevention and Conflict Resolution** analyzes the causes of ethnic, religious, and other conflicts, and seeks to identify practical ways to prevent and limit such conflicts.

The heart of the Center is its resident research community of more than 140 scholars: Harvard faculty, analysts, practitioners, and each year a new, interdisciplinary group of research fellows. BCSIA sponsors frequent seminars, workshops and conferences, maintains a substantial specialized library, and publishes books, monographs, and discussion papers.

The Center's International Security Program, directed by Steven E. Miller, publishes the BCSIA Studies in International Security, and sponsors and edits the quarterly journal *International Security*.

The Center is supported by an endowment established with funds from Robert and Renée Belfer, the Ford Foundation and Harvard University, by foundation grants, by individual gifts, and by occasional government contracts.